PUBLIC POET,
PRIVATE MAN

PUBLIC POET, PRIVATE MAN

Henry Wadsworth Longfellow at 200

Christoph Irmscher

University of Massachusetts Press • Amherst & Boston
Published in cooperation with the Houghton Library, Harvard University

Printed in the United States of America

This volume is based on an exhibition at the Houghton Library and was originally published as a special issue of the *Harvard Library Bulletin*, Volume 17, Numbers 3-4 (Fall/Winter 2006).

LC 2009010277
ISBN 978-1-55849-584-5

Library of Congress Cataloging-in-Publication Data

Irmscher, Christoph.
Public poet, private man : Henry Wadsworth Longfellow at 200 / Christoph Irmscher.
p. cm.
"Published in cooperation with the Houghton Library, Harvard University."
Based on an exhibition at the Houghton Library and was originally published as a special issue of the Harvard Library Bulletin, Volume 17, Numbers 3–4.
Includes bibliographical references and index.
ISBN 978-1-55849-584-5 (pbk. : alk. paper)
1. Longfellow, Henry Wadsworth, 1807–1882.
2. Poets, American—19th century—Biography.
3. Longfellow, Henry Wadsworth, 1807–1882--Exhibitions.
4. Longfellow, Henry Wadsworth, 1807–1882—Anniversaries, etc.
I. Houghton Library. II. Harvard Library bulletin. III. Title.
PS2281.I77 2009
811'.3—dc22
[B]

2009010277

British Library Cataloguing in Publication data are available.

For my mother,
Elisabeth Irmscher

Contents

Preface

This book tells the story of a poet, Henry Wadsworth Longfellow, and his things: the manuscripts, drawings, books, pencils, and photographs that belonged to him or his family and friends. Each of the following eight chapters corresponds to one of the eight display cases in an exhibition I curated for Harvard's Houghton Library in 2007, "Public Poet, Private Man: Henry Wadsworth Longfellow at 200." The aim of the exhibition was to honor, on the occasion of the bicentennial of his birth, a poet who was both immensely cosmopolitan and deeply rooted in the New England region. I wanted to paint a portrait of Longfellow as a professional writer and editor, devoted friend, and family man. Above all, I wanted to highlight his rather democratic conception of authorship—a trade that one can pursue even in winter, as Longfellow's daughter Annie once pointed out, to his infinite delight. In its first incarnation, this book served as an exhibition catalog of sorts, a guidebook adding depth, nuance, and historical and personal context to the objects I had chosen from the extensive collections of Houghton Library and the Longfellow National Historic Site in Cambridge. Much revised, *Public Poet, Private Man*, thanks to the many illustrations I was able to include, can now be read independently, as an unconventional introduction, in both words and images, to America's most popular poet as well as the world that shaped him and that he helped shape in turn.

Many people collaborated to make both the exhibit and the book a reality. First and foremost, thanks are due Leslie Morris, curator of modern books and manuscripts at Houghton, who conceived the idea of a Longfellow exhibit and brought her expertise and organizational skills to bear on its implementation; to Jim Shea, the manager of the Longfellow National Historic Site, who knows more about Longfellow than anybody else and whose imagination, creativity, and gift for getting people to work together I envy; and to Matthew Battles, the former coordinating editor of the *Harvard Library Bulletin*, without whom this book would never have happened. I would also like to thank Dennis Marnon, the current coordinating editor of the *Bulletin*, and William Stoneman, the Florence Fearrington Librarian of Houghton Library, who graciously allowed me to reuse and adapt the text of my original catalog. I would not have been able to complete my work without the active support of my friend Thomas Ford, photographic liaison for Houghton Library, who reproduced countless sources for me, ordered and compiled the illustrations, and shared his knowledge of native cultures with me. Lauren Malcolm, of the Longfellow National Historic Site, was a superb editor, checking facts, correcting errors, and providing additional leads. David Daly, collection manager of the Longfellow National Historic Site, cheerfully (and with lightning speed) fielded all my queries and supplied me with beautiful scans of objects in his collection. Victor Gulotta, the dean of Longfellow collectors, patiently answered my questions. My wife, Lauren Bernofsky, read several versions of my manuscript and offered detailed suggestions for improvement at every stage. Peter Accardo of Houghton Library, with grace and unfailing good humor, saw the book through the publication process, and Duncan Todd produced the beautiful design.

The range of Longfellow's interests is reflected in the number of people one needs to ask for help. I can only mention three colleagues here, to each of whom I owe a particular debt of gratitude: Solveig Brunholm of the University of Southern Denmark, who guided me through the Hans Christian Andersen material (all the translations of Andersen's texts are hers); Stewart King, elder of the Wasauksing First Nation, who discussed Longfellow's use of the Ojibway language with me; and Adriana Proser of the Asia Society of New York, who helped me understand the Asian material in the exhibit. My former research assistant, Kathleen Connors, saved me from several blunders. In its final form, the text owes much to the eagle eye of Robert Arbour, a fine young scholar in his own right, who spotted numerous inconsistencies and solved many transcription problems. I am delighted to acknowledge also the substantial award I received from the Office of the Vice Provost for Research at Indiana University, which paid for the cost of the color images, and the substantial support given by my exemplary department chair, George Hutchinson.

A group of extraordinary students inspired me with their enthusiasm. Seasoned high school teachers from all over the nation, they came to spend their summer at Longfellow's alma mater, Bowdoin College, Maine, where they attended an institute sponsored by the National Endowment for the Humanities, "Hawthorne and Longfellow: A Literary Friendship." I am grateful to Charles Calhoun, Longfellow biographer extraordinaire, who directed the institute on behalf of the Maine Humanities Council, to the NEH, for sponsoring it, and to Peter Coviello, my co-instructor, who has significantly shaped my own thinking about nineteenth-century culture.

It is a special pleasure for me to acknowledge the Friends of the Longfellow House, who awarded me a grant to allow me to travel to Cambridge several times during the last year. At "Castle Craigie," as Longfellow liked to call it, the spirit of hospitality that once attracted visitors from all over the world is still alive and well today. It is, in a sense, to Longfellow's house that I have to give tribute for this publication, too. My editor at the University of Massachusetts Press, Bruce Wilcox, grew up in Cambridge, cycled up Brattle Street every morning to school at Shady Hill, and spent, as he told me, many an afternoon playing touch football in the park right across the street from Craigie House. How fortunate for me that, many years later, our paths would cross!

Christoph Irmscher
Bloomington, Indiana
December 2008

A Note on Quotations

All quotations from Longfellow's journals are from the unpublished manuscripts in the Longfellow Papers (MS Am 1340) at Houghton Library, Harvard University. To save space, entries will only be referenced by dates, not by the call number of the volume in which they appear. In my transcriptions of manuscripts by Longfellow I have sought to represent, when important and relevant, the author's revisions and corrections. Transcriptions of manuscripts by authors other than Longfellow usually only represent the final version of the text.

Quotations from Longfellow's published works follow the "Craigie" edition, *The Complete Writings of Henry Wadsworth Longfellow*, eleven vols. (Boston: Houghton, Mifflin, 1904), and are identified by parenthetical references, citing only the number of the volume and the page. Longfellow's letters (cited as *Letters*) are taken from Andrew Hilen's edition, *The Letters of Henry Wadsworth Longfellow*, six vols. (Cambridge, MA: Belknap, 1966-1982). Longfellow's anthology *Poems of Places*, thirty-one vols. (Boston: Osgood; later Houghton, Osgood & Co., 1876-1879), will be abbreviated as *Places*. References to Samuel Longfellow's biography (*Life of Henry Wadsworth Longfellow, with Extracts from his Journals and Correspondence*, three vols., Boston: Houghton, Mifflin and Company, 1891) are abbreviated as *Life*. *ML* is shorthand for *Mrs. Longfellow: Selected Letters and Journals of Fanny Appleton Longfellow (1817-1861)*, ed. Edward Wagenknecht (New York: Longmans, Green, and Co., 1950). LNHS indicates that a document or artifact is housed at the Longfellow National Historic Site on Brattle Street in Cambridge, MA.

Throughout, my discussion of the artifacts is based on ideas I have first presented in my book *Longfellow Redux* (Urbana, IL: University of Illinois Press, 2006; revised paperback edition, 2008).

PUBLIC POET, PRIVATE MAN

Introduction

On a dark and cloudy Saturday afternoon in April 1854, Henry Wadsworth Longfellow took his two boys, nine-year-old Charley and eight-year-old Erny, to town. At Galliani's "European Hotel" on Sudbury Street (the choice of the establishment speaks volumes about Longfellow's cultural preferences), they dined on macaroni and pigeon.[1] Their European meal finished, the father and his sons got up and did something profoundly American: they walked over to Moses Kimball's "Boston Museum" on Tremont Street. There they watched a performance of *Hot Corn*, a play that, in different versions, had been a rousing success in the Bowery and at Barnum's Museum in New York as well as at the National Theatre in Boston and was now in its first week at Kimball's establishment.[2] Based on Solon Robinson's vastly successful exposés of the life of the poor published in *The New York Tribune*,[3] the play, fortunately forgotten, depicted the evil effects liquor has on people, including a poor girl named Katy, who is forced to hawk roasted corn on the streets of New York in order to support her alcoholic and abusive mother. At one point during the play, a lady (whose fashionable dress identifies her as of a better class than the rest of the sorry cast) holds a red-covered book in her hand, declaring it to be "her dear Henry W. Longfellow's Poems." She then asks her milliner, "ironically," which poet she prefers, "Longfellow or Tennyson" (22 April 1854).

Longfellow was surely right when he wrote in his journal that same night that *Hot Corn* was "wretched stuff"—an assessment that apparently didn't hinder him or his kids from sampling future offerings at Kimball's Museum, among them *Uncle Tom's Cabin* (27 February 1856) and *Ali Baba and the Forty Thieves* (8 March 1856). Incidentally, the book on which *Hot Corn* was based sported chapter headings like "One Bottle Too Many, and the Catastrophe," "I Never Kiss Any But Those I Love," and "A Voice from the Grave." But what this episode, ephemeral as it seems, conveniently recalls for us is that Longfellow was a literary superstar, part of the popular culture of his time, so much so that his name would appear in a "wretched" temperance play featuring hot corn girls and legless flower-sellers, a play performed in an establishment where most of Longfellow's more high-minded contemporaries would prefer not to be

1 Charles Galliani's "European House," 91 Sudbury Street, is listed under "Public Houses in Boston" in Damrell Moore and George Coolidge's *Boston Almanac for the Year 1855*, II (Boston: Jewett, 1854) 117.

2 See "Letter from 'Acorn,'" *Spirit of the Times* 24:11, 29 April 1854: "At Kimball's Museum, during the past week, a version of 'Hot Corn' has been presented to very fair houses. It was dramatized by Charles M. Saunders."

3 The book version, titled *Hot Corn, or Life Scenes in New York Illustrated*, was published by De Witt & Davenport in 1854.

seen (Kimball and his friend, America's "Greatest Showman" P. T. Barnum, were co-perpetrators of the famous "Fejee mermaid" hoax).[4]

Longfellow doesn't tell us what answer, if any, the milliner gave (the passage doesn't appear in the novel and must have been added specifically for the play). But it wouldn't have been completely unlikely for a New York milliner to have heard of, and perhaps even to have read, Longfellow. The bulging files of Longfellow's correspondence, preserved at Houghton Library, show that his readers came from all walks of life, including a farmer from Michigan, a nine-year-old girl from Ohio, a schoolteacher from Brooklyn, and a sign-painter from Indiana (who would later become known as the "Hoosier poet" James Whitcomb Riley). Longfellow's class-transcending appeal amazed and worried many of his more fastidious contemporaries, notably Margaret Fuller, who declined to review his *Ballads and Other Poems* for *The Dial* but later lashed out against him, no holds barred, in *The New York Tribune*.[5] In her "bilious attack,"[6] published on 10 December 1845, Fuller mocked Longfellow as "a person of moderate powers," in whose poetry no "wild flowers" were allowed to grow. Edgar Allan Poe had led the way by denouncing Longfellow as "the great Mogul of the imitators,"[7] but Fuller, with biting irony, insinuated that Longfellow didn't even deserve to be called a "plagiarist." Speaking from the secure vantage point of the first person plural, she suggested that there was a consensus among all readers of refined taste and intellect about Longfellow's deficiencies: "We have been surprised that anyone should have been anxious to fasten special charges of this kind upon him, when we had supposed it so obvious that the greater part of his mental stores were derived from the work of others." Originality was unattainable to someone like Longfellow: "He has no style of his own, growing out of his own experience and observation of nature. Nature with him, whether human or external, is always seen through the windows of literature." Longfellow was so attached to "foreign" literature, and had been quoting so freely from it, declared Fuller, that in the stale world of his poetry no one could breathe freely anymore—least of all the author himself, who seemed to be acting as if he were under

4 A letter to the editor in the *Christian Enquirer* published on 18 February 1854, page 3, declared that *Hot Corn* was "unfit for family reading where there are young persons, because the mind is more occupied with the disgusting details of vice, than it is benefitted by the *shorter* moral precepts deduced therefrom."

5 Margaret Fuller to Ralph Waldo Emerson, 9 April 1842, *"My Heart Is a Large Kingdom": Selected Letters of Margaret Fuller*, ed. Robert N. Hudspeth (Ithaca, NY: Cornell, 2001) 154.

6 See Longfellow's journal, 11 December 1845. Longfellow forgave Fuller. By 1852, he was reading Emerson's *Memoirs of Margaret Fuller* with rapt attention ("extremely interesting," 12 February 1852).

7 See Poe's review of Longfellow's *Poems on Slavery, Voices of the Night, Ballads and Other Poems* and *The Waif* in *The Aristidean*, April 1845, reprinted in Poe, *Essays and Criticism*, ed. G. R. Thompson (New York: Library of America, 1984) 761.

some kind of compulsion: "He borrows incessantly, and mixes what he borrows, so that it does not appear to the best advantage."[8]

Designating him a poet solidly of the "middle class," Fuller set the stage for future disparagements of Longfellow as a writer who would appeal only to those readers who just didn't know any better. A few decades later, Alice James fired a nurse who tried to impress her by calling Longfellow "such a *deep* poet." James found the lapse unforgivable: "we parted shortly most amiably and expensively," because "to continue on so high a key was too great a strain." Her brother Henry, who called Longfellow "not quite a Tintoretto of verse," would have approved.[9]

The very fact that Longfellow's work has unleashed attacks like those by Fuller and Alice James proves, ironically, that it is far from uncontroversial. Even today, Longfellow's poetry still seems to compel some academics to offer an apology first before they devote time to reading it.[10] Shaped by the Romantic myth of the author as the lonely, heroic battler against convention, the godlike creator of inspired, irreproducible works of literature,[11] we are apt to find unacceptable the advice Longfellow gave a colleague who is now as firmly a part of the literary canon as Longfellow himself isn't (at least, not anymore). In June 1846, Nathaniel Hawthorne, "weary of most men and things," met Longfellow in town and walked with him back to the Charles River and half-way across the bridge. Worried about the toll his new office as a Salem Custom House inspector would take on his writing, Hawthorne declared that he would write "no more Tales." Longfellow would hear none of it, suggesting that Hawthorne should continue to write his stories, "up to one hundred in all," and "then give them a good round title such as 'The Hundred Tales' or 'A Century of Tales' and let them go at that" (1 June 1846).

Longfellow's recommendation—safe, practical, useful, and disappointingly materialistic—flies in the face of all we still associate with a writer's lofty calling. Thank

8 Margaret Fuller, "Review of Henry Wadsworth Longfellow, *Poems*," *New-York Daily Tribune*, 10 December 1845, reprinted in *Margaret Fuller, Critic: Writings from the New-York Tribune, 1844-1846*, ed. Judith Mattson-Bean and Joel Myerson (New York: Columbia University Press, 2000) 285-92. I am also including here a section from Fuller's later essay, "American Literature: Its Position in the Present Time, and Prospects for the Future," from her *Papers on Literature and Art* (1846), in *Margaret Fuller, American Romantic: A Selection from Her Writings and Correspondence*, ed. Perry Miller (New York: Anchor, 1963) 229-50.

9 See Alice James's entry for 13 February 1890; *The Diary of Alice James*, ed. Leon Edel (Harmondsworth: Penguin, 1964) 86. Henry James's comment was apropos of Longfellow's *Divine Tragedy*; see James to Charles Eliot Norton, 4 February 1872, in James, *Selected Letters*, ed. Leon Edel (Cambridge, MA: Belknap, 1987) 92.

10 For an interesting illustration of this dilemma, see John Seelye, "Attic Shape: Dusting off *Evangeline*," *Virginia Quarterly Review* 60.1 (Winter 1984): 21-44.

11 Janice Radway, *A Feeling for Books: The Book-of-the-Month Club, Literary Taste and Middle-Class Desire* (Chapel Hill: University of North Carolina Press, 1997) 217-18.

God, some might say, that Hawthorne didn't heed the advice. And yet, what Longfellow had said to his friend was entirely in line with his own definition of the writer's business. A few months before his walk with the despondent Hawthorne, he had read a "high-strung" article in a newspaper "stating that the Age was 'still looking for its Poet.'" And how exactly was one supposed to know, asked Longfellow sardonically, when that new poet had arrived? Were there going to be fireworks? Would the great poet's advent be "heralded by signs and wonder"? Or would he come "like a thief in the night"? (11 February 1846).

Ralph Waldo Emerson, to be sure, thought he would be able to recognize the longed-for "American bard" when he saw him, or rather *read* him: a poet "with tyrannous eye," bold enough to address the full reality of American life, from "northern trade" to the southern plantations to Oregon and Texas.[12] Longfellow, who liked Emerson and dutifully attended his public lectures when he could, was puzzled by such ideas. When he heard Emerson hold forth on "Poetry" in 1854, he made no attempt to hide his consternation: "It was full of brilliant and odd things, but not very satisfactory, at first hearing. I hope to read it one day, and perhaps understand it better" (27 April 1854). If Longfellow did read it, which seems doubtful (the lecture wasn't published until 1872, and then under a different title, "Poetry and Imagination"), we can imagine that he would have been hard pressed to recognize his own understanding of the poet's role in sentences such as these: "In the presence and conversation of a true poet, teeming with images to express his enlarging thought, his person, his form, grows larger to our fascinated eyes. And thus begins that deification which all nations have made of their heroes in every kind, —saints, poets, lawgivers and warriors."[13]

Writing, for Longfellow, was heroic only in that it required infinite, interminable discipline, the careful honing of a craft that wasn't all that different from work pursued by other people. He very much liked a remark his little daughter Annie made when they had discussed how hard it was for the fishermen of Nahant to be outside in the winter: "The trade of Poet is better, because you can do it all winter" (18 January 1861). For Longfellow, writing poetry was a civic duty, a task that depended on an audience not deifying the writer as a person but appreciating (and paying for) the services he or she rendered. Some people might fool themselves into believing that the pen is mightier than the sword, Longfellow told Richard Boyd Davy. He, for one, knew that it wasn't a "particularly safe staff to lean upon," not safe enough at any rate for the poet not to care about what his readers might think of his work.[14] When the famous Comte de Buffon sat down to work on his *Histoire Naturelle*, as Longfellow explained to James Fields, he did so in "full dress," an expression of deference for his readers. The poet should

12 Ralph Waldo Emerson, "The Poet" (1844), *Ralph Waldo Emerson*, ed. Richard Poirier (Oxford: Oxford University Press, 1990) 212-13.

13 Emerson, "Poetry and Imagination" (1875), *Emerson*, ed. Poirier, 447.

14 Longfellow to Richard Boyd Davy, 5 February 1872, *Letters* 5: 502.

do likewise, even when answering letters, felt Longfellow. Let us, he added, always be "courtly and polite" and say "handsome things to each other." In fact, as he was writing these lines he was wearing, he told Fields, "my dress-coat, with a rose in my button-hole" (17 March 1871; *Letters* 5: 409).

Writing, as Longfellow saw it, wasn't about self-revelation. When he came across a volume of Robert Southey's letters, he was appalled by how many "private thoughts" there were in them (3 August 1856). By the same token, a writer had no business telling the public what to think either. In Longfellow's view, the poet wasn't the "legislator of the world," in Shelley's famous phrase, but the patient administrator of shared cultural goods. And while the market for which he wrote was, first and foremost, American, Longfellow always remembered that many of the goods he was using had come to him from abroad—and that quite a few, if not all of them, having been re-used and refined by him, would end up being exported back again.

This book, written on the 200th anniversary of Longfellow's birth, seeks to represent Longfellow as he really was: not as the bogeyman of modernists who wanted to exorcize the pale ghosts of their Victorian past, but as a consummate literary professional who became the most popular poet America has ever had. By foregrounding the "private" Longfellow (the drawings made by and for his children, his journals, and letters sent by and to him) as well as the international, multilingual, and widely-traveled Longfellow, I hope to show

(1) how Longfellow invented poetry as a "lingua franca" in the United States, as a forum for *everyone's* private feelings; and

(2) how, along with the distinction between "public" and "private," he also overturned another opposition just as it was in the process of being solidified by some of his more nationalistic colleagues: the distinction between what is typically and purely "American" and all that is not.

Despite some recent efforts, Longfellow, who once commanded the largest audience poetry has ever had both here and abroad, is still waiting to be rediscovered.[15] The very fact that that so few of Longfellow's poems are surrounded by the "aura" (to use the term coined by Walter Benjamin) readers have been told to associate with the literary work of art means that we can approach them without the reverence that more universally accepted canonical writers sternly demand from us. For Longfellow, poetry came from a *shared* source; infinitely repeatable by future generations of writers, any given poem should not, and cannot, claim a special status for itself.

15 See, for example, Charles Calhoun's recent biography, *Longfellow: A Rediscovered Life* (Boston: Beacon, 2004), as well as J. D. McClatchy's new edition of Longfellow, *Poems and Other Writings* (New York: Library of America, 2000), and my own *Longfellow Redux*. Much of the initial impetus for the new interest in Longfellow came from Dana Gioia's 1993 essay, "Longfellow in the Aftermath of Modernism," *The Columbia History of American Poetry*, ed. Jay Parini (New York: Columbia University Press, 1993) 64-96.

In his biography of sculptor William Wetmore Story, a work commissioned by the family, Henry James finally pushed himself to offer some grudging praise for Longfellow, a poet whom he had once regarded as "bland" and uninteresting. Now that James had lived in Europe for a while, he was able to see that Longfellow commanded some interest, if not for the quality of his poetry as such then at least "for the way in which his 'European' culture and his native culture kept house together,"[16] the way in which, we might say, given our introductory anecdote, Galliani's European Hotel and Moses Kimball's American theater are allowed to coexist. Note the faint irony James manages to attach to the word "European" here, putting quotation marks around it as if to emphasize that Longfellow's ties to Europe were imagined, invented, fabricated rather than *earned,* as James's own were, by long and continued residence abroad. But at least James seemed to recognize that a firm commitment to American literature and an equally strong passion for other, non-American, cultures didn't rule each other out.

James did not understand, however, that Longfellow's cosmopolitanism was not an affectation or the result of conscious effort. Rather, it was a matter of temperamental disposition and pervasive personal need, translated into acceptable public language. Longfellow's friend Annie Fields captured that quality well in her journal. She reports that, on a warm day in late September 1873, Longfellow burst into her house on 148 Charles Street "in one of his loveliest moods," full of excitement and hoping to talk her husband "Jamie" into joining him on one of his walks to the harbor. "Come," exclaimed Longfellow, "let us go to the tea stores and smell the tea; the warm atmosphere will bring out all the odors and we can get samples." And when that failed: "Come, let us go to the wharves and see the vessels just in from Italy or Spain. It will be a lovely sight in this soft sky, and we can hear the men speaking in their native tongues."[17]

Throughout his life, Italian opera supplied Longfellow with a much-needed window into cultures other than his own, and he attended performances whenever he could. Sometimes he would even see the same opera twice within a week. Incidentally, this was a passion he shared with Walt Whitman. But unlike the latter, he was less interested in the athletic feats performed by the singers, the physical extremes to which they went and the illustrations of the power of the human voice they supplied, than in the sensuous experience of the opera as a whole, the capacity both language and music had of transporting him beyond the narrow limits defined by Bostonian propriety. "Alboni was sublime in Norma, last night," he wrote to the closest friend he ever had, Charles Sumner, on 15 February 1853. "Would you had been with us, in our snug box" (Sumner had moved to Washington in November 1851, and Longfellow had gone to the opera in the company of Sumner's brother George). And in front of Marietta Alboni,

16 Henry James, *William Wetmore Story and His Friends* (Boston: Houghton, Mifflin, and Co., 1903) 311.

17 Annie Fields, Journal, 24 September 1873, Massachusetts Historical Society.

superstar of superstars, there "glittered the cold summits of Boston Society, unmelting, unmoved, glacial, sending back neither warmth nor sound. We, who do not pretend to be above the line of vegetation, condescended to applaud, and cry 'Bravo!'" Longfellow was pleased that he had two more performances to look forward to that week, the *Barber of Seville* on Wednesday and *Don Pasquale* on Friday (*Letters* 3: 374).

For the "glacial" Bostonians, interest in things non-American carried the whiff of impropriety, of indulgence in pleasures other than those of the mind. When Longfellow tried to convince his Harvard colleagues to sign a petition for cheaper international postage, he discovered that no one "cared a pin" about the issue. In fact, James Walker, Harvard's president, proudly announced that "he had never had but one letter from Europe and he hoped that he should never have another" (Longfellow to Charles Sumner, 27 March 1852; *Letters* 3: 336-37). One of the characters in Longfellow's *Tales of a Wayside Inn* (published in several installments between 1863 and 1873), the Theologian, makes the connection between nativism and xenophobia abundantly clear when he says that he prefers the poet who wears "homespun brown" to the one "decked with fanciful array / Of cockle-shells from Outre-Mer" (4: 275). Longfellow, of course, had once written a book called *Outre-Mer*, and so it comes as no surprise when another character in *Tales of a Wayside Inn*, the Student, takes issue with that statement. The "all-encircling" literary sun doesn't set in one's backyard only, the Student says, a point accentuated by the very existence of *Tales of a Wayside Inn* itself, a book that Longfellow had intended to be an American response to Chaucer's *Canterbury Tales*.

Brief readings of three poems by Longfellow might help illustrate the premise of this book that for Longfellow—to an extent that makes him unique among his contemporaries—the native and the foreign, the new and the old, the public and the private were not opposites. Consider first a poem in which Longfellow addressed—without ever mentioning him by name—his infant son Charley. "To a Child" (1: 230-237) was written in October 1845, a month before Longfellow's second child, Ernest, was born. In loving detail, the poem recreates a boy's look at the world as it appears to him on the pictures in his nursery:

Thou gazest at the painted tiles,
Whose figures grace,
With many a grotesque form and face,
The ancient chimney of thy nursery!
The lady with the gay macaw,
The dancing girl, the grave bashaw
With bearded lip and chin;
And, leaning idly o'er his gate,
Beneath the imperial fan of state,
The Chinese mandarin.

In the child's nursery the whole globe congregates, represented by the mandarin from China, the Turkish pasha ("bashaw"), and the parrot from South America. The work of the tides went into the making of the coral rattle the child clutches in his hand, and ages of sedimentation created the silver that was used for the bells it swings:

Thousands of years in Indian seas
That coral grew, by slow degrees,
Until some deadly and wild monsoon
Dashed it on Coromandel's sand!
Those silver bells
Reposed of yore,
As shapeless ore,
Far down in the deep-sunken wells
Of darksome mines,
In some obscure and sunless place,
Beneath huge Chimborazo's base,
Or Potosí's o'erhanging pines!

After the poet has thus taken us, swiftly and casually, to Bolivia and Ecuador, he goes on to imagine, at some length, how the silver used for the child's rattle was discovered when a peasant pulled at the shallow roots of a tree. This seemingly irrelevant detail underscores what Longfellow has been trying to establish from the beginning, that the child is, indeed, the god of its world. With the arrival of each newborn babe, space and time shrink to the size of a nursery, blurring the differences between things far and near, big and small:

For thee in foreign lands remote,
Beneath a burning, tropic clime,
The Indian peasant, chasing the wild goat,
Himself as swift and wild,
In falling, clutched the frail arbute,
The fibres of whose shallow root,
Uplifted from the soil, betrayed
The silver veins beneath it laid,
The buried treasures of the miser, Time.

Margaret Fuller would have had a field day with the last line, which indeed shows up in somebody else's poem, namely Wordsworth's "On the Power of Sound."[18] But

18 Longfellow, Journal, 15 September 1850. See lines 113-14 ("Oblivion may not cover / All treasures hoarded by the miser, Time") in Wordsworth's "On the Power of Sound" (1828/1829); William Wordsworth,

the borrowing, whether inadvertent or not, doesn't invalidate Longfellow's case here. Rather, the fusion of South American mining and American restlessness with British poetry helps bring into focus the theme of the poem, which is, after all, the crossing of boundaries. Longfellow's child, a natural cosmopolite, breaks out of the confines of the nursery, "restlessly, impatiently" striving to be free, free also of the writer-father's attempts to confine him within his metaphors. Discarded is the rattle; the past means nothing to him. Here, Longfellow, referring to George Washington, the "Father of His Country," reveals that his poem is indeed autobiographical and that the setting is his own Craigie House, a patriarchal environment if ever there was one. The house resounds with the weight of grave authority and responsibility, mirrored in Longfellow's switch to ponderous catalectic trochees:

> Up and down these echoing stairs,
> Heavy with the weight of cares,
> Sounded his majestic tread;
> Yes, within this very room
> Sat he in those hours of gloom,
> Weary both in heart and head.

Note the neat effect created by the dactylic "echoing," which introduces an element of rhythmic instability into the line and thus puts us right into the resounding stairwell of the old house. But the child in his voyage towards self-discovery, a tyrannous Tamerlane rather than a meek disciple of American history, cares little about a past that to him is a burden rather than an opportunity. And the father-speaker now learns that his speculations about the "undiscovered land" of his child's future ("By what astrology of fear or hope / Dare I to cast thy horoscope") have as little relevance as his attempts to place his child in a context rife with associations of the days of yore: "Thy destiny remains untold," he admits at the end of the poem. Still, he cannot resist another nod to the past, this time to the Sicilian bowman from Virgil's *Aeneid* whose forcefully discharged arrow caught on fire as it flew:

> For, like Acestes' shaft of old,
> The swift thought kindles as it flies,
> And burns to ashes in the skies.

Almost two decades later, in *Tales of a Wayside Inn*, Longfellow offered another celebration of cosmopolitanism, this time in a more satirical vein. "The Birds of Killingworth" (4: 127-35), the only tale in the entire collection not based on a written source, tells of an attempt by the residents of Killingworth, Connecticut to purge their

The Poems, ed. John O. Hayden, 2 vols. (Harmondsworth: Penguin, 1989) 2: 667.

town of all the birds, since they destroy, as they see it, their gardens and cornfields. The masterminds of the asinine scheme are a Parson with a perverse inclination towards violence, an arrogant and vain Squire, and a self-righteous Deacon. Only the Preceptor, a schoolteacher who also happens to be a poet, comes to the defense of the birds. His speech is a success with the ladies in town but fails to impress the men, who have "no faith in fine-spun sentiment" and would rather "put their trust in bullocks and in beeves" (in other words, into their bulls and their beef; 4: 133).

Significantly, the indiscriminate massacre that ensues, a veritable "St. Bartholomew of Birds," also rids the town of all the birds of passage, foreign birds that speak "some unknown language strange and sweet." The consequences are predictable. Invaded by insects and worms, Killingworth turns into "a desert without a leaf or shade," where the wild wind bemoans "the dead children of the air"—an uncanny anticipation of the introductory chapter of Rachel Carson's *Silent Spring* (1962), where she imagines a world from which the birds have departed. In Longfellow's Killingworth, the law banning the birds from the premises is repealed. In the course of the massacre, all the native birds were killed along with the "foreign" ones. Now, the denuded town, where no birds are native anymore, needs to *import* foreigners. The anti-nativist thrust of Longfellow's narrative is obvious, as is his attempt to establish a poet as the one good guy in the poem, the birds' only, if ineffective, ally in their hour of need. However, and this twist is important, even the Poet-Preceptor is not portrayed without irony. His fan base is the teenage ladies in town, especially fair "Almira in the upper class," a girl who is, as the Poet-Preceptor has said in a sonnet dedicated to her, "as pure as water, and as good as bread" (4: 129). Longfellow's satire cuts both ways, and it is characteristic of his deflated view of authorship that his stand-in, the poet, would not be exempted from his mockery.[19]

Longfellow thought of the author not as prophet but as a partner in a cultural conversation across lines that usually separate the private and the public sphere or one country from another. An infinitely more serious and somber poem than "The Birds of Killingworth," Longfellow's "Hawthorne," written only a year later, might help confirm what I have been describing here as his democratically inclusive conception

19 Self-irony is a pervasive feature in Longfellow's voluminous journals. In 1849, for example, he was mightily impressed by actress Fanny Kemble's public readings from Shakespeare, weeping along with everybody else in the audience (though perhaps not quite as much as the gentleman with the red cravat he saw shedding a "waterproof hat full of tears," 7 February 1849). In fact, Longfellow was so taken with Kemble that he wrote a sonnet to commend Kemble for her remarkable interpretations: "How our hearts glowed and trembled as she read, / Interpreting by tones the wondrous pages / Of the great poet who foreruns the ages. . ." ("Sonnet on Mrs. Kemble's Readings from Shakespeare," 1: 319-20). A week later, he had Kemble over at his house for supper. When, after the meal was finished, he proceeded to read his sonnet to her, he all of a sudden felt like Molière's Tricotin, reading a sonnet "on Lady Somebody's fever" (26 February 1849). The reference is to a distinctly minor poet ridiculed in Molière's comedy, *Les Femmes savantes* (1672).

of authorship. There can be no doubt that Longfellow, barely recovered from his wife's terrible death a few years earlier, was in deep anguish when he wrote his elegy for his friend Hawthorne. On 23 May 1864, in Sleepy Hollow Cemetery in Concord, Massachusetts, Longfellow was watching, along with Emerson, James Fields, Holmes, Lowell, Whittier, and Franklin Pierce, Hawthorne's close friend and the former President of the United States, as Hawthorne's coffin was slowly lowered into the ground. The manuscript of *The Dolliver Romance*, unfinished at the time of his death, went into the grave with him. Like the other men, Longfellow had bared his head when the carriage bearing the grief-stricken Sophia Hawthorne passed by. A few weeks later, he sent Fields a poem he had written to commemorate the funeral. Of course, he said, he had only recorded his own impressions of that day. But, then, he asked Fields, "Did you not feel so likewise?" (*Letters* 4: 417).

I will come back to Longfellow's question later, and I would like to do so by taking a detour through another well-known but very different poem of mourning. There is no reason to assume that Herman Melville's famous "Monody" was indeed written, as previous generations of critics have suggested, for his friend Nathaniel Hawthorne, just as there is no compelling reason to believe that it wasn't.[20] Melville's poem was a *cri de cœur*, a shout from the depths of despair to be released from grief, if only temporarily, through the soothing power of words:

To have known him, to have loved him
    After loneless long;
And then to be estranged in life,
    And neither in the wrong;
And now for death to set his seal—
    Ease me, a little ease, my song!

By wintry hills his hermit-mound
    The sheeted snow-drifts drape,
And houseless there the snow-bird flits
    Beneath the fir-trees' crape;
Glazed now with ice the cloistral vine
    That hid the shyest grape.[21]

Melville's image of the vine glazed with ice, the grape hindered from ripening by wintry death, is a startling, memorable, concentrated one, a good way of bringing

20 See Corey Evan Thompson, "Melville's 'Monody': Possibly for Malcolm?" *ANQ* 19.2 (Spring 2006): 41-46.

21 *Selected Poems of Herman Melville: A Reader's Edition*, ed. Robert Penn Warren (1970; Boston: Godine, 2004) 334.

home the finality of death. By comparison, Longfellow's poem seems, as Hawthorne's biographer James R. Mellow has said, run-of-the-mill—graceful, yes, but thoroughly "conventional."[22] Longfellow, too, talks about pain, an "omnipresent" one, in fact, but his elegy seems concerned less with the speaker's personal grief than with the nature of the loss itself:

How beautiful it was, that one bright day
  In the long week of rain!
Though all its splendor could not chase away
  The omnipresent pain.

The lovely town was white with apple-blooms,
  And the great elms o'erhead
Dark shadows wove on their aërial looms
  Shot through with golden thread.

Across the meadows, by the gray old manse,
  The historic river flowed:
I was as one who wanders in a trance,
  Unconscious of his road.
(3: 137)

Melville has eyes for nothing but the feeling of deprivation itself—the sentence that begins the first stanza of his poem is never concluded, petering out in a plea for help that the next stanza tells us has no chance of success. In "Hawthorne," Longfellow, by contrast, fills his lines with seemingly extraneous detail and unremarkable imagery. Longfellow is, at heart, a narrative poet: we hear about the unexpectedly sunny, "bright" spring day on which the funeral took place, right in the middle of a rainy week, the blossoming apple trees that make the lovely, white Concord seem even whiter, the elm trees that look like gigantic looms, the "historic" Concord River flowing serenely by the house Hawthorne had once rented from the Emersons—in fact, we are tempted, as my paraphrase shows, to supply even more detail. Were it not so sad an occasion, we would almost expect the wandering poet to be dancing with the daffodils (or apple-blossoms) soon. But we know he won't. All this mundaneness, of course, serves to drive home the point that nothing is at it once was. In fact, the speaker is confused—familiar sights and voices change their meaning for him, because the one voice needed to make sense of it all is gone. Ironically, the very everydayness of the scenery jolts the speaker into shocking awareness of the loss that has befallen him and all others, in terse lines almost free of distracting imagery and dominated by the reiterated words "one" and "only."

22 James R. Mellow, *Nathaniel Hawthorne in His Times* (1980; Boston: Houghton Mifflin, 1982) 582-83.

For the one face I looked for was not there,
        The one low voice was mute;
Only an unseen presence filled the air,
        And baffled my pursuit.

This stanza comes at a pivotal point in the elegy, separating the first four stanzas from the last four. Now it becomes evident to both speaker and reader that the spatial coordinates established in the first half of the poem (Longfellow quickly reviews them again: "meadow," "manse," and "stream") are no longer relevant. They yield to what is the real center of the poem, the unavoidable grave itself, surrounded by the pine trees. And here Longfellow takes the extraordinary step of revisiting the poem whose origin he owed to Hawthorne, *Evangeline*, where the "murmuring pines" of the forest carry on and preserve the lost traditions of the Acadians:

I only hear above his place of rest
        Their tender undertone,
The infinite longings of a troubled breast,
        The voice so like his own.

There in seclusion and remote from men
        The wizard hand lies cold,
Which at its topmost speed let fall the pen,
        And left the tale half told.

Ah! who shall lift that wand of magic power,
        And the lost clue regain?
The unfinished window in Aladdin's tower
        Unfinished must remain!

Longfellow was, if the term is permitted here, a sucker for the pathetic fallacy, ascribing human qualities to nonhuman beings and things whenever and wherever he saw fit. But to him it was a device rather than a vice. In "Hawthorne," the trees also assume the voice of the deceased, expressing, in a "voice so like his own," what he would have said if he were alive. But what in *Evangeline* marked the beginning of a tale here turns into a reminder that death is indeed final—that whatever we might have left is only a "likeness," not the real thing.

Hawthorne, the author of tales "twice told" has left the world with his tale "half-told" (a reference to the *Dolliver Romance* that Fields had placed on the coffin). The great wizard is dead—no magical storytelling can make warm again the cold, rigid hand in the grave; no genie will, at Aladdin's beckoning, complete the bejeweled window in the palace, and Aladdin won't go on to live in peace for many more years. The tautology in the last two lines of Longfellow's poem is deliberate: "The unfinished window" is, well, "unfinished." What is interesting here is that the private, personal loss described at the beginning of the Hawthorne elegy—the kind of loss that dominates Melville's poem—has now become inseparable from the public one. Hawthorne was an author, an extraordinary one, and his death deprives not only Longfellow of a friend but every member of the American reading public of further books that only Hawthorne could have written.

"Did you not feel so likewise?" Longfellow had asked Fields.[23] And herein lies, arguably, the reason for Longfellow's success in his own time as well as for the slow decline of his reputation later in the century. Melville's starkly individualistic approach to grief, the rawness of his emotional appeal, is more familiar to us today than Longfellow's dream of emotional transparency, of "mutual legibility."[24] In Melville's "Monody," we get the feeling that we are witnessing someone who is exposing himself, nakedly, undisguisedly, to our intrusive eyes, someone who is almost shocking in the intensity of his grief, someone with whom we converse only privately, where no one else can hear us. Longfellow's poem for Hawthorne, on the other hand, revolves around the idea—the hope, rather—that there is no categorical difference between a public poem and a private feeling. This vision of mutual legibility is perfectly explained in a letter from actress Fanny Kemble to Longfellow written in June 1851 (see my discussion in Chapter 6 pages 133-134). Thanking Longfellow for his poetry that has helped *her* bear her own grief, she promises to help *him* in *his* time of need.

If Longfellow's work seems strange to some of us today, this might be so because we have forgotten that there is more than one kind of feeling, more than one way of grieving. Oddly enough, we may be more comfortable today sharing an emotion that makes us uncomfortable and we tend to prefer a literary text that draws us into a selective, *private* form of intimacy with an author, simply because it seems more "authentic," even subversive, since it seems to pit itself against the structures of society

23 Fields apparently did "feel likewise," ending his chapter on Hawthorne in *Yesterdays with Authors* (1871; 7th ed., Boston: Osgood, 1873) with a stanza from Longfellow's "beautiful poem" which "will always be associated with the memory of Hawthorne" (124).

24 I have taken this term from Peter Coviello, "The American in Charity: 'Benito Cereno' and Gothic Anti-Sentimentality," *Studies in American Fiction* 30.2 (Autumn 2002): 155-81; see especially page 165. In Coviello's reading of Melville, this dream of complete emotional transparency is unmasked as a terrible deception, a fantasy which, for all its benevolence, prolongs rather than helps end a history of racism. For Melville, Delano is a sentimentalist and therefore also a *bad* reader. As I am suggesting here, the example of Longfellow might help us question this easy equation of sentimentality and readerly incompetence, at least in so far as it serves as a hiding place for the elitist idea that literature *must* be complex and can only be understood by qualified readers attuned to such complexity.

at large. Longfellow will not provide us with such tortured inwardness. Where we seek therapy, Longfellow offers catharsis in the classical mode—an experience communal in its means, public in its effects. But Longfellow's poetry doesn't really engage in "public sentiment" either, to use a term that has been tossed around in recent discussions of literary sentimentality. Quite unspecific when it comes to describing actual emotions and their causes, Longfellow's poems don't seek healing by performing normally intimate experiences on a national stage.[25] Modern literary critics usually associate "sentimentality" with ways in which audiences can be controlled and/or manipulated. But the attractiveness of Longfellow's poetry came from the open invitation it extended to the reader actively to recognize him- or herself in what the poet had written ("Did you not feel so likewise?"). Its implicit message was that, were it not for the craftsmanship and the learning that really good poetry requires, anyone who felt "likewise" and had been present at the funeral could have written that elegy for Hawthorne.

Longfellow was experienced in grieving—he had lost both of his wives, as well as one of his six children. Nevertheless, he never let personal trauma cloud what he perceived as the real purpose of his elegy. One of the most poignant truths about "Hawthorne" is that Longfellow's authorship is almost incidental to the poem. The only writer who matters here is Hawthorne, and his literary "wizardry" has ended. Along with his readers, Longfellow assumes the posture of the bereaved admirer, stunned by an unspeakable loss—that is, a loss not merely to the writer's "intimate" friends but to anyone who cares about American literature.

The nineteenth century was the golden age of private life, according to Michelle Perot. This was the time "when the vocabulary and reality of private life took shape."[26] We can see the effects of that in Longfellow's notes about his children, his and his wife's desire to save every scrap of paper their children had drawn on as well as, later on, in the adult Charley Longfellow's wish to turn his room in the Brattle Street house into his personal museum of travel souvenirs, an index to the places all over the world he had been. As a writer, Longfellow's intention, strange as it now seems, was to find a poetic language in which this new idea of a private realm might not be seen as opposed to, or even different from, the public sphere: the world of shared, communal discourse. This has put him at odds with a development in literary history in which the literary is relegated to the sphere of private, individual enjoyment—and in which the authenticity of literary communication is measured by the extent to which it separates itself from mass consumption.

25 Glenn Hendler, "Bloated Bodies and Sober Sentiments: Masculinity in 1840s Temperance Narratives," *Sentimental Men: Masculinity and the Politics of Affect in American Culture,* ed. Mary Chapman and Glenn Hendler (Berkeley: University of California Press, 1999) 125-48.

26 See Michelle Perot, "Introduction," *A History of Private Life: From the Fires of Revolution to the Great War,* ed. Michelle Perot, trans. Arthur Goldhammer (Cambridge, MA: Belknap, 1990) 2-3.

In Longfellow's world, the writer is a seemingly diminished figure—a mediator rather than a legislator, someone who doesn't "make it new" but *re*-makes it, whatever that "it" might be, again and again and again: a far cry from the "liberating God" of Emerson's 1844 essay. Poetry, insists Longfellow, is everybody's business. The latter is the guiding idea behind this book, which demonstrates how intensely invested Longfellow was in family, fatherhood, and friendship (Chapters 1, 3, 4). It also shows how these supposedly "private" aspects of his life constantly intersected with the more public aspects of his understanding of authorship, his collaborative projects (*The Poets and Poetry of Europe*, *Evangeline*, *The Divine Comedy*), and his commitment to his readers (Chapters 5 and 6). Longfellow's provocative conception of American literature as deeply "transatlantic" manifested itself in his penchant for travel (Chapter 2), his passion for translation (Chapter 7), and his interest in establishing American literature as part of Goethean "Weltliteratur" ("grand cosmopolitan literature"; Chapter 8). In Longfellow's poetry, public speech and private feeling, Galliani's European restaurant and Kimball's American theater, are two sides of the same coin, which is why his readers from both here and abroad, though strangers (as they readily admitted), felt they could readily enter into a personal conversation with Longfellow, if only for the length of a few lines, the space of a letter.

Chapter 1: From Portland to Cambridge

HENRY WADSWORTH LONGFELLOW, the most popular poet America has ever known, was born on 27 February 1807 under rather unspectacular circumstances, in his aunt's three-story frame house at the corner of Fore and Hancock streets, right on the waterfront of Portland, Maine. He was the second son of Stephen Longfellow, a promising Harvard-educated lawyer originally from Gorham, Maine, and the memorably named Zilpah Longfellow, née Wadsworth, from an established Portland family. A few weeks after his birth, the family moved into the house on Congress Street where Zilpah had grown up and which had been left to the young family by Zilpah's father, the distinguished Revolutionary War veteran and congressman Peleg Wadsworth, when he retired to the family farm in Hiram, Maine. For medical services in connection with Henry's birth, Dr. Shirley Erving of Portland charged the stately sum of $17.50.[1]

Longfellow's childhood in Portland was, by all accounts, a happy one. Although not a wild child, he wasn't a bookworm either and seems to have fit in easily, a quality that must have stood him in good stead in a family that kept growing, filling the rooms of a house that had already seemed too small to Zilpah when she lived there as a girl. By 1819, Stephen and Zilpah had eight children: after Stephen Jr. and Henry came Elizabeth, born in 1808, Anne (1810), Alexander (1815), Mary (1816), Ellen (1817), and, finally, Samuel, the poet's future biographer, who was born in 1819.

The Portland Henry Longfellow knew as a child was feeling the effects of the Embargo Act of 1807, which prohibited trade with the British, and the War of 1812. In "My Lost Youth" (3: 39-42), the ode to his hometown in which Longfellow later remembered (and romanticized) his childhood experiences, the gun battle between the American brig *Enterprise* and the British brig *Boxer* off Monhegan Island, thundering "o'er the tide," still plays a prominent role. But so does the ocean, "the sheen of far-surrounding seas." Longfellow came from a family of seafarers. His uncle, Samuel Stephenson, was a shipmaster, and Henry was named for his mother's brother, Lieutenant Henry Wadsworth of the U.S. Navy, who served on the *U.S.S. Constitution* and died a hero at the Battle of Tripoli in 1804. With its wharves, merchant vessels, and bearded sailors, the "beautiful city ... seated by the sea" would leave its traces everywhere in Longfellow's poetry. Throughout his life, an "almost irresistible attraction" drew Longfellow to the ocean (18 July 1847). Arguably, he was as sea-savvy as some of the writers more often

1 "Dr. Shirley Erving's bill at birth of Henry W. Longfellow, 1807," Maine Historical Society (Coll. 185, Box 2, fl. 17). The bill can also be viewed on the Maine Memory Network (www.mainememory.net), no. 12370.

mentioned, such as Herman Melville or Richard Henry Dana, except that his preferred vantage point, the position from which he liked to watch the tides and the sudden shifts in the weather, more often than not was the beach. Henry David Thoreau, not given to praising people unless there was ample reason to do so, in one of the chapters of *Cape Cod* called Longfellow a "weather-wise" writer (he went on to quote his poem "Seaweed").[2]

Longfellow would return to Portland regularly, catching his breath every time he approached and could see the city of his birth from a distance. This is what happened, for example, on a splendid August morning in 1838: "A glorious scene—with market-boats rowing city-ward—rocks—promontories—light-houses—forts and wooded islands." A less poetically inclined fellow passenger commented, "That 'ere hill takes off the heft of the city." Yes, Longfellow said to himself, quietly: "so it did, thou commonplace individual, but couldst thou not wait patiently till we rounded the point yonder and the break-water and the city rose before thee beautiful as Venus from the bath?" (1 August 1838). A few years later, while vacationing in Portland's Back Cove, he watched a couple of children chasing and then catching a screaming sea-bird, a scene that powerfully brought back memories of what that closeness to the water had meant to him when he was a boy. The bird's capture was loudly celebrated by an assortment of "little savages" on the shore: "Show him for a sight and ask a cent apiece!" A boy with a somewhat gentler disposition, "the young poet of the rising generation," sang out as he ran past Longfellow: "It was a crane / Flew down the lane." Longfellow recorded this little poem and was instantly taken back to the time when he roamed the streets of Portland: "I remember, when I was a boy of his size, as with two companions I dashed through the street on a stick, crying out: 'We three / Champions be'" (1 August 1846).

Portland was where Longfellow became a poet, long before he had written a line—a tangle of sounds and sights, as he recalled in an undated fragment, a misty backdrop to feelings he would be able to articulate fully only much later:

> Out of my childhood now rises in my memory the recollection of many things, rather as poetic impressions than as prosaic facts. Such are the damp mornings of early Spring, with the loud crowing of cocks, and the cooing of pigeons on roofs of barns. Very distinct in connection with these are the indefinite longings incident to childhood; feelings of wonder and loneliness, which I could not interpret, and scarcely then took cognizance of. But they have remained in my mind.
> ("Materials on Childhood," Longfellow Papers, MS Am 1340 [145] folder 4)

2 *Cape Cod* was published in its entirety only after Thoreau's death, in 1865. For the reference to Longfellow, see Henry David Thoreau, *A Week on the Concord and Merrimack Rivers, Walden, or Life in the Woods; The Maine Woods; Cape Cod*, ed. Robert F. Sayre (New York: Library of America, 1985) 896-97.

Longfellow's father was, judging from the letters that have survived, stiff but not unkind. Zilpah considered him her "dear friend"; on the day of Stephen's funeral, Henry wrote in his journal that he had lost an "excellent father."[3] Indeed, Stephen Longfellow's letters reveal a man intent on dispensing useful advice to his children, in ponderous prose weighed down by his good intentions. Under the polished surface, however, Stephen was unhappy, dissatisfied with his apparent failure as a lawyer (unlike his father, he never became a judge) and fearful that the political duties he had assumed to compensate for his lack of professional advancement would soon overwhelm him. In 1821, Stephen suffered his first attack of epilepsy, and in 1823, just after he had been elected to the United States Congress, he confessed to Zilpah that he could hardly go on: "I am uncommonly feeble & exhausted .... I have lost all confidence in myself."[4] Outwardly, he continued to play his part. When Longfellow's second wife Fanny met Stephen Longfellow in 1843, she called him "stately" (she also found "no trace of Henry" in either of his parents).[5]

Longfellow's father wasn't home much, either because he worked long hours in court or because he was traveling on political business. Zilpah, battling a variety of health problems, came to rely more and more on the help of her sister Lucia, who also lived in the house, "one of those," as Longfellow would later say about Sally Manchester in *Kavanagh*, "who are born to work, and accept their inheritance of toil as if it were play" (8:365). In 1814, Stephen was elected representative to the General Court of Massachusetts in Boston, a position that required that he spent even more time away from home. On 23 January 1814, he sat down and wrote a letter to his six-year-old son Henry, apparently in response to a note he had received from him. Stephen's brief letter marks the beginning of many later exchanges in which he would lecture his son about the benefits of good epistolary skills.[6] Tantalizing Henry with the prospect of a fabulous gift, a "pretty drum," he then said he might not be able to get that for him after all, either because it was too expensive or because the problems caused by the war would prevent

3 Zilpah Longfellow to Mary Longfellow Greenleaf, 2 February 1850, LNHS; Longfellow, Journal, 5 August 1849. My account of Stephen Longfellow is indebted to Joyce Butler's excellent essay, "The Longfellows: Another Portland Family," *The Maine Historical Society Quarterly* 27.4 (1987): 20-41.

4 Stephen Longfellow to Zilpah Longfellow, 20 September 1823, LNHS.

5 After he died, however, Fanny would gratefully recall that Stephen had always treated her with "tenderness" (*ML* 156).

6 See, for example, Stephen Longfellow to Henry Wadsworth Longfellow, 26 December 1824: "a literary man must remember that taste & scholarship are as much displayed in correspondence as in any exercise—you should also recollect that ease & elegance of composition in letters affords great pleasure to friends" (Letters to Longfellow, Houghton, bMS Am 1340.2 [3516]). Longfellow answered somewhat indignantly that he *would* write to his friends with greater pleasure "if they as correspondents would give me fairer opportunities" (*Letters* 1: 99).

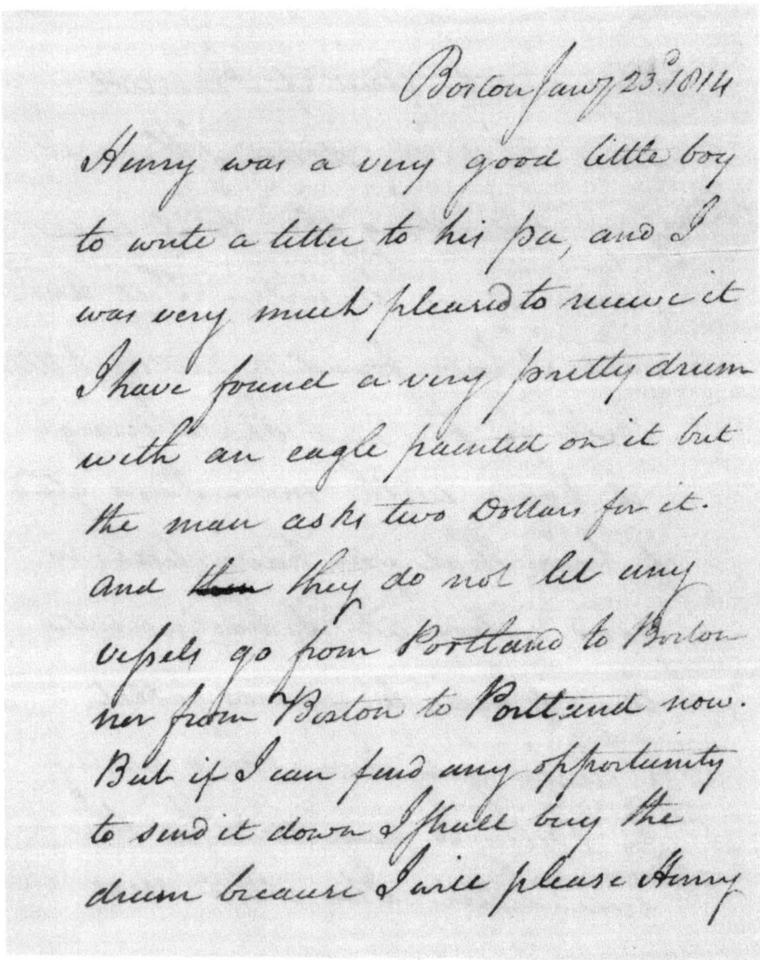
Boston Jany 23. 1814
Henry was a very good little boy
to write a letter to his pa, and I
was very much pleased to receive it
I have found a very pretty drum
with an eagle painted on it but
the man asks two Dollars for it.
and ~~then~~ they do not let any
vessels go from Portland to Boston
nor from Boston to Portland now.
But if I can find any opportunity
to send it down I shall buy the
drum because I will please Henry

Figure 1. Stephen Longfellow to Henry Wadsworth Longfellow, 23 January 1814, "Materials on Childhood," Longfellow Papers, Houghton, MS Am 1340 (166)

him from sending it to Portland. But Henry would get *something*, and so would his sisters Anne and Elizabeth:

> Henry was a very good little boy to write a letter to his pa, and I was very much pleased to receive it I have found a very pretty drum with an eagle painted on it but the man asks two Dollars for it. And they do not let any vessels go from Portland to Boston nor from Boston to Portland now. But if I can find any opportunity to send it down I shall buy the drum because I will please Henry very much. And if I cannot send down the drum I shall buy something else that

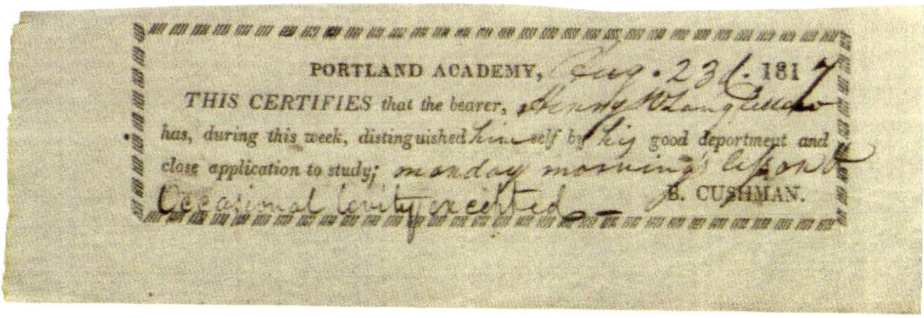
PORTLAND ACADEMY, 181
THIS CERTIFIES that the bearer,
has, during this week, distinguished self by good deportment and
close application to study;
B. CUSHMAN.

Figure 2. School certificate for Henry Wadsworth Longfellow, Portland Academy, 23 August 1817, "Materials on Childhood," Longfellow Papers, Houghton, MS Am 1340 (166)

will please him as will [sic]. Tell Ann [sic] that I have found a pretty little Bible for her, and shall bring it home with me—I am glad to hear that you have been so good a boy at School, and are likely to get a billet—I shall get something pretty for Betsy to pay her for the nice letter she sent me you must save all your billets until I come home & then I shall know how good a boy you have been—If I can get time I shall write you & Stephen an other letter Still about the State House & the Theatre & other things that there are in Boston. Give my love to Betsy and Ann & tell them I shall write to them next time—

S. Longfellow.

("Materials on Childhood," Longfellow Papers, Houghton, MS Am 1340 [166], FIGURE 1)

When Henry Longfellow was five, his parents sent him to the Portland Academy, a private institution where his older brother, Stephen, was also enrolled:

Portland Academy *Aug. 23d.* 1817
This certifies that the bearer, *Henry W. Longfellow* has, during this week, distinguished *him*self by *his* good deportment and close application to study; *monday morning's lesson & Occasional levity excepted.—*
("Materials on Childhood", Longfellow Papers, Houghton, MS Am 1340 [166], FIGURE 2)

At age fourteen, Henry was admitted to Bowdoin College in Maine, a campus safely removed from the potential depravities of urban life. Henry at first remained at home, studying under the supervision of a tutor. A year later, his parents allowed him to move to Brunswick. Pleased with Henry's aptitude for serious study, Stephen Longfellow unrelentingly pushed him to become a lawyer. Henry's far less manageable brother Stephen, an unruly student at Bowdoin where Henry was now near the top of his class, did end up working in his father's practice. Stephen's desire that Henry, too, join the fold, instead of fruitlessly seeking "future eminence in literature" (*Letters* 1: 94), led to a number of pointed exchanges in their correspondence. "I can be a lawyer," Longfellow wrote on 24 January 1825, when he had reached the height of exasperation, "for some lawyers are mere simpletons" (*Letters* 1: 104).

Stephen spared no efforts for the cause. In a letter sent from Washington, he reiterated an argument that he must have made many times before—namely that there wasn't enough wealth in America to "afford encouragement and patronage to mere literary men"—and then zeroed in on a poem he had seen printed in a newspaper, which he suspected to have been written by his son. As if to underline his contention that literature wasn't a profession but a pastime anyone with a little education could pursue, Stephen pointed out a metrical error in the second line of the sixth stanza, which had too many feet. He felt it would be "improved by substituting *lonely* for *motionless*." (The poem, "Autumnal Nightfall," was indeed by Henry Wadsworth Longfellow; it had appeared in *The United States Literary Gazette* of 1 December 1824, and Stephen's criticism was right on target.)[7]

Longfellow met his father half-way; rather than seeking to live a "literary life," he became a professor of modern languages, first at Bowdoin College, his own alma mater, and then at Harvard College, positions for which he prepared himself with periods of extensive and intensive travel in Europe. Although he took his teaching seriously and went to bat for his students and the department, Longfellow's journals show that, at least in his darker moods, he considered teaching a "laborious plough-share" (22 March 1838). At Harvard he was, he wrote in his journal, "working in the crypts of life"; no wonder that he felt entitled to mock all those who observed "education only from afar" and therefore spoke of it in unrealistic terms of wonder and praise: "You see the great picture only hanging in the light, not the grinding of the oil and paint, nor the pulling of hair from the camel's back for the brushes" (3 April 1848). At the same time, he often felt he needed his professorial "harness" (11 January 1855) to write poetry; indeed, he did not resign his Harvard professorship until it had become abundantly clear that he would be able to make a living solely as a writer.

Stephen Longfellow spent the last years of his life reading, taking naps, and going for walks in the neighborhood. Even he was now ready to admit that his world-famous son's works were a significant improvement over, say, "Autumnal Nightfall." Zilpah, his less restrained mother, told Longfellow, in a letter written in 1845, that the words from his pen went "directly to my heart and made me happy."[8] But happiness had not been Stephen's lot. He died on 3 August 1849, aged seventy-three. After his father's funeral,

7 See the letter by Stephen Longfellow to Longfellow, 26 December 1824 (see note 6), LNHS.

8 Zilpah Longfellow to Mrs. Bartlett, 7 August 1843, LNHS. "I feel exceedingly glad, that my books find so much favor in your sight," Longfellow writes to his father on 16 January 1840, after *Voices of the Night* has been in the stores for a few weeks (*Letters* 2: 209).

Henry briefly revisited the life that could have been his: "Went to Father's Office—the dusty—deserted, silent place—where he toiled so day after day—The ledger showed his reward in page after page of unpaid charges! Alas! for a lawyer in a little town" (9 August 1849). As Henry was heading back to Portland, the train passed Portland's Western Cemetery, the stones "gleaming white" in the ocean air. In an extraordinary scene, Longfellow imagined his "poor, old father" in his shroud, waving "a last adieu" to him (25 August 1849).

In February 1854, Longfellow resigned from Harvard. He had come to enjoy greatly his pleasant life in "Castle Craigie," the Georgian mansion his father-in-law, the wealthy industrialist Nathan Appleton, had bestowed upon his daughter Frances Elizabeth ("Fanny") on her wedding to Professor Longfellow on 13 July 1843. He loved the large rooms of the house in which he had first lived as a lodger, the comfortable bed, the buttercups in the grass outside, the lilac bushes, and the omnipresent associations with the colonial past, specifically George Washington, who had resided there from 1775 to 1776.[9]

Longfellow had met Fanny Appleton in July 1836 in Switzerland, barely six months after his first wife, Mary Potter, had died from a miscarriage in Rotterdam. Zilpah had liked Mary, the daughter of a Portland judge, very much and was delighted with Henry's marriage, "far more so, than if Henry had introduced us to a city lady of fortune, with her airs & graces & expensive habits, as our future daughter-in-law."[10] Longfellow's new love interest was, in some ways, Zilpah's worst nightmare come true. Initially, Fanny rejected all of Henry's advances, casting a dark shadow over his first years as the new Smith Professor of Modern Languages at Harvard. Longfellow's journal entries—the ones he didn't delete—reveal the tortures he suffered during that time, when his mind was, as he put it, occupied by "one only thought" (10 June 1838). Finally, Fanny relented. On 10 May 1843, she sent the man she had been calling "the Professor" a note in which she accepted his love. Thus began what Longfellow deemed his "Vita Nuova of happiness" (10 May 1844). Fanny now regretted her coldness during the past few years. In January 1844, to make amends, she began reading Longfellow's old journals, reliving his life during the years she had rejected him: "I am thankful to glean any part of it that was lost to me—how much through my own strange blindness.... I regain my birthright in him, as it were, by reading these faithful pages" (*ML* 104-5). Longfellow supplied what he thought was missing by compiling an account of the circumstances under which he

9 See 15 May 1848 ("How delightful the large rooms, the comfortable bed") or 1 June 1850 ("The old house looks delightfully [sic]—the green grass waving in the wind and a whole California of buttercups, like scales of gold in the rolling waves of the sacraments").

10 Zilpah Longfellow to Stephen Longfellow, 14 July 1833, LNHS.

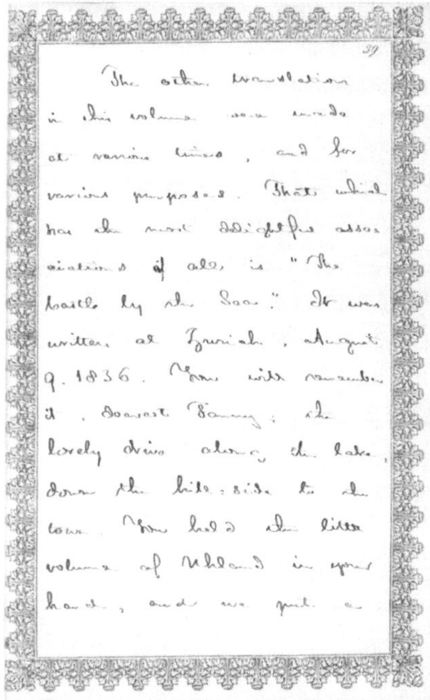

Figure 3. Longfellow, "Manuscript Gleanings" ("To Fanny, the Beloved, 6 October 1846"), p. 39, Longfellow Papers, Houghton, MS Am 1340 (146)

had written his earlier poetry. He inscribed the little volume, a commercially produced commonplace book,[11] "To Fanny, the Beloved, October 6, 1846."

Some of the entries in the little book seem self-serving, as if the 39-year-old professor still needed to convince Fanny that she had made the right choice. "The book has gone through eleven editions, besides the cheap edition in New York and the illustrated one in Philadelphia," he writes about *Voices of the Night*, for example. "Together these several editions make between nine and ten thousand copies; and adding the cheap Boston edition, afterwards united with the New York, between eleven and twelve thousand." As if he suddenly realized how this must sound to Fanny, Longfellow then stopped himself: "But these are details of business; and surely I did not think of them when I began these brief notes, dear Fanny, for our amusement." Perhaps the most important passage, from Fanny's point of view, was contained in a

11 According to the publisher of the commonplace book, "No attempt has hitherto been made … to supply the World of Literature and Fashion, and more especially the Fair portion of it, with an elegant and suitable Depository for those Selections which the reading of even the passing hour offers to its votaries. It is under such an impression, and wishing to remedy the defect just pointed out, that this Specimen of an entirely new Literary Scrap Book is here submitted to the attention of the public at large."

Figure 4. Fanny Appleton Longfellow, carte-de-visite, ca. 1860; photographer: J. W. Black, 173 Washington Street, Houghton *2001M-8, box 2

short note on pages 39 to 40 about the translations Longfellow had included in *Voices of the Night*:

> The other translations in this volume were made at various times, and for various purposes. That which has the most delightful associations of all is "The Castle by the Sea." It was written at Zurich, August 9. 1836. You will remember it, dearest Fanny; the lovely drive along the lake, down the hill-side to the town. You held the little volume of Uhland in your hand, and we put a stanza or two into verse and we drove along in the spacious traveling Carriage. In the evening we completed it; you recording as I translated. Some of the best lines are yours. ("Manuscript Gleanings," Longfellow Papers, Houghton, MS Am 1340 [146], FIGURE 3)

For Longfellow, this particular passage recalls the beginning not just of their shared emotional but also their intellectual life. As he remembered it, Fanny's and his first experience together was a *collaborative* translation—in this case, of a rather spooky ballad by the German poet Ludwig Uhland (6: 267-68)—an activity in which Fanny was able to hold her own or maybe even do the language professor one better: "Some of the best lines are yours." Apparently, Longfellow here wanted to redeem himself, after the rather different and not consistently flattering portrait of Fanny he had painted in *Hyperion* (see Chapter 5, pages 119-21), where she appears as the Englishwoman "Mary Ashburton," "not beautiful, but very intellectual." In the novel, Longfellow's alter ego, Paul Flemming, eager to impress Miss Ashburton with his fluency in German, indeed reads Uhland's "The Castle by the Sea" to her. But there is no indication here that he is ready to share: "Do you repeat the German after me," Flemming tells Mary somewhat condescendingly, "and I will translate to you."[12]

Unsurprisingly, Fanny Appleton was at first none too pleased with Longfellow's novel and, by implication, its creator. In a letter to her close friend Emmeline Austin, she said *Hyperion* was "a thing of shreds and patches like the author's mind" *(ML* 58). She wasn't a fan of Longfellow's poetry either, offering, in another letter to her friend, the following devastating but funny assessment of Longfellow's *Ballads and Other Poems*, a rather slim volume: "The Professor has a creamy new volume of verses out—rather meager *selon moi*, the cream of thought being somewhat thinner than that of the binding" (*ML* 79).

In a widely circulated image of her, the book Fanny carries in her hand is most certainly not a prop (Fanny Appleton Longfellow, carte-de-visite, 1860; Houghton *2001M-8, box 2, FIGURE 4). Fanny's intellectual abilities were at least equal to her husband's. Although she never put her skills to use apart from her letter-writing or journalizing, she refused to be limited to the role of the Victorian "angel in the house." She wasn't "terribly fussy" when it came to domestic duties, she readily admitted, and always liked to leave her house behind, even for extended periods of time (*ML* 180). But she was no bluestocking either. The actress Fanny Kemble, she felt, should give up the fight against her abusive ex-husband, rather than being "dashed in two" by him: "a woman cannot contend with a man" (to Emmeline Austin Wadsworth, *ML* 181). And like most Bostonian bluebloods, she didn't approve of *The World's Own*, Julia Ward Howe's play about a peasant girl wronged by, and then seeking revenge on, her aristocratic lover: "there is tragedy enough in life to inspire a drama without descending to vice" (*ML* 209). However, Fanny did show sympathy for the woman in New York who got acquitted after stabbing the man who had seduced her, welcoming that men now "begin to feel for women in these matters" (Journal, 9 February 1844; *ML* 107).

12 See *Hyperion* III, chapter 4 (8: 209). Longfellow's journal for 9 August 1836 corroborates the account given in *Hyperion*. "I translated Uhland's ballad," wrote Longfellow, while Fanny Appleton "was scribe on the occasion."

Figure 5. Longfellow, Craigie House, watercolor and pencil on paper, early 1850s, LONG 4168, LNHS

Not afraid to admit the "strong passion" she felt for Henry, she also freely expressed her jealousy when he took her to Portland, where she saw the "green snake" of his past romantic associations lurking in Deering Woods, as if she felt the need to guard "her domain from intruders" (27 July 1843; *ML* 90-91). Fanny had her own opinions about Longfellow's literary contemporaries, such as Bronson Alcott ("Plato-Skimpole," *ML* 190), Ralph Waldo Emerson ("Where has his humanity gone, I wonder?" *ML* 151), and Nathaniel Hawthorne, whose silence reminded her of "Dante's poor sinners" and their inability "to weep through their frozen lids" (*ML* 112). She loved her children, or "chicks," as she liked to refer to them, unconditionally, meticulously keeping track of their doings in a document she called "The Chronicle of the Children of Craigie Castle" (LONG 21576). At the same time, she seems to have accepted her children's more uncomplicated relationship with their father and was grateful for Henry's ability to contain Charley, who was often abusive to her: "Charley struck me with a stick and the pain made me cry like a baby. He has grown very insolent, but a few words from his papa softened him and he begged my pardon very penitently" (*ML* 144).

Displeased with the pronounced Calvinistic bent of many American children's books, she briefly contemplated becoming an author herself: "I often thought of writing some myself, knowing so well what pleased best my own children. They liked always stories of simple truth, without being spiced with horrors or with fairy fancy, but as they get older their tastes are less innocent" (*ML* 186). An even stronger pacifist than Longfellow, she was less inclined to tolerate Charley's obsession with guns: "the truth is that I do not like to have little boys play soldiers though I don't mind their playing with them" (*ML* 196). In her reading, she seemed to gravitate towards women writers, Charlotte Brontë's *Shirley*, for example ("wonderfully good," *ML* 163), the poetry of Elizabeth Barrett Browning, whose "prodigious genius" she greatly admired (*ML* 178), and Harriet Beecher Stowe, whose *Uncle Tom's Cabin*, her husband's efforts notwithstanding, she pronounced to be "the most American book we have had" (to Samuel Longfellow, 10 May 1852; *ML* 189). But she was not an undiscriminating reader by any means: she had doubts, for example, about Alice Cary's poetry ("it rings, like the mocking-bird of too many other songsters, as do most of her sister and brother poets"; *ML* 189).

Fanny's journals and letters show her to be an accomplished writer and careful observer, with a gift for pithy metaphors (the preacher she hears on Thanksgiving Day does not, she writes, "boldly venture upon the great sea of Truth, but plays well on the shore"; *ML* 145). Her descriptions are concise and witty. Visiting the Shakers in New Hampshire, for example, she memorably evokes their way of dancing, "knees bent, with a sort of galvanized hop, hands paddling like fins, and voices chanting these wild airs" (*ML* 62). On the whole, however, Fanny Appleton Longfellow remains somewhat inscrutable, a quality that she admits she cultivated. On 28 December 1855, she wrote in her journal that, growing older, she was coming to enjoy "more and more my *shell*," and she compared herself to one of the turtles she had found in Louis Agassiz's "wonderful" new book, the second volume of his *Contributions to the Natural History of the United States of America*, where their "physiognomies are so accurately painted" (*ML* 213).

Fanny and her husband greatly enjoyed company, especially visitors from abroad who reminded them of the "easy, delightful pleasure" of life in Europe (Fanny Longfellow to Emmeline Austin Wadsworth, 15 May 1860, *ML* 221). At the same time, Craigie House remained the center of their lives. Here it is featured in one of her husband's watercolor and pencil drawings from the early 1850s (LONG 4168, LNHS, FIGURE 5). Fanny and Henry are portrayed on the right, in front of the east porch or "piazza," as the Longfellows would have called it, while Charley, Erny, and possibly Alice can be seen peering out of one of the windows on the second floor. Technically, the watercolor is perhaps less accomplished than other work produced by Longfellow (the outlines are static, the people frozen in their poses), but it is so radiant with color—the yellow paint of the house, the green shutters, the lawn, the red curtains of the study and the patterned ones of the parlor, the flushed cheeks of the boys in the upstairs nursery[13]—that it effortlessly conveys the happiness felt by the inhabitants.

13 The nursery had been Henry's study and was surrendered to "noisy Charley" in 1846 (see Longfellow's journal, 22 June 1846).

Henry's and Fanny's marriage was an exceedingly fulfilled one. Longfellow's journals are replete with passages in which he expresses his delight at seeing his wife's face, at night, for example, in the lamplight, as she is bending over a book (26 May and 22 June 1846). And he never forgets to acknowledge the special anniversary they celebrated every year on 10 May, their own personal "Easter" (9 May 1847). Aware of the "plight of women," he arranged for Fanny to become the first woman in the United States to give birth (to their daughter Fanny) under the influence of ether. Longfellow had to enlist a dentist to administer the drug, since "no physician has tried it in cases of *accouchement*; nor seems very much disposed to try it" (6 April 1847). The next day, 7 April 1847, Fanny "heroically inhaled … the great nepenthe" and a healthy baby girl was born. "While under the vapor, there was no loss of consciousness" and "no pain," a result that Longfellow thought extremely important: "Women have so much to suffer. I told [Fanny] that she could congratulate herself upon having had it in her power to show her countrywomen how some of their agony might be safely avoided" (9 April 1847). One would be hard pressed to find passages like these in the diaries of his contemporaries. It is remarkable, too, that Longfellow observed his daughter's birth himself, instead of lingering somewhere else in the house, where most of his male friends and contemporaries would have been found. Think of Cassy's father in Elizabeth Stoddard's novel *The Morgesons*, who is waiting outside as his son is born, smoking meditatively by the fire.[14]

Some rumors to the contrary aside (Fanny once got extremely upset when it was alleged "that Henry and I were among the unhappy slaves of the matrimonial oar"—an "impossibility," she told her brother),[15] the Longfellows were so widely known to be blessed with happiness that when disaster finally struck, the shock waves rippled through the entire community, if not the country. On 9 July 1861, Fanny Longfellow was in the library, sealing a small paper package containing a lock of Edie's curls, when her light muslin dress suddenly caught fire.[16] She ran into the adjoining study, waking Longfellow, who, hoping to extinguish the flames, wrapped her in a rug and burned himself quite severely in the process. Fanny died the next morning and, on July 13, was buried in Mount Auburn Cemetery, with Longfellow still too ill to attend. A day later, her father, Nathan Appleton died, too. Afraid that he was "growing idiotic," Longfellow begged his friend Cornelius Felton that he not be sent to an asylum (C. C. Felton to Charles Sumner, 10 July 1861, *ML* 242). "How I am alive after what my eyes have seen, I know not," a dazed Longfellow wrote a month later to Fanny's sister Mary, struggling for words to describe the end of the "beautiful life" that he and Fanny had led together: "I never looked at her without a thrill of pleasure; she never came into a room where I

14 Stoddard, *The Morgesons* (New York: Carleton, 1862) 29.

15 Fanny Appleton Longfellow to Thomas Gold Appleton, 28 February 1847 (*ML* 127).

16 There are different accounts of how the fire started; see Calhoun, *Longfellow* 216-18.

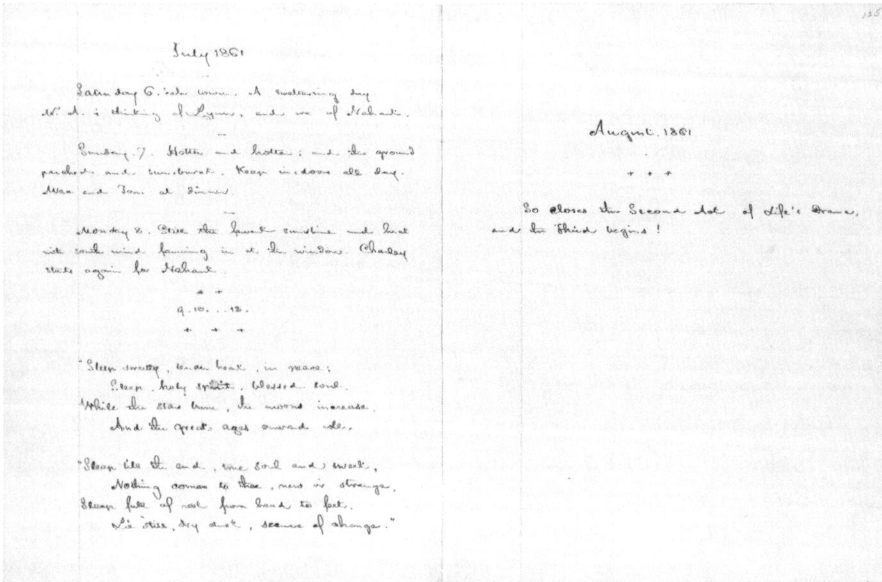

July 1861

9. 10. . . 12.

"Sleep sweetly, tender heart, in peace;
Sleep, holy spirit, blessed soul,
While the stars burn, the moons increase,
And the great ages onward roll.

"Sleep till the end, true soul and sweet,
Nothing comes to thee new or strange.
Sleep full of rest from head to feet;
Lie still, dry dust, secure of change."

August 1861

So closes the Second Act of Life's Drama,
and the Third begins!

Figure 6. Longfellow, entries for July/August 1861, from Journal, 1 Jan 1860-25 Dec 1862, pp. 124-25, Longfellow Papers, Houghton, MS Am 1340 (209)

was without my heart beating quicker, nor went out without my feeling that something of the light went with her" (*Letters* 4: 242). A few months after Fanny's death, six ballet dancers in Philadelphia burned to death after a flame from a gas jet had ignited the light gauze dress of one of them, a horrific accident that prompted *The Medical and Surgical Reporter* to condemn the "existing fashion of hoop skirts," which had already claimed several lives: "Among these we may mention Mrs. Longfellow." The authors of the editorial called not only for better guards to be placed over open fires but also for more experiments with chemical solutions that would help render "the light material of ladies dresses blaze-proof."[17]

The Victorian obsession with hair, which had, in a sense, cost Fanny her life, also impelled someone, in the last hours of her life or right after her death, to cut off one of her curls. Longfellow saved the sad memento in an envelope and, in understandable distress, wrote the wrong year on the envelope (1862). The actual wrapping, however, dates the curl as having been obtained on 10 July 1861. Among Houghton's holdings is a lock of Longfellow's hair, too, given to Fanny in August 1849 (MS Am 1340 [51][18]).

For the next few weeks, the pages in Longfellow's journal, faithfully kept throughout the years, remained empty. The only entry for the months of July and August 1861

17 "A Sad Lesson," *The Medical and Surgical Reporter*, 21 September 1861, 564-65.

18 Shelved with MS Am 1340 (231).

consists of the two final stanzas of a poem by Tennyson, "To J. S." (1832), an elegy for Edward, the brother of Tennyson's close friend James Spedding:

"Sleep sweetly, tender heart, in peace;
Sleep, holy spirit, blessed soul.
While the stars burn, the moons increase,
And the great ages onward roll.

"Sleep till the end, true soul and sweet,
Nothing comes to thee, new or strange,
Sleep full of rest from head to feet.
Lie still, dry dust, secure of change."
(Longfellow Papers, Houghton, MS Am 1340 [209], FIGURE 6)

It is revealing that Longfellow, who was so skeptical of self-revelation that he once called the "I" that "objectionable pronoun," would turn to somebody else's lines for comfort.[19] His pain was too deep for his own poetry or, for that matter, his journal: "The thoughts that are in my heart and brain I cannot record" (19 September 1861). "The Cross of Snow," the starkest expression of his grief for Fanny, was written eighteen years later and remained unpublished during Longfellow's lifetime.

Longfellow tried his best to carry on and to avoid becoming a recluse, if only for the sake of the children. Eventually, work on his Dante translation and on *Tales of a Wayside Inn* as well as a stream of visitors helped him out of the depths of grief in which he had been hurled. A wine list from 1870, "Wines in cellar," written in an agenda book, shows that at least his interest in good wine had not waned. Emerson, who believed that the poet should be "tipsy with water,"[20] cited Longfellow's wine connoisseurship as one of the reasons why he didn't feel very comfortable at Craigie House: "Longfellow, we cannot go & talk with; there is a palace, & servants, & a row of bottles of different colored wines, & wine glasses, & fine coats."[21] Other visitors, however (a good example is Louis Agassiz—see Chapter 4, pages 95-97), were attracted rather than repelled by the extent and the refinement of Longfellow's supplies.

Italian Wines:
Barolo
Nebiolo Secco

19 Longfellow to Mary Neal Sherwood, 14 September 1877, *Letters* 6: 300.

20 "The Poet" (1844), *Ralph Waldo Emerson*, ed. Richard Poirier (Oxford: Oxford University Press, 1990) 209.

21 *Emerson in His Journals*, ed. Joel Porte (Cambridge: Belknap, 1982) 443.

— Spumante
Moscato

Capri Bianco
— Rosso
Lagrima Christi Bianco
— — Rosso

Falerno Bianco
— Rosso
Greco Gerace Bianco
— — Rosso

Segestano
Vino di Pergola. Sweet.
Marsala. Florio
— Vergine.
Vino di Zucco
(Longfellow Papers, Houghton, MS Am 1340 [216])

As William Dean Howells later said about Longfellow, "He tasted history and poetry in a precious wine."[22]

Longfellow liked living well, and he had learned to accept the celebrity status that came with commercial success. But it cannot be said that he particularly relished it. In December 1851, for example, he attended a performance of *The Winter's Tale* and found his presence and "warm applause" reported the next day in *The Boston Transcript*. "A fine state of things this," he sighed in a letter to Charles Sumner, "when a man cannot clap his hands without having it put into the papers" (*Letters* 3: 322). This was only the beginning. As Longfellow's bearded face became one of the most recognizable images of the poet both here and abroad, the house he lived in acquired iconographic status, too. For example, a beautiful oval portrait of "Castle Craigie" was included in a collection of 198 albumen photographs compiled for the Harvard class of 1869 (Houghton *2001M-8, box 2; photographer: King & Pearson, Harvard Square).

Lucky was the photographer who managed to get a photograph not only of the house but its famous inhabitant, preferably in one and the same image. In September 1873, one such individual coerced a reluctant Longfellow into having his picture taken

22 William Dean Howells, *Literary Friends and Acquaintance: A Personal Retrospect of American Authorship*, ed. David F. Hiatt and Edwin H. Cady (1900; Bloomington: Indiana University Press, 1968) 170.

Figure 7. Longfellow and daughter Edith in front of Craigie House, September 1878, photographer: A. E. Alden, Boston; Houghton *2001M-8, box 2

right in front of the main entrance, a red-letter day in the early annals of paparazzidom. The day had been a particularly annoying one, Longfellow complained in a letter he wrote the same night to his friend Eunice Farley Felton (20 September 1878; *Letters* 6: 385-86). First there had been that box of blank cards that arrived from Chattanooga, "with the request that I would write my name on each" (had anyone but a Bank President, Longfellow asked, signed his name so many times in a row?). Later, John Owen, Longfellow's former publisher and now his assistant, burst in, laden with proof sheets for *Poems of Places*. Then the editor of *The Princeton Review* showed up (Longfellow doesn't say what he wanted). After that, Longfellow himself had to leave, on an errand he had inflicted on himself: he had agreed to procure a pulpit bible which he was going to give, suitably inscribed, to a very grateful Unitarian congregation in Brunswick, Maine. Back at Craigie House, he was dismayed to see even more proof sheets drifting in, delivered this time by Charlotte Fiske Bates (see page 151). His daughter Edith was waiting, too, hoping that her father would join her for a walk. It was then that the final interruption took place, the most momentous of all: "As we went out of the door, there stood another photographer with his deadly instrument aimed at us, and insisting upon taking us as we stood on the steps. Such are the impediments in my way!"

The result of that final, aggressive picture-taking was the stereoscopic view of Longfellow and daughter Edith in front of Craigie House (Stereoscopic view of Longfellow and daughter Edith in front of Craigie House; photographer: A. E. Alden, 63 Court St. Boston; Houghton *2001M-8, box 2, FIGURE 7). Annoying as he was, Mr. Alden, the photographer, knew what he was doing. He placed the reluctant Longfellow squarely in the middle of his composition, as if he had just emerged from the house, frozen in the frame provided by his famous doorway. Alden must have asked Longfellow to remain standing on a higher step than his daughter, which makes him appear much taller than his daughter. Edith is standing below him, portrayed in profile and turned towards Longfellow, though not actually looking at him, thus prefiguring the mode in which the viewer should approach the photograph—respectfully, adoringly. But the actual subject of the photograph is Craigie House itself. Cut off on both sides, Alden's photograph insinuates that the House is much larger than it really is, especially to viewers not from Cambridge who haven't seen the original. The windows, some of them shut, others open, endow the scene with life, as do the overgrown bushes on either side of the walkway.

This stereoscopic view, produced for mass consumption, marked only the beginning of the commodification of the Longfellow House. Soon mere images were no longer enough. The first known full replica was the 1883 "Gladisfin" in Newcastle, Maine, followed in 1887 by a house in Evanston, Illinois. Other copies of "Castle Craigie" were erected in Great Barrington and Lincoln, Massachusetts, Aberdeen, South Dakota, and Warrenton, Virginia. By 1918, Craigie House, more evocatively renamed "The Magnolia," could be ordered by mail, for up to $6,000. Proudly featuring their top-of-the-line product on the cover of their "Homebuilder's Catalogue," Sears, Roebuck & Co. taunted their readers with "the close resemblance" of their house-in-a-box to "the famous residence in Cambridge, Mass., where the poet Longfellow composed his immortal works."[23] In 1907, the Minneapolis entrepreneur and showman "Fish" Jones commissioned a two-thirds replica of Craigie House to be built at the corner of Minnehaha Parkway and Hiawatha Avenue. The gardens surrounding the house included a zoo and a miniature train as well as a sandstone statue of Longfellow himself, of whose poetry Fish was said to have been a great admirer. Though the house has since been moved, the statue is still there. Longfellow would have been amused to learn that among the various functions the fake Craigie mansion in Minneapolis has had over the years was that of a "haunted house."

23 See Katherine Cole Stevenson and H. Ward Jandl, *Houses by Mail: A Guide to Houses from Sears, Roebuck & Co.* (New York: Preservation Press, 1986) 285, as well as Matthew Gartner, "Longfellow's Place: The Poet and Poetry of Craigie House," *New England Quarterly* 73: 1 (2000): 32-57; see 48n34.

Chapter 2: Travel

In a letter to his father, written on 11 January 1824 while he was home from college for the winter vacation, Longfellow announced that he would travel to Boston. His classmate Eugene Weld had offered him "a seat in his sleigh." Somewhat reproachfully, Longfellow added, "I would inform you that I was never fifty miles from Portland, in all my life, which I think is rather a sorrowful circumstance in the annals of my history .... I often wish I had not been so fond of a sedentary life" (*Letters* 1: 71). That would soon change. As the story is usually told, Bowdoin College offered the eighteen-year-old Longfellow a teaching job in modern languages, but with the stipulation that he acquire the knowledge necessary for his teaching by spending time traveling in Europe. This sounds so patently absurd (why offer a position to someone so obviously unsuited for it that one must insist he acquire the necessary training first?) that one suspects Longfellow senior, delighted that an avenue for gainful employment had opened up for his son, had more than a hand in the arrangement. In fact, he bankrolled the entire expedition, to the tune of over $2,604.24.[24]

Stephen's idea was that his son would quickly acquire a good knowledge of French and Spanish and then hasten home to become a college professor and settle down. The letters exchanged between father and son during the latter's European sojourn have a whiff of the comical because it was so clear that, far from Portland, Maine, the mission was spinning out of control. And it did so right from the beginning. In a letter from Paris, sent when he had been there only about five weeks, Longfellow called himself "Henri" and described how he would deck himself out for a stroll in the Jardin du Luxembourg:

> I ... have decorated my outward man with a long-waisted thin coat—claret-coloured—and a pair of linen pantaloons:—and on Sundays and other fête days—I appear in all the glory of a little hard French hat—glossy—and brushed—and rolled up at the sides—it makes my head ache to think of it. In this garb I jostle amongst the crowds of the Luxembourg ....
> (*Letters* 1: 173-74).

Longfellow's detailed description clearly irked his father, who promptly responded: "You will allow me to doubt the expediency of conforming your dress to the fashion of the country in which you may reside for a short time .... You should remember that you are an American, and as you are a visitor for a short time only in a place,

24 Calhoun, *Longfellow* 42.

you should retain your own National Costume."[25] Longfellow didn't take his father's advice seriously—his previous self-description, he said, had been just a joke, anyway (to Stephen Longfellow, 19 November 1826; *Letters* 1: 205).

One of Longfellow's journals from these years almost defiantly quotes the lines Shakespeare's Rosalind addresses to the melancholy Jaques, who boasts of the experiences he has gained abroad: "Farewell—Monsieur Traveller: Look you lisp and wear strange suits: disable all the benefits of your own country:—be out of love with your own nativity, and almost chide heaven for making you that countenance you are:—or I will scarce think that you have swam in a gondola" (*As You Like It* IV.i.33-38; Houghton, MS Am 1340 [178]). Swim in a gondola Longfellow did, but not before he had traveled extensively in France. He visited Rouen, Auteuil, Limoges, and Bordeaux, and hiked through the Loire Valley. In March 1827, he left for Spain. En route, there were the inevitable little skirmishes with his father in Portland about where to go and when to leave and how much to spend, with Longfellow usually insisting that he lived as frugally as possible: "you will find my writing almost illegible upon such thin paper—but [it] is the thickest,—best,—and most economical that my port-folio affords" (*Letters* 1:216). A self-portrait from his "Journal in Spain" (Longfellow Papers, Houghton, MS Am 1340 [172], FIGURE 8) shows Longfellow still unconcerned about his "National Costume." Astride his horse on the road from Malaga to Granada, an image of determination and speed, he now seems to be copying his new hero, the widely-traveled Lord Byron. The caption comes from Byron's *Childe Harold's Pilgrimage* (1812–1818), a poem about a world-weary man seeking rejuvenation in foreign travel: "To horse—to horse—he quits, forever quits / A scene of peace though soothing to his soul."[26]

Byron's poetry accompanied Longfellow wherever he went during his European travels—*almost* everywhere, that is. He accidentally left his well-worn copy of *Childe Harold* in Rome when he traveled to Venice in December 1828, not expecting that Byron would catch up with him in a different way. Longfellow arrived in Venice on a lovely, moonlit night.[27] As he was floating along the Canal Grande, his eyes feasted on what he saw: "What an enchanting scene!—so calm—so beautiful—with the long curve of lamps around the wide basin at the entrance—and here and there a little gondola flitting across the water, and darting into a little alley" (14 December 1828). While in Venice, Longfellow met Toni Toscan, a gondolier and prolific popular poet (a so-called "improvvisatore") who had once also worked for Lord Byron, taking him to his trysts

25 Stephen Longfellow to Henry Wadsworth Longfellow, 24 September 1826, Longfellow Papers, Houghton, bMS Am 1340.2 (3516).

26 Byron, *Childe Harold's Pilgrimage* I, 28, in Byron, *Complete Poetical Works*, ed. Frederick Page and John Jump (Oxford: Oxford University Press, 1970) 185.

27 See his Journal in Italy and Germany, Longfellow Papers, Houghton, MS Am 1340 (178).

Figure 8. Longfellow, self-portrait, p. 29 from "Journal in Spain," 1827, Longfellow Papers, Houghton, MS Am 1340 (172)

with married Venetian women and acting as his messenger.[28] Longfellow was excited about this opportunity for vicarious participation in his admired precursor's exploits. In his journal, he sketched Toscan's memorable face (hat pulled down to his forehead, a profusion of black curls spilling out from under it) and asked that the author sign it himself, in Venetian: "Poeta Natural che venizian / ch' el so nome xe un Tal / Toni Toscan." ("The Venetian folk poet, whose name is a certain Toni Toscan"; "Journal

28 At least one of these occasions can be independently verified; see Donald H. Reiman and Doucet Devin Fischer, eds. *Shelley and His Circle, 1773-1822*, vol. 7 (Cambridge, MA: Harvard University Press, 1986) 320.

Figure 9. Longfellow, portrait of Toni Toscan, p. 60, from "Journal in Italy and Germany," December 1828, Longfellow Papers, Houghton, MS Am 1340 (178)

in Italy and Germany," 1828-1829, Longfellow Papers, Houghton, MS Am 1340 [178], FIGURE 9).

Opposite the portrait appears a tribute to the "famous poet" ("famoso poeta"), "Ottova Al Nobil Sig.r Erico Mericano," in Toscan's handwriting. The poem, a rather loosely handled "octave," was, as Longfellow admitted, "une composition bien curieuse" (he was assiduously practicing his languages, and parts of this journal were written in French).[29] Consider the curious nexus of relationships here, between Henry Longfellow, a fledgling poet and would-be professor from Maine, and the scandal-ridden English aristocrat Lord Byron, whom Harriet Beecher Stowe would later assail as the "Nebuchadnezzar" of modern poetry,[30] and, finally, the half-mad 16th-century Italian poet Torquato Tasso, whose *Gerusalemme liberata* was a favorite with the rough-hewn gondoliers of Venice and whose poetry had inspired Byron's own poem, "The Lament

29 See Longfellow, "Journal in Italy and Germany," Longfellow Papers, Houghton, MS Am 1340 (178).

30 Harriet Beecher Stowe, *Lady Byron Vindicated: A History of The Byron Controversy, From Its Beginning to the Present Time* (Boston: Fields, Osgood, and Co., 1870) 100.

of Tasso" (1817). And in this crazy city where, as Longfellow would later describe it, the streets are rivers and the sidewalks shadows created by the sun,[31] all these figures meet through Toni Toscan, who is not a poetic construct, but a living, breathing presence, an urban and urbane folk poet who is not at all modest about his own powers.

In his "Ottova," Toscan refers to Byron in the present tense ("ch' està"); either he simply didn't yet know that Byron had died on 19 April 1824 in Greece, or Byron was still alive to him, and would always be so. Quoting Tasso, one of Byron's favorite authors, to this Byron-adoring American, Toscan takes evident delight in his role as a cultural mediator:

> Dal caso un dì a Venezia
> à stando al uno Traghetto
> ma domandà un sogietto
> ch' giera American
> C' mi ò Risposo a Sù
> con pronta servitù
> che so Toni Toscan
> à sto Famoso poeta
> chè giusto Merican
> Subito me Riscercà
> del Nobile biron
> ch' està el mio bon Patron
> quando a venezia [sic] està
> Col Tempo material
> zirando el gran canal
> sempre ma Riscercà
> e do stanse del Tasso
> subito gho cantà
> Pien de umiltà e Rispetto
> me cavo al mio cappello
> de cuor che inchino al capo
> A Erico Longfello

Like Byron, who thought it sounded especially pleasing out of the mouth of pretty women,[32] Longfellow loved the Venetian language, "the most beautiful of all the Italian

31 "White phantom city, whose untrodden streets / Are rivers, and whose pavements are the shifting / shadows of palaces and strips of sky . . . ." ("Venice" [1876], *Places* 13: 208).

32 Thomas Moore, *Letters and Journals of Lord Byron: With Notices of His Life*, 2 vols. (London: John Murray, 1830) 2: 253.

dialects."[33] A few years later, he used Toscan's poem in his lengthy scholarly essay "History of the Italian Language and Dialects," which appeared in 1832 in *The North American Review*. He had yet to publish a volume of his own poetry, which is probably why he eliminated the flattering reference to the famous poet "Longfello" from the version of Toscan's poem he printed here.[34] He also omitted—whether for reasons of modesty or because he wanted to maintain the impression of scrupulous scholarly objectivity—his own name from the final line of the poem.

Such reticence goes well with the tone of scholarly objectivity Longfellow adopts throughout his *North American Review* essay, the most extensive study of Italian dialectal varieties any American had undertaken up to that point, complete with tips for proper pronunciation and copious examples of vernacular poetry. The freshly minted Bowdoin professor Longfellow had not only familiarized himself with the most ephemeral linguistic details, he had also assiduously collected songs, poems, and prayers from each of the major dialects or varieties of Italian. Most of these appear not only in their original form but also with translations by Longfellow himself, completed with the active help of Charles Folsom, a classical scholar and an editor for the University Press in Cambridge.[35] Here is Longfellow's translation of Toscan's effusive poem:

> To the Noble signor — American.
> By chance one day at Venice,
>   as I stood at the Ferry
>   there asked for me a person
>   who was an American.
> And I replied to him
>   with ready service,
>   I am Toni Toscan,—
>   to this famous stranger,
>   who is exactly the American.
> Forthwith he inquired of me
>   concerning the noble Byron,
>   who is my good Patron
>   when he is in Venice.

33 Longfellow, "History of the Italian Language and Dialects," *The North American Review* 35 (October 1832): 283-342.

34 From a "famoso poeta," the unnamed addressee of the poem (though "Longfello" still resonates, as a rhyme word corresponding to "cappello") has been demoted to "famoso foresto," a "famous stranger."

35 After a stint as chargé d'affaires in Tunis, Folsom (1794-1874) was a librarian at Harvard (1823-1826) and at the Boston Athenaeum (1845-1856). From 1826, he worked for the University Press in Cambridge (the firm of Folsom, Wells & Thurston) as a proofreader and editor.

At our own time and leisure
    floating along the grand canal,
    he did again request me,
    and two stanzas of Tasso
    I forthwith sang to him.
Full of humility and respect
    I take off my hat
    to — —
("History" 324)

In his journal, Longfellow also inserted a page with yet another sample of Toscan's work, "All' Destinto Merito del Signor Erico Longfello [sic]."[36] Here Toscan thanks Longfellow, the "Poeta stima molto bon" ("poet of great esteem"), for the portrait he has made of him and slyly claims that they both—the American traveler as well as the "half-mad" Venetian gondolier—are animated by the same great passion for poetry ("Conoso quanto è granda la Pasion").[37]

Longfellow returned home in August 1829, tired of the unsettled life he had been leading and on the brink of accepting his father's belief in the "charlatanism of literary men" (to Stephen Longfellow, 15 May 1829, *Letters* 1: 310). But the professorship at Bowdoin turned out to be less of a prize than anticipated, and Longfellow's mail over the next few years shows how desperately he wanted to get out: among other things, he was considering founding a girls' school in New York, made inquiries about a position with the American Legation in Madrid, and had some of his friends nominate him for a professorship in Spanish at New York University that turned out to be completely unpaid (the previous incumbent had made his money by "teaching the Spanish guitar,—an instrument which I do not play upon"; *Letters* 1: 442).

Meanwhile, Longfellow was publishing anthologies and grammars and losing confidence in his creative powers: "*fine-writing*," he complained to George Washington Greene, required vastly more courage than the making of textbooks for college boys. Eventually, however, he did complete a book, a kind of memoir of his European travels, comprised of "scenes in France, Spain, and Italy" (*Letters* 1: 310). At the end of one of the chapters of *Outre-Mer: A Pilgrimage Beyond the Sea*, the irrepressible Toni Toscan reared his curly head again. After some conventional travel book prose exhorting the reader to follow in the author's footsteps, Longfellow allowed Toscan to speak in his own voice, quoting the very words he had used to autograph his portrait in Longfellow's journal:

36 "Erico" is the Venetian form of "Enrico" or "Henry."

37 For more on Longfellow's encounter with Toscan, which has escaped the notice of biographers, see Christoph Irmscher, "Mediterranean Metamorphoses: 'Enrico Longfello's' Contribution to Multilingual American Literature," *America and the Mediterranean*, ed. Massimo Bacigalupo and Pierangelo Castagneto (Turin: Otto editore, 2003) 23-42, as well as Irmscher, *Longfellow Redux*, 159-75.

> Should you ever want a gondolier at Venice to sing you a passage from Tasso by moonlight, inquire for Toni Toscan. He has a voice like a raven. I sketched his portrait in my note-book; and he wrote beneath it this inscription:
>
> Poeta Natural che Venizian,
> Ch' el so nome xe un tal Toni Toscan.
>
> (7: 319)

Outre-Mer is a journey back in time through the literary history of Europe as much as a record of things seen and heard during the author's travels abroad. Dripping with the influence of Washington Irving's *Sketch Book* (1820), Longfellow's *Outre-Mer* joyfully exoticizes Europe as a misty world beyond the sea where the American traveler's ardent desires and a reality too wonderful to be contained in the language of conventional travel-writing meet. "The cities of our dreams are not more enchanting," Longfellow sings about Cadiz, for example, the "city of beauty and of love" (7: 257), where he stares at Spanish women while daring lines from John Fletcher's play *Monsieur Thomas* (1619) swirl through his excited brain: "What eyes, what lips, what everything about her! / How like a swan she swims her pace, and bears / Her silver breasts" (I.1.97-99).

Longfellow based *Outre-Mer* on his European journals, often *verbatim*. But intent on establishing himself as the "pilgrim of Outre-Mer," he carefully edited out many experiences that would have seriously disturbed the "haziness" he evoked in his introductory chapter, the attitude of expectant admiration with which he had approached (as the reader now will, too) the "Holy Land" of his imagination. Gone are the beggars of Genoa, for example ("The poor—the maimed—the blind!—Such splendour and magnificence seen side by side with poverty and rags") or the wretched inmate of an asylum at Granada who tells Longfellow that he has "very clear eyes." He doesn't mention either the French woman, who, unconcerned about propriety and to the consternation of his travel companion George Washington Greene, simply held her child out of the window "pour faire l'eau." [38] The poet's roving eye, darting quickly through many a passage in the journal, is contained and the young American's infatuation with Mediterranean women remains visible mostly through the veil of literary allusion or quotation: "She is a maid of artless grace / Gentle in form and fair of face" (7: 173; see also 6: 209-210).

Longfellow's *Outre-Mer* strays far beyond the parameters of the sketchbook genre as Washington Irving had established it. Everything seems to have gone into this book: sketches that Longfellow had written for *The New England Magazine*, passages from his journals, translations, and even a few of his scholarly articles from *The North American Review*—a jumble of quotes, allusions, reflections, pronouncements. *Outre-Mer* was a cut-and-paste job, arbitrarily ending "on the sands of Holland" (7: 322) when the

38 "Journal in Spain," 1827, MS Am 1340 (172) p. 24; Journal, 16 Dec. 1827-24 April 1829, Longfellow Papers, Houghton, MS Am 1340 (173) pp. 2, 20.

author had run out of steam. *Outre-Mer* remained a work-in-progress even after it was officially published. In the first American edition, for example, readers would have found Longfellow's essay-length review of Sidney's "Defence of Poetry," which Longfellow later removed.

Like other American tourists, Longfellow felt powerfully drawn to ruins, but in the case of *Outre-Mer* the unfinished or broken things he describes (the Château de Chambord, the Coliseum, the Alhambra, the feudal castles along the Danube) carry more personal significance. Throughout his life, Longfellow was particularly interested in the architect's work, the vision and knowledge of material it requires, and the comforting anonymity that seems to come with it: "Strange enough," he wrote in his journal after reading an article about the Cathedral of Cologne, "that the name of the architect of this greatest work of Gothic Architecture should be irretrievably lost" (10 December 1846). When he was traveling through the Loire Valley in October 1826, he was instantly intrigued by the Château de Blois. Later, under King Louis-Philippe, the old castle would be declared a historic landmark and turned into a museum (see the description in chapter IV of Henry James's *A Little Tour in France*), but Longfellow still saw it in the dilapidated state in which it had been left by the French Revolution:

> It seems as if the strong hand of the builder had been arrested in the midst of his task by the stronger hand of death; and the unfinished fabric stands a lasting monument both of the power and the weakness of man,—of his vast ~~purposes~~ desires, ~~and~~ his ~~disappointed~~ sanguine hopes, his ambitious purposes,—and of the unlooked for conclusion ~~which the goal at where which~~, where all these desires and hopes and purposes are so often arrested . . .
> (Autograph ms. of *Outre-Mer*, p. 23, Longfellow Papers, Houghton, MS Am 1340 [68], FIGURE 10)

The section of Longfellow's autograph manuscript featured here illustrates dramatically how haphazardly put together Longfellow's *Outre-Mer* really was. The inserted sheet (on which the quoted passage appears) is tucked in and folded over. *Outre-Mer* as a whole is built around an architectural metaphor, that of the pilgrim seeing "afar the spire which rises above the shrine of his devotion" (7: 19) and then entering, and worshipping in, the vast cathedral of European culture that houses so many different languages and traditions. But it is a cathedral that, upon closer inspection, turns out to be patchwork. And so was Longfellow's manuscript, notes written on loose pieces of paper or discarded envelopes, scraps glued to other scraps, all barely held together by Longfellow's burning desire to be recognized as a serious writer. But the loose shape of the "sketchbook" gave Longfellow the freedom to experiment with his capacities as a writer. The book was his "tailor's drawer," a name the Spanish give—as he explains in one of the chapters—"to a desultory discourse, wherein various and discordant themes

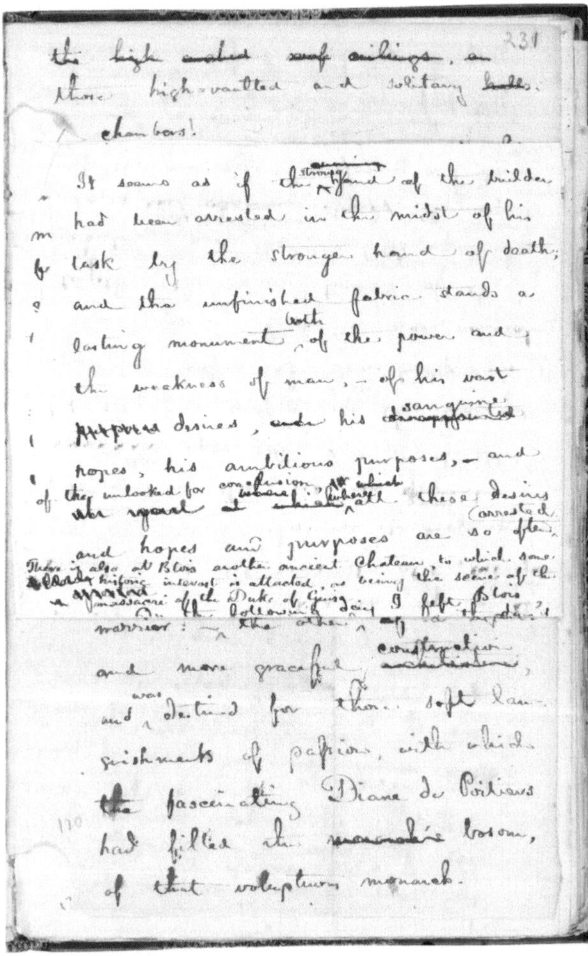

Figure 10. Longfellow, p. 23 from autograph ms. of *Outre-Mer*, ca. 1833, Longfellow Papers, Houghton, MS Am 1340 (68)

are touched upon, and which is crammed full of little shreds and patches of erudition" (7: 168).

Outre-Mer was printed but not yet bound when Longfellow, his wife Mary Potter, and her friend Clara Crowninshield sailed for Europe. This time Longfellow wanted to devote himself to the study of the Scandinavian languages. Their first stop was London, where Longfellow contracted with Richard Bentley—"*the* great—or *one* of the great London Publishers," as he told his father proudly (6 June 1835, *Letters* 1: 492)—to publish an English edition of his travel book. Half of the profits from *Outre-Mer: Or, A Pilgrimage to the Old World. By an American*, as the book was re-titled to make it more palatable to a European audience (Harry Elkins Widener Collection, Harvard University, HEW 7.2.21 v.1), were supposed to go directly to Longfellow, but it is unclear whether or not he ever saw any of the money.

By September, however, when he was in Copenhagen, the American chargé d'affaires, Mr. Jonathan Woodside, had a copy of the London edition. At first not aware of who Longfellow was, he criticized *Outre-Mer* and proceeded to slam the book, pointing out that the chapter on Old English Prose Romances was "too trivial." By now, Longfellow felt confident enough about his achievements to retaliate. Having swallowed the "bitter pill" of criticism and now feeling as if he wanted to swallow the doctor, too, he snapped back: "I put this paper [i.e., Old English Prose Romances] in my book as you put a Chinese ornament on your mantle-piece, not for its intrinsic value, but because it illustrates manners, customs, and feelings of another age or country" (21 September 1835). Among the readers of *Outre-Mer* was also the young Fanny Appleton, who, probably to the author's great relief, had liked the book better than Mr. Woodside. (She also assumed that it had been written by a "venerable gentleman" [*ML* 32].) Houghton Library's copy was owned by Julie Hepp, the daughter of Frau Hepp, the Heidelberg landlady of Longfellow's travel companion, Clara Crowninshield. The inscription reads: "Miss Julia [sic] Hepp with the kind regards of the author. Heidelberg. Aug. 23 1836." Longfellow would order books from Bentley in London during his European sojourn,[39] and Miss Hepp probably received her copy shortly after Longfellow returned from his trip to the Swiss Alps, during which he met Fanny Appleton. On August 27 Clara and he "took leave *auf ewig* [forever] from the Hepp family" (they sailed from Le Hâvre on 12 October 1836).[40]

Although Longfellow had just lost his wife, he did attempt to make the most out of his stay in Heidelberg, the small university town he found both quaint and a little appalling, especially from a sanitary point of view. "Every front entry smells worse than a stable," he wrote in his journal, "and I know more than one that stinks like a pig stye [sic]." Lads walked through the streets in the evening "with their arms around the waists of girls … and I seldom come home at night without finding some boor or other squeezing a servant maid against a wall" (26 May 1836). Some form of deprivation might be speaking through these lines—it had not even been a year since Mary Potter's death. But a moonlit night, when the air was as "soft as in Italy" and the fireflies "hung their tiny lamps in the great trees," was all that Longfellow needed to reconcile himself with his surroundings (23 June 1836). Clara Crowninshield, by contrast, was cold and lonely much of the time and remained a bit frightened by the prospect of having to speak German all the time. Julie Hepp acted as Clara's German tutor, but she soon decided that she wanted to learn English, too, a request to which

39 See *Letters* 1: 511-12; 1: 535.

40 *The Diary of Clara Crowninshield: A European Tour with Longfellow, 1825-1836*, ed. Andrew Hilen (Seattle: University of Washington Press, 1956) 292.

Clara did not respond generously: "she has so little shame about boring us to hear her read and try to say the half dozen sentences she has learnt ... that I feel not the least desire to help her."[41] It is possible that Miss Crowninshield, the exact nature of whose relationship with Longfellow can no longer be determined, was also a little envious of the rather involved conversations about Goethe and Schiller Julie was having with her newly-single traveling companion.

Longfellow stayed in touch with the Hepp family. On 28 September 1840 he wrote to Julie in German, introducing one of his friends, Joseph Coolidge Shaw, to her and sending her also, "als ein Hauch von meiner Seele" ("as a whisper from my soul"; *Letters* 2: 250), a copy of his *Stimmen in der Nacht* (German for *Voices of the Night*). When he was back in Germany in the summer of 1842, Longfellow immediately dashed off a few lines to Julie, the "liebe Freundinn" [sic], promising to visit her "so bald als möglich" ("as soon as possible"), which he in fact did, on 27 September of the same year (*Letters* 2: 412).

In the following two decades, Longfellow would reminisce about his European travels and long for Italy but would never muster up the courage to actually go. Having married Fanny Appleton in 1843, Longfellow found the pleasures and comforts of home too irresistible and his responsibilities as a college professor, husband, and father too pressing to consider another transatlantic trip. His travels were now by the fireside only, where he enjoyed other people's poems about the places *they* had been. In "Travels by the Fireside" (1874), he praised the flexibility of mind and the breadth of perspective such imaginary voyages induce even in those who merely read about them:

> I journey on by park and spire,
>   Beneath centennial trees,
> Through fields with poppies all on fire,
>   And gleams of distant seas.
>
> I fear no more the dust and heat,
>   No more I feel fatigue,
> While journeying with another's feet
>   O'er many a lengthening league.
>
> Let others traverse sea and land,
>   And toil through various climes,
> I turn the world round with my hand
>   Reading these poets' rhymes.

41 *Diary of Clara Crowninshield* 255-56.

Figure 11. Longfellow, "Mr. Peter Quince going up in a balloon," ca. 1860, Longfellow Papers, Houghton, MS Am 1340 (163)

From them I learn whatever lies
    Beneath each changing zone,
And see, when looking with their eyes,
    Better than with mine own.
(3: 86)

In a series of drawings he produced for the entertainment of his children, he invented Peter Quince, a character for whom travel became synonymous with accidents. See FIGURE 11, "Mr. Peter Quince going up in a balloon" (Longfellow Papers, Houghton, MS Am 1340 [163], no. 4 in the complete series) and FIGURE 12, "Mr. Quince falls out

Figure 12. Longfellow, "Mr. Quince falls out of his balloon into the sea," Longfellow Papers, Houghton, MS Am 1340 (163)

of his balloon into the sea" (Longfellow Papers, Houghton, MS Am 1340 [163], no. 6 in the series). Longfellow's capacity for self-irony is abundantly evident here. Quince, who might have been named after the clumsy carpenter in Shakespeare's *Midsummer Night's Dream*, is also a character very much like Longfellow himself. The parallels would not have been lost on Longfellow's children. For starters, Quince likes to relax at home. One of the installments shows him in delicious after-dinner repose, smoking his pipe in a rocking chair right by the fireside. But he also has a craving for adventure, which he satisfies by embarking on a hazardous balloon voyage, a perennially popular theme for children's books.[42]

42 Charley Longfellow, for example, owned "Theodore Tinker's" *The Balloon and Other Stories. With Illustrations for Children* (LONG 8349), which had been given to him by his father.

As these two pictures demonstrate, Quince likes to travel dangerously, but he isn't very good at it.[43] Perhaps Longfellow might have been ironically alluding to the homespun moralism and blatant nationalism of such books as *The Balloon Travels of Robert Merry and His Young Friends, over Various Countries in Europe* (1855), by Peter Parley (i.e., Samuel Goodrich). Led by Mr. Merry, Parley's juvenile balloon travelers survey the world from their high vantage point and find reason enough to congratulate each other on being Americans. France especially doesn't stack up to their own superior nation, the United States: "How little is a nation which has no other thought than to live to-day, to eat, to drink, and to die, compared with a nation which looks beyond to-day, which considers itself God's missionary, charged with the duty of improving, elevating, and blessing mankind," declares Mr. Merry.[44] By contrast, there is not much elevating going on in Longfellow's story. His American protagonist, Mr. Quince, tumbles into the ocean, and rather ignominiously so. No room for superiority here: the drawing shows him falling head first, a helpless, beetle-sized miniature human headed for a big, graceless plunge into the great wide ocean, which Longfellow skillfully indicates by only a few horizontal lines and a couple of sailboats.

In 1868, seven years after Fanny's death, Longfellow let himself be persuaded to undertake one last trip to Europe. The ostensible reason was that Longfellow was to receive an honorary law degree from Cambridge University in England. But the size of Longfellow's party, which left New York on 27 May 1868 aboard *The Russia*, made the undertaking seem like an official state visit. Apart from Longfellow himself, there were his three daughters, his son Ernest and his new wife, Harriet Spelman, his son Charley, Longfellow's sisters Anne Longfellow Pierce and Mary Longfellow Greenleaf, his brother Samuel, and his brother-in-law Thomas Gold Appleton, as well as the former governess Hannah Davie, who came along as a family friend. They landed in Liverpool on 6 June, spent several months in England and France and then went to Italy for the winter.

This time Europe didn't seem to be working its usual magic: "You may be sure," he wrote to his friend Louis Agassiz, a Swiss by birth, "that I grow every day more Protestant, more Republican and more American if possible" (31 December 1868; *Letters* 5: 270). In Sorrento, near Mt. Vesuvius, Longfellow was, for a brief period of time, buoyed by the sight of the sea: "a thin, tender haze along the horizon; a sail or two here and there; and dolfins [sic] disporting themselves in the water. This is more

43 The series, 27 installments of which have survived, ends dramatically: Quince is thrown off his gig, his friends carry him home, and a doctor is called in.

44 *The Balloon Travels of Robert Merry and His Young Friends, over Various Countries in Europe, Edited by Peter Parley* (New York: J. C. Derby, 1855) 74.

Figure 13. "The Longfellow Family in Italy, 1869," photograper: Antonio Sorgato, S. Zaccaria, Venice; Houghton *2001M-8, box 2

like the home of the Sirens, than anything we have seen" (11 April 1869).[45] But here as elsewhere, the enforced "idleness" of travel he found hard to cope with.

It was in Venice that Signor Antonio Sorgato, a well-known photographer of traveling celebrities, took a photograph of the Longfellow traveling party ("The Longfellow Family in Italy," 1869; photographer: Antonio Sorgato, S. Zaccaria, Venice; Houghton *2001M-8, box 2, FIGURE 13).[46] Featured are, from left to right, Samuel Longfellow, Alice Longfellow, Thomas Gold Appleton, Ernest Longfellow, and Harriet Spelman Longfellow. Seated, left to right, framed by the two Longfellow sisters, Mary Longfellow Greenleaf and Anne Longfellow Pierce, who look like the embodiments of mournful widowhood, are Edith Longfellow, Henry Wadsworth Longfellow, and Anne Allegra Longfellow. Longfellow sits enthroned in the middle of his clan; it almost seems as if his head were resting against the considerable stomach of his fun-loving brother-

45 Longfellow Papers, Houghton, MS Am 1340 (212). Longfellow in fact wrote this journal into a specimen copy (a dummy prospectus) of the large-paper edition of the *Works of Francis Bacon*, edited by James Spedding.

46 Antonio Sorgato (1825-1885) opened his studio in 1860; the Massachusetts Historical Society owns several portraits by Sorgato of the expatriate writer Hermann Jackson Warner (Hermann Jackson Warner photograph collection, ca. 1845-1905).

in-law, Tom Appleton, the only one among the group so plainly marked as given to the pleasures of the flesh. He seems to be all body, his head stuck on, no neck visible, almost as an afterthought.

One of Longfellow's most faithful friends and admirers, the Sicilian Luigi Monti, had met up with the group during their Italian sojourn. Deeply involved in the Italian revolution of 1848-1849, Monti (1830-1914) had come to the United States as a refugee and worked as an instructor at Harvard from 1854 to 1859. With some help from Longfellow, he then secured an appointment as the U.S. consul in Palermo, where he served from 1861 until 1873. Longfellow used him as the model for the young Sicilian in *Tales of a Wayside Inn.*[47] In his unpublished autobiography Monti later distinctly remembered a night in Florence, "one of those balmy Spring evenings of Italy," when Longfellow and his party had been invited to a reception and Longfellow didn't really want to go. He tried to persuade his friend to join, but Monti politely declined. "How fortunate you are," said Longfellow. "You can refuse without giving offence, I cannot!" Then, as they were getting ready to go, Longfellow whispered, "Can't you come and wait for me outside of the house to which we are going? I will try to get out early, at ten o'clock, and we will take a stroll together." Which is what they agreed to do, like schoolboys arranging to go out after curfew. When they met, punctually at ten, Longfellow took Monti's arm, and they walked along the Lung' Arno, on to the Ponte Vecchio:

> There, leaning on the parapet, and watching the river as it silently glided down reflecting in rippling streaks the lights of both shores and the other bridges, he said, "How many times Dante must have crossed this very bridge and stood on this very spot revolving in his mind the various historical events connected with it; of Taddeo Gaddi who built it, the old broken statue of Mars that stood at its head, under which Buondelmonti was murdered, and the civil strife between the Guelphs and the Ghibellines which derived from it!" Thus musingly we lingered a long while, and then slowly returned by Oltrano and Ponte St. Trinita to the Hotel where the ladies had long before returned and retired. –It was long after midnight!—He looked at me; then smiling said: "How dissipated we have been! How deceitful is this bewitching climate of Italy! I do not wonder at your people turning night into day![48]

47 Among Monti's publications are, besides numerous translations, *A Grammar of the Italian Language* (Boston: Little, Brown, and Co., 1855), *The Adventures of a Consul Abroad* (1878), and *Leone*, a novel (1882). Houghton owns two autobiographies by Monti, an earlier and shorter sketch and a later book-length manuscript, both of which have remained unpublished (Houghton *2001M-8, box 1).

48 Luigi Monti, autobiography, Houghton *2001M-8, box 1, pp. 26-27 (in file marked "Personal Reminiscences"). This is the earlier, and shorter, of two drafts (the second, begun, according to a note by Monti himself, in 1897 and finished in 1902, is 297 pages long).

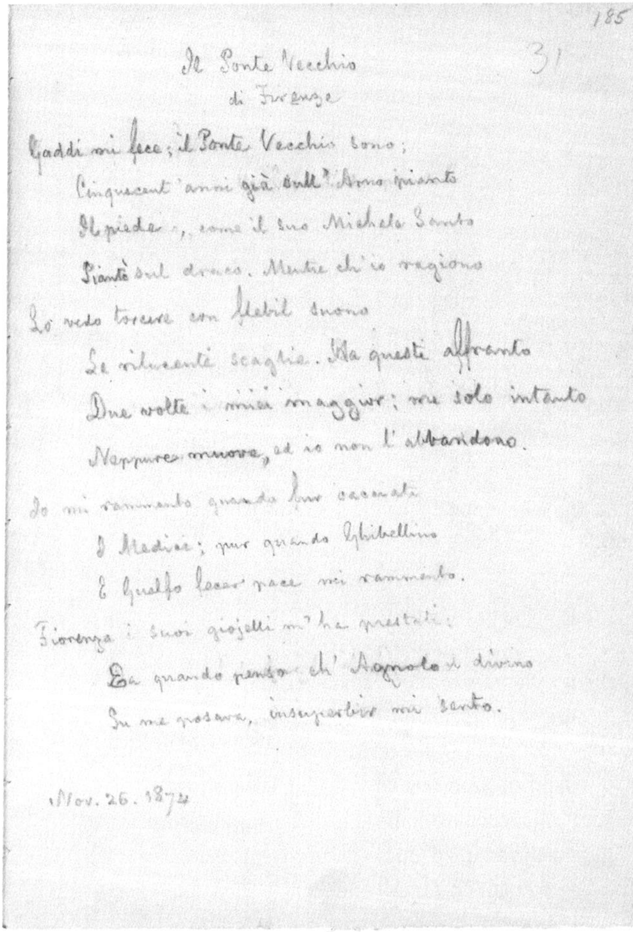
185 31

Il Ponte Vecchio
di Firenze

Gaddi mi fece; il Ponte Vecchio sono;
Cinquecent' anni già sull' Arno pianto
Il piede, come il suo Michele Santo
Piantò sul draco. Mentre ch'io ragiono
Lo vedo torcere con flebil suono
Le rilucenti scaglie. Ha questi affranto
Due volte i miei maggior; me solo intanto
Neppure muove, ed io non l'abbandono.
Io mi rammento quando fur cacciati
I Medici; pur quando Ghibellino
E Guelfo fecer pace mi rammento.
Fiorenza i suoi gioielli m'ha prestati;
E quando penso ch' Agnolo il divino
Su me posava, insuperbir mi sento.

Nov. 26. 1874

Figure 14. Longfellow, ms. of "Il Ponte Vecchio di Firenze," 26 November 1874, p. 185 from autograph ms. of *The Masque of Pandora and Other Poems*, 1874-1878, Longfellow Papers, Houghton, MS Am 1340 (129)

A few years later, Longfellow wrote a poem remembering exactly that experience, "The Old Bridge at Florence," one of his most accomplished Petrarchan sonnets:

Taddeo Gaddi built me. I am old,
    Five centuries old. I plant my foot of stone
    Upon the Arno, as Saint Michael's own
    Was planted on the dragon. Fold by fold
Beneath me as it struggles, I behold
    Its glistening scales. Twice hath it overthrown
    My kindred and companions. Me alone

It moveth not, but is by me controlled.
I can remember when the Medici
Were driven from Florence; longer still ago
The final wars of Ghibelline and Guelf.
Florence adorns me with her jewelry;
And when I think that Michael Angelo
Hath leaned on me, I glory in myself.
(3: 226)

He let the poem sit for a while, but then he rewrote it in Italian, calling it "Il Ponte Vecchio di Firenze":

Gaddi mi fece; il Ponte Vecchio sono;
Cinquecent' anni già sull' Arno pianto
Il piede, come il suo Michele Santo
Piantò sul draco. Mentre ch' io ragiono
Lo vedo torcere con flebil suono
Le rilucenti scaglie. Ha questi affranto
Due volte i miei maggior; me solo intanto
Neppure muove, ed io non l' abbandono.
Io mi rammento quando fur cacciati
I Medici; pur quando Ghibellino
E Guelfo fecer pace mi rammento.
Fiorenza i suoi giojelli m' ha prestati;
E quando penso ch' Agnolo il divino
Su me posava, insuperbir mi sento.
Nov. 26. 1874
(Longfellow Papers, Houghton, MS Am 1340 [129], p. 185, FIGURE 14)[49]

Both versions he sent, along with a recent photograph of his "rather sad and wrinkled face," on 25 January 1875, to a young American admirer in Florence, Arabella Duffy, explaining that the poem had come to his mind when he was thinking of Florence, "as I very often do." We may assume that Duffy would have made the connection between, on the one hand, the old bridge, reminiscing about the past and boasting, "like an old man, of its victory over the turbulent river" and, on the other hand, the aging man who had produced the poem.[50] As Longfellow explained in his letter, translating his own

49 The poem first appeared in *The Masque of Pandora and Other Poems* (1875).

50 Duffy's reply doesn't indicate deep comprehension of Longfellow's poetry or, for that matter, anything else: "You speak so lovingly of Florence, that I am sorry to think of your having no intention to

poem into Italian was "one way of visiting Florence, and I fear the only one for me" (*Letters* 5: 12). Dreaming about travel had become preferable to actually doing it, and metaphor had superseded experience.

On a superficial level, Longfellow's decision to make a bridge the speaker of his poem reflects, of course, an old man's desire for permanence, for victory over the vicissitudes of life, represented by the dragon with its glistening scales. But especially when we take into account the bilingual existence of the poem, another symbolic implication becomes even more important, and the Ponte Vecchio begins to speak to Longfellow's lifelong commitment to transatlantic exchange, his desire to build bridges between different nations and speakers of different languages, as a translator, as an editor of *Poems of Places*, and as a multilingual poet. It is significant that Longfellow represents himself here not as a builder of bridges but as the bridge itself, not as the producer (Taddeo Gaddi) but as the product that has outlasted the one who made it.

Conspicuously absent from the group photo taken in Venice was the most worldly and reckless member of the Longfellow family. Charley Longfellow, bored with the prospect of celebratory dinners and sightseeing, skipped out soon after their arrival in France. He went as far away as he could. When Longfellow, later that year, told Charley in a letter sent from Venice that he was done with traveling and that he longed to be home again (*Letters* 5: 284), he knew that his son was already in India. For years, family members, embarrassed by Charley's restless life, would invoke the wounds he sustained in the Civil War as a justification for his lack of interest in living as they did, for the prolonged state of excited adolescence in which he had gotten stuck. It is hard not to notice the immaturity of the letters Charley sent home. He refers to his father as "the governor" and to himself as "the child," takes "an awful shine" to the places he visits, finds the Japanese language "beastly hard," and calls the people he meets "tip-top" or "swell" or "capital." He is particularly proud of his accomplishments as a sailor, claiming to have "licked" every other boat in Yokohama.[51] The truth is, of course, that Charley's

come here again," she wrote on 5 March 1876, "I wish I cd. think that one day *soon* I might cross the broad seas, to know you in your own home—a charming one, I am sure." She went on to chat about a popular science book she had read recently and rather liked, John Fiske's *Outlines of Cosmic Philosophy* (which she misquotes as *Cosmic Forces*), and then congratulated Longfellow on being a poet: "It must be a great thing to be a poet, dear Mr. Longfellow, & not to … seek in the hard facts of science for the best answers to the 'problems that perplex us'" (A. J. Duffy to Longfellow, Letters to Longfellow, Houghton, bMS Am 1340.2 [1706]).

51 Charles Appleton Longfellow, *Twenty Months in Japan, 1871-1873*, ed. Christine Wallace Laidlaw (Cambridge, MA: Friends of the Longfellow House, 1998) 28, 36, 122, 126. As a child, Charley wasn't inclined to "sit down to his books," as Longfellow wrote to Anne Longfellow Pierce (29 May 1862, *Letters* 4: 285). His erratic spelling continued to be a family joke; when he was living in Japan, his sister Alice encouraged him to think of becoming a writer ("You are quite capable") after the model of his equally peripatetic uncle, Thomas Gold Appleton. But then she revealed the real reason for the suggestion: "Nothing would please me more

temperament and intellect were unsuited to the stability his father, despite his interest in things far away, craved more than anything else. Charley did not fit into any of the niches provided by a society his father himself once defined as "glacial" (see pages 6-7). Just how Puritan Boston still was Charley found out in 1863 when, home from the war to recuperate from an infection, he and a friend went bathing in the nude on the Nahant beach and were observed by none other than the wife of the former western explorer John C. Frémont. One would like to imagine an almost Whitmanian scene here—with the lady "handsome and richly drest" hiding while water is splashing over the slim bodies of the young men—were it not for the fact that Mrs. Frémont had them arrested for public indecency. But perhaps there was more to it than she cared to admit: Charley's lawyer won the case when he got Mrs. Frémont to admit she had her opera-glass turned on the young men.[52]

Charley would eventually settle down, in Tokyo, where he built the only house he would ever own, but even that period in his life would last for less than two years. He always returned to Craigie House but, as his sister Edith humorously noted, he always felt compelled to "dash away" as soon as reality set in.[53] Between 1875 and 1891, he went to Cuba, Mexico, Scotland, Ireland, the Canary Islands, Madeira, Italy, North Africa, Turkey, France, the West Indies, Egypt, Scandinavia, Spain, Portugal, Wales, Colombia, England, the Netherlands, Japan, Peru, Chile, Argentina, Uruguay, Brazil, the Seychelles, China, Tahiti, Fiji, Samoa, Hawaii, and Australia. He very much wanted to go to the North Pole with the De Long expedition ("I hope that you are not thinking of joining any Arctic expedition," his anxious father wrote to him; *Letters* 6: 382), but luckily he wasn't selected. Most of the members of the expedition perished in a blizzard somewhere north of Siberia.

From his various trips abroad, Charley wrote home more or less regularly, corresponding with his sisters rather than with "the governor" himself. When he did write to Longfellow, money was never far from his mind. Like Longfellow did when he was in Europe, his son Charley kept assuring his father that he was being careful. He said that he wouldn't enter into business transactions "without the profit [being] nearly a sure thing"; that he was "going to try to travel on a strictly economical basis," and, none too subtly, that he was writing a letter with a pencil since he had broken his only pen. Sometimes, however, despair over his never-ending financial predicaments got the better of him and "Charley-san" expressed himself in a blunt postscript: "Please don't forget the money" (*Twenty Months* 142). As Charley kept drawing on funds that were not

than to have my finger in the pie in the way of punctuating and spelling." In her eyes, his letters had been getting worse: "I must say the climate of Japan has a rather more unhealthy effect on those two virtues than ever India had" (*Twenty Months in Japan* 117).

52 *Walt Whitman's* Leaves of Grass: *The First (1855) Edition*, ed. Malcolm Cowley (New York: Viking, 1955) 34; Calhoun, *Longfellow* 226.

53 Edith Longfellow to Mary King Longfellow, 5 November 1875, LNHS.

or not yet available, Longfellow scrambled to get the money together by selling bonds: "Do you not see that, at this rate, you will soon have nothing left?" (*Twenty Months* 183). History was repeating itself, but with a difference. Charley Longfellow could not even boast of literary aspirations as a justification for demanding his father's support. But, fortunately for him, Henry Longfellow, unlike his father Stephen, required no explanation when it came to someone else's "thirst for foreign travel" (16 June 1846).

Chapter 3: Family

"MY DARLING CHARLEY," wrote Longfellow in his journal on 19 April 1846, after watching his then almost two-year-old son play outside, "always aims for the street and the largest freedom. He is a splendid boy, notwithstanding his waywardness and willfulness." Charley already had a distinct taste for hearing stories, but he wouldn't allow them to be read from a book: "Improvised must they be, and instantly, or he will kick" (19 April 1846). And Longfellow, a very hands-on father, was happy to oblige. He was deeply involved in the lives of his children—Charles Appleton Longfellow (1844–1893), Ernest Wadsworth Longfellow (1845–1921), Alice Mary Longfellow (1850–1928), Edith Longfellow (1852–1915), and Anne Allegra Longfellow (1855–1934)—in practical ways but also emotionally. His third child, Fanny Longfellow, died on 11 September 1848, when she was only 17 months old, a loss that completely devastated Longfellow and made him wonder if this "had paralyzed my affection for my other children" (16 September 1848). Weeks later, he could hardly control his "inappeasable longing" to see "my dear little Fanny" (12 November 1848).

American Victorians emphasized gentleness rather than stern discipline in their dealings with children and would rather play on a child's guilt or appeal to his better nature than use the rod. "If I am merely willful," reflected Ralph Waldo Emerson about his relationship with his young son Waldo, he "sets his will against mine, tit for tat." But if he was kind to him and acted "for the soul," Waldo would begin to act likewise: "his young eyes look with soul also; he reveres & loves with me."[54] Gender roles were in fact often more fluid than one usually assumes. James Russell Lowell, for example, after the birth of his daughter Blanche in 1845, became the "the personification of the maternal principle," as he put it himself, lamenting those fathers who saw their children as after-dinner enjoyment, "an additional digestif to the nuts and raisins."[55] But even for a time when fathers were becoming more actively involved in family matters,[56] the depth of Longfellow's investment in his children's lives is striking. So is the sheer amount of time he spent with them. Many entries in his journals report on activities he pursued with them, from pushing them around in a wheelbarrow and rowing on Cambridge's Fresh Pond to taking them to Boston for dinners and opera performances. Longfellow carefully noted the trips to town he undertook for the purpose of acquiring toys for his

54 *Emerson in His Journals*, ed. Joel Porte (Cambridge, MA: Belknap, 1982) 215. The entry was presumably made around 12 January 1839.

55 See Martin Duberman, *James Russell Lowell* (Boston: Beacon, 1966) 89.

56 See Shawn Johansen, *Family Men: Middle-Class Fatherhood in Early Industrializing America* (New York: Routledge, 2001) 86.

children (see, for example, 25 March 1848: "Went to town; and attended to sundry little matters; of which the most important was buying two hoops, for Charley and Erny; which gave infinite delight"). After his wife's death, when the world was, in the words of his friend Felton, "strangely changed for him," he had to be both mother and father to his children, especially to his girls, with whom he developed a close bond (*ML* 243). He took Erny and Charley on a trip to Niagara Falls in the summer of 1862, but he missed Annie and Edith so much that the sight of a strange little girl holding her father's hand at Trenton Falls moved him to tears, as he admitted in a letter to his two daughters (8 June 1862; *Letters* 4: 289).

The Longfellow children were, from the beginning, the center of their parents' lives. Scores of photographs were taken of them; their lives were chronicled, in great detail, in letters and journals, and countless scraps of paper on which they drew, doodled, or wrote were saved, often with notes that identify the artist and date the work. With Erny, the future painter, Longfellow seems to have worked diligently on his drawing, numbering and labeling each of the boy's efforts, sometimes even providing a story to go with the picture. For example, to an abortive drawing of a bookcase by the six-year-old Erny (LONG 4160, LNHS, FIGURE 15), Longfellow added the note: "Attempt and failure of Erny to draw a Book-case which caused tears and despair. March 5. 1851." A more successful attempt on Erny's part to record an outdoor scene he had witnessed comes with an even more elaborate explanation on the reverse: "Erny went with me to Hovey's Garden, and on his way back standing on a pile of boards saw the train pass. April. 26. 1851" (LONG 19962, LNHS).

Despite or perhaps because of the attention lavished on them, the Longfellow children did not always conform to the period's standard of "good" behavior. Probably one of the best known images is a daguerreotype, attributed to the studio of Southworth and Hawes and taken in 1849, which shows Longfellow and his grim-faced wife Fanny herding their two boys, Charley and Erny, into sitting still for the camera. Albert Sands Southworth and Josiah Hawes had a reputation for producing "natural portraits," but this one might have come out a bit too natural even by their own standards.[57] Granted, in the late 1840s having one's portrait taken was a serious affair and especially no fun for the kids, and of course it is impossible to freeze a natural-looking smile for an exposure that takes thirty seconds.[58] Given all that, the two Longfellow boys still look extraordinarily unhappy, staring straight and not at all cheerfully into the camera. Fanny's wrist is visible behind Charley's neck, maintaining a steady grip on him to make sure that this opportunity for a family portrait was not wasted. Her left hand rests

57 *Photography in Nineteenth-Century America*, ed. Martha A. Sandweis (New York: Abrams, 1991) 328-29. The daguerreotype is preserved in a maroon leather case with two hook-and-eye latches, the front and rear of which are embossed with a floral bouquet in a serpentine border.

58 John Monroe and Earle G. Shuttleworth, Jr., *First Light: The Dawn of Photography in Maine* (Portland, ME: Maine Historical Society, 1999) 13.

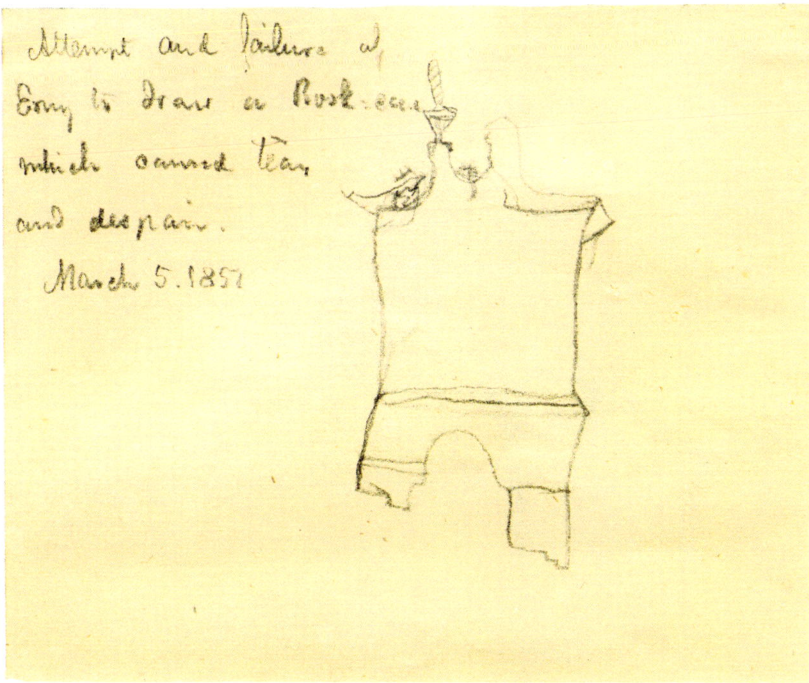

Figure 15. Ernest Wadsworth Longfellow, Bookcase, with annotation by Henry Wadsworth Longfellow in top left section ("Attempt and failure of Erny to draw a Book-case which caused tears and despair"), pencil on (torn) paper, LONG 4160, LNHS

lightly against Erny's belly, preventing him from moving forward, as does Longfellow's leg, the ultimate barrier, in the foreground (LONG 4807, LNHS, FIGURE 16).

The three Longfellow girls fared a little better with the image that would preserve their faces for posterity, an oil painting by the painter and poet Thomas Buchanan Read (1822-1872), which still hangs in the dining-room of Craigie House and was frequently reproduced in the form of inexpensive cartes-de-visite (Houghton *2001M-8, box 2, FIGURE 17). Or at least they would have fared better had it not been for Read's evident limitations as a painter. In the portrait, the four-year-old Annie appears in the right foreground, the six-year-old Edith to the left, and Alice, aged nine, to the right rear. Because Read had been trained as a sign-painter and not as a portraitist, he made Annie look as if she had been born without arms, a rumor that spread like wildfire. When James Russell Lowell heard a woman chatting on a Cambridge omnibus about the poor Longfellow girl who was so courageous in the face of adversity, he felt compelled to intervene, adding that he was an "intimate friend" of the family. The lady who had told the story was unfazed. Giving Lowell "an injured look," she snapped back:

Figure 16. The Longfellow family, half-length daguerreotype portrait in maroon leather case. Attributed to Southworth and Hawes, Boston, ca. 1849, LONG 4807, LNHS

"I have it, sir, from a lady who got it from a member of the family."[59] On the battlefield at Gettysburg, when the fighting had ended and the bodies of the dead as well as their scattered belongings were being retrieved, someone found a locket with an engraving made after Read's portrait of the three Longfellow daughters. No Longfellow relative is known to have fought at Gettysburg, so we must assume that one of Longfellow's "perfect strangers" (see Chapter 6) had carried the image with him, inside his shirt, a substitute for the family he no longer or perhaps never had.[60]

Read's painting was widely regarded as a suitable illustration for Longfellow's poem "The Children's Hour," the poem in which Longfellow describes an evening ritual that involves his three daughters: "Grave Alice, and laughing Allegra, / And Edith with golden hair." As the light declines, they invade his study and wrap their arms around him, while he is trying to embrace them, too, promising never to let go. Longfellow's editor, James Fields, was enthusiastic about the poem, predicting that "the parental

59 George Lowell Austin, *Henry Wadsworth Longfellow: His Life, His Works, His Friendships* (Boston: Lee and Shepard, 1833) 340.

60 The locket, to which I was alerted by Charles Calhoun, was part of the exhibition "Longfellow: The Man Who Invented America," Maine Historical Society, Portland, Maine, 12 April-31 December 2002.

Figure 17. Longfellow's daughters, after Thomas Buchanan Read, carte-de-visite, Houghton *2001M-8, box 2

public" would like it hugely.[61] Subsequent critics have pointed to "The Children's Hour" as an example of Longfellow's "masscult poetry," a poem written when he was at his sentimental worst.[62] But the poem is in fact better than its reputation. What Longfellow wanted to accomplish in "The Children's Hour" was, above all, to find a public language for the powerful affection he felt for his daughters, a love that pushed the conventional boundaries of such relationships.

The poem has a somewhat troubling subtext that would have confounded the average American reader, the story of the medieval Bishop Hatto of Bingen in Germany, as it is hinted at in the seventh stanza of the poem. Hatto, featured also in a grisly ballad by Robert Southey, "God's Judgment on a Wicked Bishop," stole food from the poor and then holed himself up in his tower, only to be found there and eaten alive by an army of invading mice. The allusion is casual and lighthearted, of course, but the reader familiar with the legend will almost automatically associate the father-speaker with the

61 James T. Fields to Longfellow, 1 August 1860, Letters to Longfellow, Houghton, bMS AM 1340.2 (1972).

62 Newton Arvin, *Longfellow: His Life and Work* (Boston: Little, Brown, 1963) 328. For an extended reading of the poem, see my *Longfellow Redux* 72-80.

greedy Bishop and the girls with the carnivorous mice. As if he wanted to take the edge off such a reading of the poem, without discouraging it entirely, Longfellow cut a stanza that, while still playful, shows the father in the poem in a rather unappealing light:

> They do not know I am watching,
>   That every motion I mark,
> For they in the light are standing,
>   While I am hid in the dark.
> (Longfellow Papers, Houghton, MS Am 1340 [128], FIGURE 18)

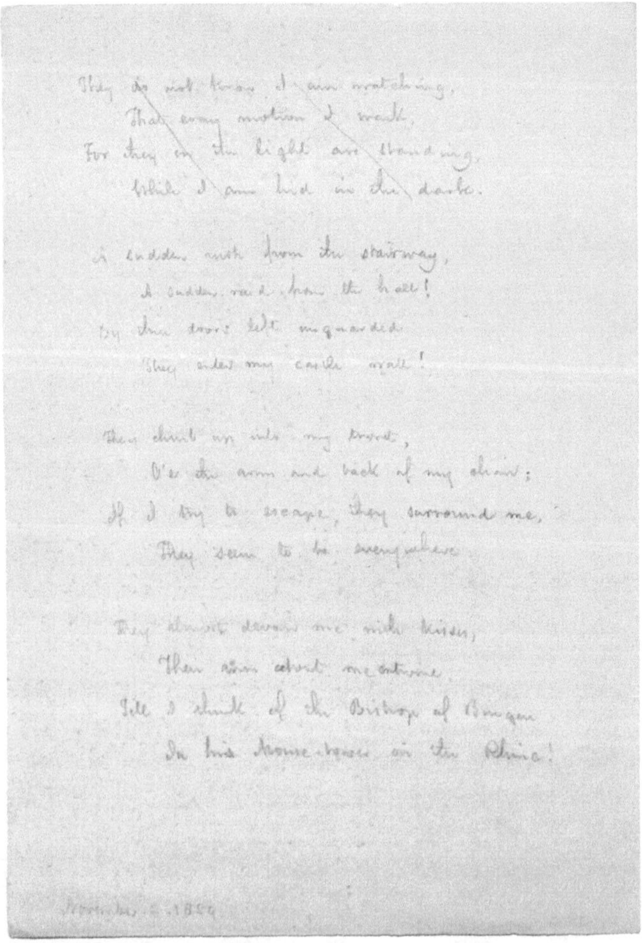

Figure 18. Longfellow, draft of "The Children's Hour," 2 November 1859, from autograph ms. marked "Poems from *Birds of Passage, flights second, third, fourth, and fifth*," Longfellow Papers, Houghton, MS Am 1340 (128)

Mindful of his lawyer-father's interventions into his own life, Longfellow the writer never seems to have forced his children into an appreciation of the delights of the literary life. Which is not to say that he didn't eagerly seize the opportunity when one of his children came to him with an idea that corresponded to his own interests. See, for example, the entry for 3 February 1862: "Evening, Dante's Purgatorio, with Miss Davie, Charlie [sic], Erny, and Alice. Charlie has taken up this idea, from attending Lowell's lectures in College; not from any suggestion of mine ...." Those Dante readings don't seem to have lasted long. On 6 March 1862, Charley's friend "Willie" Fay asked him to sail with him to Ship Island, Mississippi, and Longfellow gave his consent, although not without misgivings: "It is a great tug at the heart-strings this parting with a son for the first time."

Generally, Henry and Fanny did what they could to foster an atmosphere that would allow their children to express themselves, verbally, visually, or (especially in the case of "wayward" Charley), physically, through the activities they liked, such as fishing, rowing, and sailing. Books were, of course, ubiquitous, too. In a household where reading aloud was a daily activity, Don Quixote and the Constant Tin Soldier were familiar after-dinner guests.[63] Longfellow's library includes over 70 books specifically for children (obviously, Cervantes and Andersen were enjoyed by the adults, too—see Chapter 6). Among the books that Charley, Erny, Annie, Edie, and Alice read were poetry, novels, adventure books, primers, and anthologies in English and other languages. Examples of books that can be traced back to Longfellow himself include "Oliver Optic's" (i.e., William Taylor Adams's) *The Boat Club; or, The Bunkers of Rippleton, a Tale for Boys* (1856; LONG 8347), a gift from Longfellow to Charley; "Theodore Tinker's" *The Balloon and Other Stories, With Illustrations for Children* (1850; LONG 8349), also given to Charley by his father; an edition of Grimm's *Kinder- und Hausmärchen* from 1826, which Longfellow purchased in Europe in 1836 (LONG 12658); and an English translation, published in 1839, of Grimm's fairy tales, *Gammer Grethel or German Fairy Tales and Popular Stories from the Collection of M. M. Grimm* (LONG 11830).[64]

When Longfellow collaborated with his children, he did so without imposing his own superior knowledge on their attempts to express themselves. A particularly salient example is two journals kept by Charley, one recorded by his father when he was just five years old, and a second one, this time in Charley's hand, when he was nine (Houghton, MS Am 1340 [161] and [162]).[65] From the first page of the five-year-old's

63 See, for example, 30 January 1860: "Evening. Fanny read Don Quixotte [sic] aloud with the boys, who are delighted with it. This has been the evening reading for some time."

64 The five-year-old Charley Longfellow's diary, for example, contains a reference to listening to "Ellen" read from *Gammer Grethel*, 26 May 1850 (Longfellow Papers, Houghton, MS Am 1340 [161]).

65 For an excellent reading of Charley's diary, see the senior thesis by my former student Elizabeth Ann Greenwood, "Declarations of Independence: American Children's Diaries, 1820-1860," Thesis, A.B. Honors in History and Literature, Harvard University, 2001.

journal, there is ceaseless activity, each entry a metaphorical slap in the face of the Victorian notion of the angelic child. Charley plays on his drum, rakes the paths in front of the house, plays soldier and printer, digs a hole in the ground of the carriage house, pays a visit to the toy store (where he acquires a shovel—for more digging, we may assume), and colors pictures in his father's issues of *Punch* magazine. When it is raining outside, he quickly transforms his nursery into a great ship, using a pile of building blocks and boxes for a mast. And these are only the events of the first week described in the journal. When Charley embarks on "artistic" endeavors, such as the writing of poetry ("It is very sorrowful / To sail away in a ship! It is very sorrowful / When you get there," runs one of his songs, inspired by a picture on a screen in his room), Longfellow takes him seriously—even, in the instance of the latter product, setting Charley's "poem" to music and singing it to him while accompanying himself on the piano (29 April 1850). A "very large" picture that Charley paints on brown paper, featuring "steamers, and ships and bridges and wharves," Longfellow hangs up in his dressing-room. "Mama" plays a marginal role throughout the journal, limited to the giving of presents: a new book for Charley or a puzzle for his birthday. "Papa," on the other hand, is constantly active, showing Charley the new-born kittens in the cellar or "curing" him by putting a wet towel on Charley's nose when it begins to bleed "because I worked so hard on my pictures." Above all, Longfellow *makes* countless things for him and his brother Erny: moulds for lead-casting (for a dog, a sportsman with his gun, and, especially important, for a cow), a watch out of a wafer box ("with hands and a pin key to wind it up"), a paper knapsack, and a wooden roll for an endless ream of paper, which Charley wants to use for a "panorama."

There is no doubt that, in the collaborative process of composing the journal, Longfellow must have exerted some influence, either directly or through the conversations he had with Charley. There are, for example, the remarks about the weather, a common feature in adult diaries of the period, which almost certainly originated with Longfellow *père* and not with Charley. Nevertheless, despite the fact that the entries in Charley's first journal are in his father's handwriting, they do, for the most part, faithfully reflect a child's way of thinking, especially in terms of what is included and what is omitted. Consider Charley's account of a trip to New York the family undertook in May 1850. Watching the city from his horse-drawn car, Charley notices mostly the toy-shops, of course. Later, he indeed gets a boat as a present, painted blue, "with a white streak." Note the specificity here, lacking in other entries. Note also how, in the excerpt from the journal reproduced here, the first entry records the damage Charley does to his father's cane but says nothing about the latter's reaction, which we may assume wasn't positive. And finally, make a note of how the summary of the play he watched at Barnum's Museum in New York focuses on the bare bones of the story, without any understanding of what the plot might mean (provided there was any).

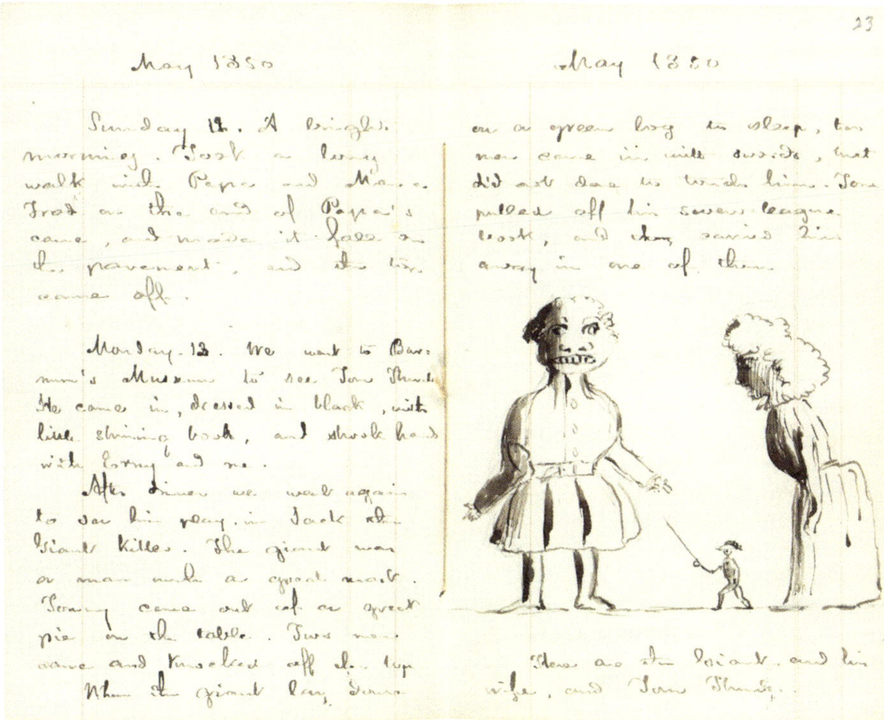

Figure 19. Charles Appleton Longfellow, “Charley’s Journal,” 1850, pp. 22-23, Longfellow Papers, Houghton, MS Am 1340 (161)

Sunday 12. A bright morning. Took a long walk with Papa and Mama. Trod on the end of Papa’s cane, and made it fall on the pavement, and the top came off. Monday. 13. We went to Barnum’s Museum to see Tom Thumb. He came in, dressed in black, with little shining boots, and shook hands with Erny and me.

After dinner we went again to see him play, in Jack the Giant Killer. The giant was a man with a great mask. Tommy came out of a great pie on the table. Two men came and knocked off the top.

When the giant lay down on a green log to sleep, two men came in with swords, but did not dare to touch him. Tom pulled off his seven-league boots, and they carried him away in one of them.

(“Charley’s Journal,” 1850, Longfellow Papers, Houghton, MS Am 1340 [161], FIGURE 19)

A drawing by Longfellow follows, with the note: “Here are the Giant, and his wife, and Tom Thumb.” Longfellow’s drawing admirably catches the scene as Charley would have perceived it, in its full absurdity and incongruity. Note the Giant's huge nose and fierce eyes, as well as Longfellow's attempt to recreate the three-dimensional drama of the scene as Charley would have experienced it by shading in the areas that would not have been illuminated on the stage. "Tom Thumb" was the name Barnum had given to Charles Sherwood Stratton, a Connecticut boy whom he discovered in 1842. At age four, Stratton was less than two feet tall and weighed fewer than sixteen pounds; he would prove to be Barnum's most profitable human "oddity." A born actor, Tom Thumb starred in plays that were little more than a series of vignettes written to highlight his smallness. No wonder that Charley had trouble grasping how the various goings-on on stage were connected.[66]

As the example of the diary shows, Longfellow was unusually keen on collaborating with his children, developing, or helping them develop, the kinds of stories and activities they needed. His daughters profited from his availability just as the boys had done earlier. He was not above contributing a story about Trap the fat family dog to *The Secret*, the monthly handwritten newspaper Annie and Edie produced from 1865 to 1866. Apparently, a girl had seen Trap from a distance and, amused by the sight, had told her parents that Trap looked "like a pig" (*Letters* 4: 492-93). *The Secret* contained stories of the Longfellow children's daily lives as well as puzzles and rebuses they composed, so Longfellow's contribution fit right in.

However, his most sustained effort at providing entertainment for his children was a series of vignettes he had begun in the late 1840s, titled *Little Merrythought. An Autobiography with a Portrait* (MS Am 1340 [165], FIGURE 20). It appears that his audience at Craigie House liked the original idea, so he continued to work on the story over the course of several years, expanding the original cast of characters beyond Charley and Erny to include Alice, "Edie", and "Annie" Allegra. Longfellow's rather loose narrative revolves around the trials of a tiny bone, "Merrythought," ripped from a Christmas turkey. Since he is so small (note the similarities between Tom Thumb and Merrythought), the former wishbone, decked out in a fancy cloak and dapper shoes, is able to comment unrestrainedly on the relations between Papa ("a rather portly man, with a bright red waistcoat") and Mama ("very beautiful") and their children: brown-eyed Erny ("a dreamy little boy, who sucked his thumb") and the older, boisterous Charley, also known as "Infant Terrible," with "grey eyes snapping like steel traps." The girls are shown at school, where Edie translates "Ma mère est aimable" as "My mother ate a marble," dropping the "r" in "marble" the way all proper Bostonians do and thus amusing "Papa" so much that tears are streaming down his face. Or we see them playing with their dolls, using chocolate wrappers or a label from a matchbox as paper money. One of the most affecting episodes shows the father ("Papa") pressing

66 Christoph Irmscher, *The Poetics of Natural History: From John Bartram to William James* (New Brunswick, NJ: Rutgers, 1999) 108-11; Alvin Goldfarb, "Gigantic and Minuscule Actors on the Nineteenth-Century American Stage," *Journal of Popular Culture* 10:2 (Fall 1976): 267-97.

Figure 20. Title page, Longfellow, *Little Merrythought*, 1847– ,
Longfellow Papers, Houghton, MS Am 1340 (165)

one of his daughters, "Panzie" (i.e., Annie Longfellow), against his heart, trying to calm her down by asking her to set the "little watch" of her heart by the "great town clock" (i.e., Longfellow's own heart). As it turns out, even that "great town clock" isn't too reliable: it "did not exactly keep time with other steady old town clocks, but struck too soon and made too much noise" (which implies also that "Papa" Longfellow isn't too much like the other adults).

Merrythought as a narrator gives Longfellow the opportunity to make fun of himself, which makes this unassuming story a particularly memorable example of Longfellow's ability (and desire) to see with eyes other "than mine own" ("Travels by the Fireside"). Most adults don't look very impressive when viewed up close from a child's perspective. For example, Longfellow's boys surprise him during his morning shave and find that soapsuds-covered Longfellow seems just like a "buffalo with his horns sawed off." Papa realizes that they have a point. In Merrythought's words, the father "could not help laughing to see what a grotesque figure he really made."

Longfellow also made an effort to include the children's pets and toys in the narrative, notably a wooden rooster, given to him as a kind of silent alarm-clock and portrayed here, life-sized, in watercolors:

> This is a true portrait of the Cockerel that little Erny gave his Papa, to wake him up in the morning. He was stationed on the top of a ~~long~~ tall Cologne box, on a table in the dressing room, at the feet of a broken statue, of which nothing remained but the bare legs. He strutted a good deal; but I never heard him crow.[67]
> (Longfellow, "Erny's Wooden Cockerel," from *Little Merrythought*, Longfellow Papers, Houghton, MS Am 1340 [165], FIGURE 21)

Erny's miniature toy rooster, carved from wood and then painted in bright naturalistic colors, his tail fanned out and head cocked to one side, has in fact survived. He was found in 1977 in the attic of Craigie House and is shown here for the first time, (NUMBER 26, LONG 13997, LNHS, FIGURE 22): one of many toys still kept at the Longfellow National Historic Site.

After Longfellow's death, Daniel Lothrop, the editor of the Boston children's magazine *Wide Awake*, made known that he was interested in publishing "Little Merrythought." Lothrop knew a good children's story when he saw one; he was married to Harriet Stone, better known as Margaret Sidney, the author of the very popular "Little Peppers" series (beginning with *Five Little Peppers and How They Grew*, 1881). However, Longfellow's heirs, when consulted by Samuel Longfellow, decided that they

67 On the importance of Longfellow's second-floor dressing room for his children, see Alice Longfellow's "Reminiscences of My Father" (unbound ms. at LNHS): "My father's dressing room was one of the earliest household resorts of the children. There we hurried first thing in the morning for the pleasure of his company, and perched on an old red sofa, watched with keen interest the mysteries of the toilet . . ." (quoted in *Historic Furnishings Report: The Longfellow House*. Longfellow National Historic Site, vol. I: *Administrative and Historical Information, Illustrations, and Bibliography* [typescript; Harpers Ferry, WV: National Park Service, 1999] 243).

Figure 21. Longfellow, "Erny's Wooden Cockerel," from *Little Merrythought*, Longfellow Papers, Houghton, MS Am 1340 (165)

felt uncomfortable with the glimpse into their private lives the little book would have afforded a larger audience. Or so the following letter in the Houghton collection, from Samuel Longfellow to an unnamed recipient, dated 12 February 1887, suggests:

> Dear Sir,
> I have delayed answering your letter till I would get from my brother's children a decision about the Story of Lettle [sic] Merrythought I find that they are

Figure 22. Wooden rooster ("cockerel"), LONG 13997, LNHS

> decidedly opposed to its being printed not merely because they figure in it, but because it is so very fragmentary & incomplete. So it must *remain* unpublished, in spite of Mr. Lothrop's very generous offer . . .
>
> Yours very truly
>
> Saml. Longfellow
>
> (Houghton *2001M-8, box 1)

The heirs' concern over the unfinished state of the manuscript seems like a pretext, given that they did not object, for example, to having Longfellow's fragmentary verse play, *Michael Angelo*, published in 1883. A more likely explanation for their refusal would be that, for them at least, Merrythought's irreverence had lost none of its edge.

"Little Merrythought" becomes doubly enjoyable when we consider the turgid little book in Longfellow's library that might have been Longfellow's source, *The Wise Boys; or Entertaining Histories of Fred Forethought, The Boy Who Looked Before He Leaped; Matt. Merrythought, The Boy Who Was Always Happy; Luke Lovebook, The Boy Who Was Fond of Learning; and Ben. Bee, The Boy Who Was Always Industrious.*[68]

68 LONG 13442. I owe this reference to Jim Shea of the LNHS.

The book, published by Edward Dunigan in New York in 1842, came from the prolific pen of Sarah Josepha Hale, editor of *Godey's Lady's Book* from 1837-77, remembered today chiefly as the author of the popular nursery rhyme, "Mary Had a Little Lamb." An inscription on the flyleaf of the book establishes that it was given by Longfellow's father Stephen to his nephew Henry, the son of Longfellow's hapless brother Stephen. Henry (or "Hen," as Longfellow's namesake was known) might have indeed needed the guidance, since his alcoholic father probably didn't have much to give him in that direction. (In 1850, Longfellow's widowed sister Anne took legal guardianship of ten-year-old Henry.) That said, the plodding meter, awkward rhymes, and treacly lessons of *The Wise Boys* explain why Longfellow might have felt inspired to try his hand at parodying Hale. Matthew Merrythought, who thinks that "cheerfulness of mind" is the best cure for all disappointments life might throw our way, is irritatingly superior to "sulky Joe," featured in the clumsy illustration that accompanies the story, who won't sit still when being washed (and therefore gets soap into his mouth and eyes), mopes in school, and has to stand in a "cold corner, / With a dunce cap on his head," for not doing his homework well. In fact, Matthew Merrythought is the polar opposite of the Longfellow boys as described in Longfellow's narrative:

> When his toys were broken, he would not,
> As naughty children do,
> Begin to fret and pout, and cry,
> In hopes of getting new;
>
> But he would hum a cheerful tune,
> Or, maybe, sit and sing,
> And try to mend them up again
> With many a bit of string.

How ironical that in Longfellow's narrative it is Merrythought himself who ends up being broken. In an outburst of unexplained rage, Charley, the "Infant Terrible," flings the little creature on the table, "with such violence, that I thought every bone in my body was broken," while exclaiming: "You ugly little fellow! I wish you were dead!" Think of Andersen's Constant Tin Soldier and his fate (he is flung into the stove by one of the little boys, though "there was no reason for his doing so"[69]). Merrythought, with one of his legs shattered, is instantly shut away in a little box. Ultimately, Charley apologizes and "Papa" repairs him, using a matchstick as a prosthetic leg: "It is round and smooth and just long enough. And then he has only to scrape it on the ground, and it will light up, and he can touch off a cannon with it." Children are violent, and

69 Hans Christian Andersen, *Wonderful Stories for Children*, trans. Mary Howitt (London: Chapman and Hall, 1846) 117.

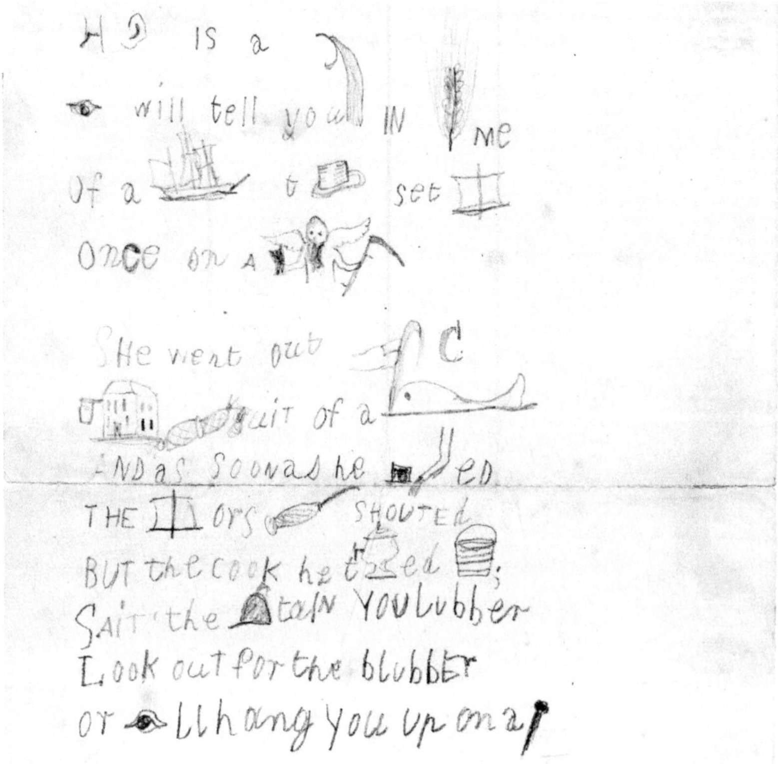

Figure 23. Henry Wadsworth Longfellow and Charles Appleton Longfellow(?), Whale Rebus, LONG 19957, LNHS

they like thinking about violence; hence the reference to the cannon Merrythought can set off with his new leg. Erny is no better than Charley—he threatens to chop his Nurse's head off, and once can be seen rolling on the floor, abuzz with anger like some great insect, over some trivial reason. The only cure for such behavior, as Longfellow, assuming for a moment the tiny mantle of Merrythought's authority as a storyteller, is genuine sympathy, not some inane prescription for cheerfulness.

In the cache of children's drawings at LNHS is also a rebus (LONG 19957, LNHS, FIGURE 23), written in a child's hand, although the illustrations suggest the skill of an adult. The sailboat in particular, since it is so reminiscent of some of the Peter Piper drawings, points to some involvement of Longfellow senior. The handwriting is strikingly similar to that in the nine-year-old Charley's journal (Houghton, MS Am 3140 [162]), who was also the Longfellow child most consistently interested in ships and the ocean. Rebuses were quite popular with Victorians (Charles Dodgson, better known as Lewis Carroll, used them to entertain his young pen pals); it is amusing to see how the word game here is made to serve the imagination of an American child who is fascinated by reckless adventure and the prospect of some violence.

The little poem that emerges from the rebus, once it has been deciphered, doesn't show extraordinary poetic talent. What it does, however, is forecast rather uncannily the penchant for dangerous travel that would come to shape the life of Charley Appleton: "Here is a tale / I will tell you in rhyme / Of a ship that set sail / once on a time. / She went out to sea / In pursuit of a whale. / And as soon as he had spouted / The sailors all shouted / But the cook he turned pale; / Sait [sic] the captain you lubber / Look out for the blubber / Or I'll hang you up on a nail."

Figure 24. Longfellow, "Peter Piper sees a whale," ca. 1860, Longfellow Papers, Houghton, MS Am 1340.9.1

Whales also play an important role in the accomplished series of drawings Longfellow made for his children involving a character called Peter Piper, of tongue-twister fame, a dapper traveler who looks like a carrot-nosed snowman in boots and has few facial expressions at all—a perfect epitome of Henri Bergson's theory that automata are almost inevitably comic (Longfellow, "Peter Piper," Longfellow Papers, Houghton, MS Am 1340.9.1, FIGURES 24, 25, 26). Longfellow allows his talents as a draftsman full sway here. Consider "Mr. Peter Piper sees a whale." Perched on the bow of his ship, dressed to the nines, swinging a cane and smoking his pipe, Mr. Piper is

Figure 25. Longfellow, "Peter Piper takes a ride on the whale," Longfellow Papers, Houghton, MS Am 1340.9.1

Figure 26. Longfellow, "Mr. Peter Piper is saved by the boat,"
Longfellow Papers, Houghton, MS Am 1340.9.1

arguably not too well-equipped to embark on a risky deep-sea adventure. The next installment, "Mr. Peter Piper takes a ride on the whale," however, suggests that the whale and his visitor have more in common than the viewer anticipated—they are both striped. The amusingly tranquil image is diminished just a little by the fact that in the middle ground, i.e., between the whale and the large ship in the background, a small boat can be seen rowing towards Piper. In the next image, "Mr. Peter Piper is saved by the boat", the inevitable has happened: the whale has gone down again, leaving Piper half immersed in the water, though he still won't let go of his ornamental cane. The whale's tail in the background serves as a comic reminder of Piper's recklessness. Note the wonderful effect Longfellow achieves by giving Piper's two rescuers a darker shade of stripes—a small trick which nevertheless focuses the viewer's attention on what is really happening.

With his interest in extreme sports, Peter Piper takes all the risks that his creator, who (in his son Ernest's unforgettable description) always thought it "wisest not to do a thing,"[70] would usually avoid. No wonder that the Peter Piper drawings particularly appealed to his children, as Alice Longfellow later remembered. Peter Piper's adventures were, she wrote, "a constant source of delight" to her and her siblings. Longfellow kept the small drawings in the drawer of one of his bookcases. New installments would appear there "from time to time, and we never knew what the wonderful Peter Piper would do next. He went traveling, with adventures in foreign lands; he went hunting, and fell from his horse; he went to sea, and was chased by a shark, and rode on a whale, and went down in a diving-bell, and all the possibilities of life were before him."[71] It would be wrong to dismiss Longfellow's drawings for his children as ephemeral products of a man who would have been better advised to use the time for his poetry. The Peter Piper and "Merrythought" drawings imagine a world in which fathers and children, like authors and readers, can be—to borrow a phrase from "The Children's Hour"—truly "matches" for each other.

70 Ernest Wadsworth Longfellow, *Random Memories* (Boston: Houghton Mifflin, 1922) 29.

71 Alice Longfellow, "Longfellow with His Children," *The Youth's Companion*, 2 September 1897, 405.

Chapter 4: Friends

Craigie house was at the center of an extraordinary nexus of relationships, the hub of a social life that, in the middle of what was then still little more than a village,[72] spanned different cultures, continents, and national traditions. Longfellow not only maintained an enormous correspondence, but he also regularly had friends over for supper and often for overnight stays. The tradition of gatherings in Craigie House began after Longfellow had moved in as a lodger and the "Five of Clubs" congregated there, a weekly dinner-group made up of Henry Cleveland, Cornelius Felton, George Hillard, Charles Sumner, and Longfellow himself. It reached its apotheosis in the 1860s with the famous Dante Club.

Longfellow's deep commitment to friendship is far more than an incidental biographical fact. Understanding how relationships fostered and shaped his writing and the writing of others in his circle helps us depart from the persistent focus in literary history on the solitary writer's "individual talent," in T. S. Eliot's phrase. If Longfellow never had, as Eliot would have put it, "his complete meaning alone," it wasn't because he made a conscious attempt to "extinguish" his personality so that he could approach the temple of literary history as a supplicant, surrendering himself to the "work that is to be done."[73] From the beginning, writing, to Longfellow, was an exercise in community-building, an exhilarating but often tedious process of reworking and filtering the ideas and sometimes even phrases he had received from past writers (whether by reading Danish poetry or Dante's *Divina Commedia*) or in conversation with contemporaries (e.g., when Hawthorne's friend Conolly passed on to him the germ of the story that became *Evangeline*). The multiple connections that existed not only between writers but between writers, poets, translators, and scientists are evident from any issue of *The Atlantic Monthly.* In January 1864, for example, readers would have found Longfellow's "Three Cantos of Dante's 'Paradiso,'" Louis Agassiz's "External Appearance of Glaciers," James Russell Lowell's poem honoring Robert Gould Shaw, "Memoriae Positum," as well as reviews of Bayard Taylor's novel *Hannah Thurston* and Agassiz's *Methods of Study in Natural History.*[74]

Longfellow went to great and sometimes inexplicable lengths to support his friends. One of the most persistent beneficiaries of his generosity was George Washington

72 The population of Cambridge swelled from 6,000 to 48,000 in the years between 1830 and 1875.

73 T. S. Eliot, "Tradition and the Individual Talent" (1919), in Eliot, *Selected Essays*, 3rd ed. (1930; London: Faber, 1986) 15, 22.

74 See Longfellow to Charles Sumner, 22 December 1863, *Letters* 4: 374-75.

Greene (1811-1883), who was, like Longfellow, both a grandson of a Revolutionary War general and a passionate Italophile. He was also an unrelentingly mediocre writer who, during the last decade of his life, depended on Longfellow's help and money and would spend large periods of time at Craigie House, clinging "tremulously" to Longfellow's arm wherever he went, as William Dean Howells remembered in his autobiography.[75] Greene's bad luck became almost proverbial in the Brattle Street household. Longfellow himself once remarked, in a letter to his sister Mary Greenleaf, that Greene had had "all calamities" and that "nothing remains for him, but to be struck by lightning." He added, mischievously, that he would have a good chance of that now "as we have on a[n] average one thunderstorm a day" (*Letters* 5: 575).

Unlike Greene, Charles Sumner (1811–1874), one of the original members of the Five of Clubs, was Longfellow's intellectual equal. He was a somewhat diffident partner in George Hillard's Boston law firm and a lecturer at Harvard Law School when Longfellow arrived in Cambridge in 1837. The friendship between Longfellow and Sumner—intense from the beginning—lasted until the latter's death. "Why have I always been in the breach?" Sumner asked Longfellow plaintively on 22 June 1870.[76] With Longfellow, there had never been the friction that Sumner, rigorous and unwilling to compromise (or so people were saying), routinely experienced with others. Longfellow admired Sumner's courage and unequivocally supported his political goals and ambitions, his opposition against the Mexican War and the Fugitive Slave Law, his unwavering commitment to the destruction of southern "slave power," and his dedication to civil rights. Sumner's complex personality, his brusqueness, alleged narcissism, and penchant for rhetorical flourishes have elicited astonishingly unsympathetic reactions even from modern interpreters who stop just short of accusing him of having started the Civil War.[77] Longfellow stood by him and trusted him implicitly, although this did not always endear him to his Harvard colleagues, especially those associated with the

75 Howells, *Literary Friends and Acquaintance* 163.

76 Charles Sumner to Longfellow, 22 June 1870, *The Selected Letters of Charles Sumner*, ed. Beverly Wilson Palmer, 2 vols. (Boston: Northeastern University Press, 1990) 2: 507.

77 Carl Sandburg's dictum that Sumner became "the most perfect impersonation of what the South wanted to secede from" (*Abraham Lincoln: The Prairie Years and the War* Years [1956; New York: Harvest, 1982] 208) has shaped much of the modern response to Sumner. See, for example David Herbert Donald's biography, *Charles Sumner and the Coming of the Civil War* (1960; Chicago: University of Chicago Press, 1980). Donald announces that he had not "felt it my proper function to sit in moral judgment" upon the subject of his biography but then writes of Sumner's "inflexible zeal," "moral terrorism," and "icy reserve" (40, 243). He describes how Sumner would become "frantic" or "frenetic" when faced with opposition or backsliding, and, by way of conclusion, outlines what Sumner might have realized had he only been given to self-criticism—among other things, that although he assumed the right to speak for the nation's conscience, he had never been "chosen by direct popular vote" (388). See also the comments provided by Sumner's editor, Beverly Wilson Palmer, who calls Sumner "rigid," "naïve," "vain," and "humorless," though, interestingly,

Harvard Law School. As Frank Preston Stearns claimed, "At a distance Longfellow's politics attracted little attention, but in Cambridge they could not help being felt."[78]

Longfellow was always excited when Sumner turned up at his house. When Longfellow was gone, Sumner would wait on the piazza or in the parlor for his friend to return. "I am delighted to see him so often," wrote Longfellow. "The face of a friend, and such a friend! is what one cannot see too much of" (12 June 1846). When Longfellow traveled to Washington, D.C. in December 1863, to help take care of his son Charley, who had been shot through the shoulder, the New York politician Caleb Lyon persuaded him and Sumner to sit for their portrait at the studio of Alexander Gardner. Gardner had just severed his ties to photographer Mathew Brady and was striking out on his own as a portrait photographer and producer of war views.[79] His double portrait of Sumner and Longfellow, titled "The Politics and Poetry of New England," gained wide circulation as a carte-de-visite (Houghton *2001M-8, box 2, FIGURE 27). Though both men are seated, the photograph amusingly highlights the physical difference between the two close friends—the average-sized Longfellow, accustomed to the sedentary life of the writer, appears to be comfortable in his chair, his hands resting idly on his hat, while Sumner, six feet and two inches tall, looks gangly, awkward, as if not sure what to do with his long arms and legs. Longfellow seems pensive, his facial expression further softened by the white beard, while Sumner's large features radiate the kind of fierce determination a man would have needed who wanted to carry, as Frank Preston Stearns put it tendentiously, "the impracticable theory of social equality to an extent beyond that of most Americans."[80] But the handy caption of Gardner's photograph suggests a strict dividing line where there was none. Sumner's interests, for example, were remarkably encyclopedic; he was multilingual and in many instances served as the first audience for Longfellow's works-in-progress, offering detailed advice on literary matters (see the proof sheets for *Evangeline* discussed in Chapter 5, pages 122-24). Inevitably, though, politics often took over. In October 1848, when Sumner was heavily involved in campaigning for the Free Soil Party he had helped found, Longfellow lamented, "Oh! Where are the genial days, when literature was the theme of our conversation!" (17 September 1848). Preston Brooks's merciless caning of Sumner on the floor of the Senate completely devastated Longfellow. "Burning with

---

she also notes that "Sumner's general arrogance does not seem to have carried over to friendship with black people" (*Letters of Sumner* 2: 291)

78 Frank Preston Stearns, *Cambridge Sketches* (Philadelphia: Lippincott, 1905) 79.

79 See Longfellow to Sumner, 18 December 1863, *Letters* 4: 372. On Gardner and the increased American appetite for images during the war, see Keith F. Davis, "'A Terrible Distinctness': Photography of the Civil War Era," *Photography in Nineteenth-Century America*, ed. Martha A. Sandweiss (New York: Abrams, 1991) 131-79.

80 Stearns, *Cambridge Sketches* 199.

Figure 27. Alexander Gardner, photographer, "The Politics and Poetry of New England," ca. 1863, carte-de-visite, Houghton *2001M-8, box 2

indignation and shame," he exclaimed, "O Southern Chivalry! O blackguardism! O scoundrelism!" (23 May 1856).

There is no doubt that both men were strongly drawn to each other, both intellectually and emotionally. Longfellow's journal entries emphasize how "handsome" Sumner was, with his flowing "dark hair and pale face" (18 February 1846). Watching his friend try out the shower bath at Craigie House, Longfellow facetiously called him "a kind of Adam."[81] Sumner, who had accompanied Longfellow even for part of his honeymoon with Fanny, immediately responded: "With all my ribs," a slight directed against women, who were, Sumner implied, not needed in the exclusive world created by their friendship (14 June 1846). But this was, of course, wishful thinking on Sumner's

81 Ernest Longfellow, perhaps embarrassed by the thought that Sumner might have been naked in his father's presence, suggested that the whole shower incident was an accident and Sumner got drenched while fully clothed (Ernest Wadsworth Longfellow, *Random Memories* 22).

part. Unlike Sumner, who was married only briefly later in life (an experience that left him an "unhappy waif," as he told Longfellow),[82] Longfellow did have a full and demanding family life. This becomes especially clear in the following episode, which pits the city-dwelling Sumner ("he who knows not grass from grain") against members of the Longfellow family, who cannot help but laugh about their awkward friend's misfortune. Interestingly, Longfellow represents himself, at the beginning of the journal entry, as the one initiating a political discussion:

> *Sumner* at dinner. Urged him to take strong ground against conditions by which the Anti-slavery doctrines of the Free Soil party may be suppressed, as in New York.
>
> After dinner we strolled in the garden. On the lawn stood tethered a calf, which Sumner wanted to pat on the head, in a bucolic moment of enthusiasm for the fascinations of rural life—he who knows not grass from grain. Accordingly he seized the rope—and pulls nearer and nearer, saying: 'Come here! come here!' when with a sudden leap away springs the idylic [sic] animal; the rope sweeps through the grass; there is a glimmer of gray gaiters high in air, and prone lies the philanthropist on the sod!
>
> Fanny, Charley and I were the spectators of this catastrophe, and could not help laughing, which Sumner rather resented by saying to Charley;
>
> "When a friend meets with an accident you ought not to laugh at him; you ought to pity, and sympathize with him!"
>
> (4 November 1849; Longfellow Papers, Houghton, MS Am 1340 [203], FIGURE 28)

Sumner's reprimand at the end seems directed not only against Charley but also at Longfellow himself and his patent lack of parental supervision.

In the last decade of Sumner's life, his precarious emotional state and declining health became a never-ending concern to Longfellow. When Sumner heard about Hawthorne's death in 1864, he wrote to Longfellow: "Life is weary & dark. I am ready to go at once."[83] But he held on for another decade, plagued by recurring attacks of *angina pectoris*. "I thought I was prepared," wrote Longfellow to George Washington Greene after he had received a telegram with the words: "Charles Sumner is dead." But he wasn't, not now, not ever. "It is terribly sudden and unexpected to me as it will be to you. I cannot write more" (11 March 1874; *Letters* 5: 727). He was a pallbearer at Sumner's funeral; incredulously, he "heard the first bluebirds singing" (16 March 1874).

82 Sumner to Longfellow, 4 October 1867, *Letters of Sumner* 2: 405.

83 Sumner to Longfellow, 21 May 1864, *Letters of Sumner* 2: 241.

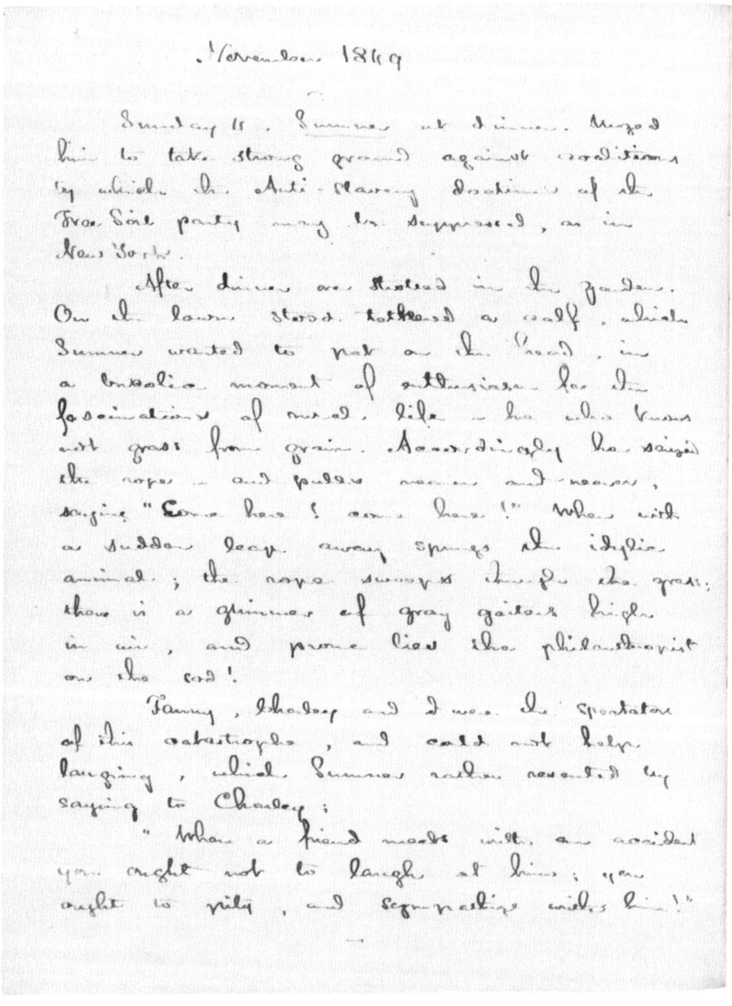

November 1849

Sunday 4. Sumner at dinner. Urged him to take strong ground against coalitions by which the Anti-Slavery doctrines of the Free Soil party may be suppressed, as in New York.

After dinner we strolled in the garden. On the lawn stood tethered a calf, which Sumner wanted to pat on the head, in a bucolic moment of enthusiasm for the fascinations of rural life—he who knows not grass from grain. Accordingly he seized the rope and pulled nearer and nearer, saying "Come here! come here!" When with a sudden leap away springs the idyllic animal; the rope sweeps through the grass; there is a glimmer of gray gaiters high in air, and prone lies the philanthropist on the sod!

Fanny, Charley and I were the spectators of this catastrophe, and could not help laughing, which Sumner rather resented by saying to Charley:

"When a friend meets with an accident you ought not to laugh at him; you ought to pity, and sympathize with him!"

Figure 28. Longfellow, entry for 4 November 1849, p. 106 from Journal 1 Jan. 1849-31 Oct. 1850, Longfellow Papers, Houghton, MS Am 1340 (203)

Longfellow memorialized the "handsome" Sumner not once but twice: first in a deeply felt but undistinguished poem included in *The Masque of Pandora* ("Charles Sumner")[84] and then in a sonnet, written on 14 June 1874, that became part of a series devoted to "Three Friends of Mine" (i.e., Felton, Agassiz, Sumner; 3: 215-217). Uncharacteristically for Longfellow, his grief here at times breaks through the detachment that marks other memorial verse written during those years, such as his

84 The poem did not satisfy Longfellow either: "I have been trying to write something about Sumner, but to little purpose. I cannot collect my faculties" (2 April 1874).

tributes to the Harvard classicist Cornelius Felton or the former Bowdoin professor Parker Cleaveland. The poet begins by asking the Charles River, Sumner's namesake, to embrace his dead friend not only literally (because it flows past Mount Auburn Cemetery, where he has been laid to rest) but also metaphorically. It is particularly poignant that, after a friendship that had lasted almost forty years, during which the salutation in their letters ("My dear Sumner"; "My dear Longfellow") had never changed, Longfellow finally musters up the courage to call his friend by his first name, but again can do so only indirectly. "Say good night," the speaker exhorts the "Charles" River, only to see, two lines later, with the reference to the dampness that gathers on the face of a corpse as the body temperature falls, the whole gesture exposed as what it really is—a clever conceit, a convenient fiction:

> River, that stealest with such silent pace
>   Around the City of the Dead, where lies
>   A friend who bore thy name, and whom these eyes
>   Shall see no more in his accustomed place,
> Linger and fold him in thy soft embrace,
>   And say good-night, for now the western skies
>   Are red with sunset, and gray mists arise
>   Like damps that gather on a dead man's face.

What the conceit accomplishes, though, and with heart-rending clarity, is to remind the speaker of the many times he and his friend actually—and not at all metaphorically!—did say good night to each other at Craigie House, in a past that now seems definitely past. But then, in another extraordinary reversal, the speaker in the last tercet of the sonnet decides to introduce and hold on to yet another fiction: namely that the past isn't over after all, that the departed friend in reality has just gone up the stairs to sleep, while he, the speaker, is staying up watching the fire burn down. The intimacy of that final scene, with the two friends interacting as if they were an old married couple, is touching and powerful, but in a poem as meandering as the river to which it is addressed, even that cannot be the final word. Milton's elegy for Lycidas had ended with the loved one's ascension to paradise. But this fantasy has no relevance for Longfellow. The "as" in the penultimate line marks the last image as yet another fiction, a final "as if," a beautiful but ultimately useless attempt to disguise the brutal fact that Charles Sumner is no more:

> Good-night! good-night! as we so oft have said
>   Beneath this roof at midnight, in the days
>   That are no more, and shall no more return.
> Thou has but taken thy lamp and gone to bed;

I stay a little longer, as one stays
To cover up the embers that still burn. (3: 217)

As problematic a person as Sumner is still made out to be, the bond between him and Longfellow remained strong and untroubled to the end.[85] Longfellow's relationship with an equally complex man, Nathaniel Hawthorne, was by contrast, anxiety-laden. Both had been members of the legendary class of 1825 at Bowdoin College, although they were not friends then and in fact belonged to different literary societies: Longfellow was a member of the more staid, more respectable "Peucinians," whereas Hawthorne was an "Athenaean," affiliations that are misleading and do not accurately characterize their political stances later in life.[86] They went their different ways after graduation until 1837, when Hawthorne, struggling to maintain himself as a writer and impressed with the apparent success of *Outre-Mer*, remembered his former classmate and, hoping for much-needed help, asked his publisher, the American Stationers Company, to put a copy of his *Twice-told Tales* in the mail to Longfellow. In a letter announcing the imminent arrival of his book, Hawthorne sheepishly conceded that "we were not, it is true, so well acquainted at college that I can plead an absolute right to inflict my 'twice-told' tediousness upon you" but then went ahead and did just that. After Longfellow had thanked him for the letter, saying how much "very great delight" previous publications by Hawthorne had given him, Hawthorne dispensed with all decorum and made no bones about his despair: "I have made a captive of myself, and put me into a dungeon; and now I cannot find the key to let myself out—and if the door were open, I should be almost afraid to come out."[87] Longfellow was happy to oblige his former classmate and, in the words of Annie Fields, "administered true consolation."[88]

He reviewed *Twice-told Tales* favorably in the July 1837 issue of *The North American Review*. After spilling much ink on generalities ("As to the pure mind all things are pure, so to the poetic mind all things are poetical") and what he considered the tradition of New England storytelling, he finally did get around to praising Hawthorne, vaguely but fulsomely, calling his prose "clear as running waters" and—here the imagery gets a bit muddled—describing his words as the "stepping stones" on which author and reader cross "the bright and rushing stream of thought" (7: 426-32). That was good enough

85 In the 1872 presidential election, Sumner endorsed Horace Greeley instead of Grant, a choice not welcomed by Longfellow, but there is no evidence that this affected their friendship. Instead, Longfellow declared that American politics in general now "puzzle[d] and annoye[d] him" (Longfellow to Sumner, 14 May 1872, *Letters of Sumner* 2: 587, n. 3).

86 See Calhoun, *Longfellow* 37.

87 Hawthorne to Longfellow, 7 March 1837, 4 June 1837; *Selected Letters of Nathaniel Hawthorne*, ed. Joel Myerson (Columbus: Ohio State University Press, 2002) 41-43; Brenda Wineapple, *Hawthorne: A Life* (2003; New York: Random, 2004) 94-95.

88 Fields, *Nathaniel Hawthorne* (Boston: Small, Maynard & Co., 1909) 39-40.

for Hawthorne, who immediately dashed off a thank-you note. Five people at least agreed with Longfellow's praise, he said, namely his mother, his aunt, two sisters, and, "the sturdiest believer of the whole five," Hawthorne himself. Hawthorne also warned Longfellow that he was going to come to Cambridge soon: "I am anxious to hold a talk." [89]

And talk they did from then on, over a period that survived Hawthorne's prolonged stay in Europe and continued until his death in 1864. Henry as well as Fanny continued to act as his cheerleaders when metaphysical despair got the better of their brooding friend, praising his work ("How admirably Hawthorne writes," 8 September 1846) as well as his "manly beauty" (27 October 1846) and inviting him to Craigie House for dinner. Hawthorne, in turn, offered career advice to Longfellow, telling him that he should "by all means give up College now, and devote these golden years of life to literature alone." Yes, said Longfellow, as he had done before, "I mean to do it." He was, he had realized just the day before, a "fool and a madman" to hang on to the life of a college professor (26 October 1846).

Not all their exchanges were anxiety-laden. A letter written on 19 March 1843, addressed to "Nathaniel Hawthorne at Dr. Peabody's West Street," shows Longfellow from a relaxed, playful side:

> Dearest Hawthornius,
> Don't forget that you are to dine with me on Tuesday next—that is to say, the day after tomorrow—at 3 o'clock.
>
> I want very much to see you, and to tell how truly delighted I was with your last story, The Birth Mark. Not the comet himself can unfold a more glorious *tail*.
>
> But you should have made a Romance of it, and not a short story only.
>
> More of that on Tuesday; till when
>
> Yours very truly
>
> H.W.L.
>
> Cambridge March 19 1843
> (Houghton *2001M-8, box 1, FIGURE 29)

Longfellow had read "The Birth-mark" in the March 1843 issue of James Russell Lowell's short-lived periodical, *The Pioneer*. The comet he mentions was the so-called "Great March Comet" of 1843, one of the most spectacular of the nineteenth century, the record-holder for the longest tail in history. Note Longfellow's pun on tale/tail, and note, too, how seamlessly the length of the comet's tail becomes part of an attempt to convince Hawthorne to write a longer "tale" (a novel) instead of limiting himself to

89 See *Life* 2: 265-66, as well as James R. Mellow, *Hawthorne and His Times* (1980; Boston: Houghton Mifflin, 1983) 78-80.

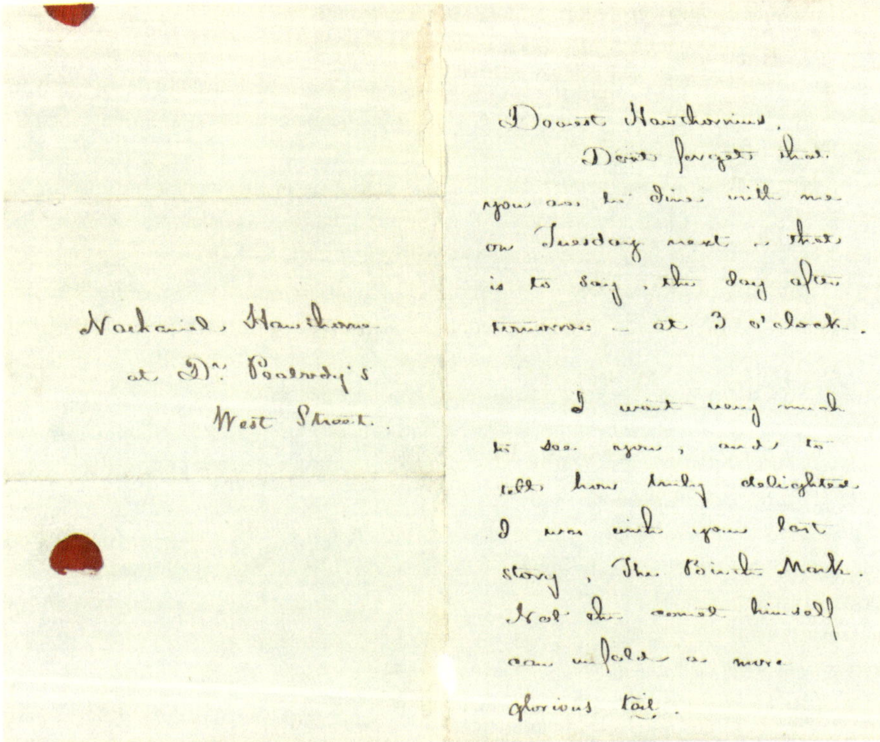

Nathaniel Hawthorne
at Dr. Peabody's
West Street.

Dearest Hawthorne,
Don't forget that you are to dine with me on Tuesday next — that is to say, the day after tomorrow — at 3 o'clock.

I want very much to see you, and to tell how truly delighted I was with your last story, The Birth-Mark. Not [illegible] himself [illegible] unfold a more glorious tale.

Figure 29. Longfellow to Nathaniel Hawthorne, 19 March 1843, Houghton *2001M-8, box 1

shorter, and presumably less profitable, works (*The Scarlet Letter* didn't appear before 1850, and then only because of his publisher's enthusiasm for the book). Longfellow must have enjoyed the veiled critique of Emersonian transcendentalism in Hawthorne's story of the scientist who is bent on removing a birthmark from his wife's cheek and ends up killing her in the process: "our great creative Mother, while she amuses us with apparently working in the broadest sunshine, is yet severely careful to keep her own secrets."[90] Whether Longfellow fully understood the "secret" of Hawthorne's creativity is another matter; the advice he dispensed to Hawthorne—write 100 stories, turn your story into something resembling a novel—certainly shows a much cannier, less broodingly introspective approach to the business of writing than that practiced by his friend.

In 1840, Hawthorne had been able to return, at least indirectly, the favors the more successful Longfellow had extended to him when he graciously allowed Longfellow first dibs on a story he had first heard from Hawthorne's Salem acquaintance, the

90 Hawthorne, "The Birth-mark," *Tales and Sketches*, ed. Roy Harvey Pearce (New York: Library of America, 1982) 769.

Reverend Horace Conolly.[91] Longfellow used the material—the tale of a young couple in French Acadia, separated by the British invaders and united only in death, after long wanderings across the continent—for the epic in hexameters that would become his runaway bestseller, *Evangeline: A Tale of Acadie*. Hawthorne, who had thus, ironically, helped his Bowdoin classmate become even more popular, continued to chafe at his own lack of commercial success. His ascension to the consulship at Liverpool, engineered by another Bowdoin classmate, President Franklin Pierce, which provided him with $5,000 to $6,000 a year, did not permanently lighten his mood.[92] "All the devotion of his publishers," wrote Annie Fields later, in a self-serving aside meant to highlight her and her husband's efforts, was needed to create an audience for Hawthorne's work, "proved by the constant reprinting of his books in varying forms, by newspaper articles, by private letters and conversations."[93] In 1860, after three more years in Italy and another year in England, he and his wife Sophia traveled back to America, in the company of James and Annie Fields, who had joined them for the return passage: "At Ticknor's found both Hawthorne and Fields, who came back in the English Steamer of Thursday," Longfellow recorded in his journal. "Both have the brown tint of the sun and the sea; and both seem a little bewildered and sad at getting back from Europe" (30 June 1860). When he heard about the death of Fanny Longfellow, Hawthorne wrote to Fields, incredulous that someone other than he should have been beset by tragedy—and worried about the effect such misery might have on *him*: "One would think that there ought to have been no deep sorrow in the life of a man like him; and now comes this blackest of shadows, which no sunshine hereafter can ever penetrate! I shall be afraid to meet him again; he cannot be the man that I have known."[94]

Three years later, Hawthorne was dead. Annie Fields inserted an autograph of Longfellow's elegy for Hawthorne into the fair copy (the final, clean version intended for use by the printer) of *The House of the Seven Gables* that she left to Harvard College. As a faint postscript to Hawthorne's neatly written manuscript, Longfellow's autograph epitomizes the relationship between the two men, a subdued but strong friendship in which Longfellow, for the most part, was content to give rather than receive. The poem (analyzed in some detail in the introduction to this book, pages 10-14) was first published in James Fields's *Atlantic Monthly* and subsequently in a small, exquisitely illustrated and bound volume which contained only thirteen pieces, Longfellow's *Flower-de-Luce* (Ticknor & Fields, 1866). The copy owned by Houghton Library (Houghton *81-162), a first edition, was inscribed by Longfellow, on 18 December 1866,

91 The exact date of the conversation with Conolly is uncertain. See *Life* 2: 70-73, as well as Calhoun, *Longfellow* 180.

92 Communications between Longfellow and Hawthorne seem to have petered out while the latter was abroad: "Do send me some news of yourself," wrote Longfellow on 5 August 1857 (*Letters* 4: 44).

93 Fields, *Hawthorne* 88.

94 Hawthorne to James Fields, 14 July 1861, in Mellow, *Hawthorne and His Times* 545.

to "Mrs. E. A. Wadsworth," Emmeline Austin Wadsworth, who had married William Wolcott Wadsworth in 1846 and had been a close friend and Beacon Street neighbor of Fanny Appleton Longfellow (see page 26).

The unlikeliest member of the innermost circle of Longfellow's friends was probably the Swiss paleontologist, marine biologist, geologist, and museum founder Louis Agassiz, now chiefly remembered because he helped popularize the idea of the "Ice Age." Agassiz was born on 28 May 1807 in Motier, Switzerland (and thus shares the 2007 bicentennial with his friend Longfellow). Longfellow first met him, "a pleasant voluble man, with a bright, beaming face," at the house of Cornelius Felton, then the Eliot Professor of Greek literature at Harvard, and soon came to enjoy Agassiz's company greatly, finding him "exceedingly agreeable" (9 January 1847; 3 February 1847). His delight increased when, at a dinner party given in Agassiz's honor at the house of Longfellow's father-in-law, Nathan Appleton, he overheard him praising his description of the Glacier du Rhône in *Hyperion*, "which is pleasant in the mouth of a Swiss, who has a Glacier Theory of his own" (4 February 1847).[95] He was impressed by Agassiz's style as a lecturer ("He warms and glows as he advances") and liked his teaching methods (Agassiz would take his students to the beach at Nahant to catch nature in the act, "pour prendre la nature sur le fait," 7 April 1848). His theory "that all animals are to be traced to one original form in the egg" reminded him of Goethe (6 February 1849). Agassiz's reluctance to attend church on Sundays, the subject of much gossip in Cambridge, did not bother him at all—Longfellow shrugged it off by quoting from the famous ode in which Horace identifies himself as a "sparse and infrequent worshipper of the gods" (11 June 1848).[96]

Agassiz's fiftieth birthday was celebrated in Cambridge as if it were a national holiday, with a surprise concert, organized by his students, in front of his house the night before and a dinner the next day given to Agassiz by the "Saturday Club." Longfellow, normally reluctant to deliver poems-made-to-order, wrote a few lines for the occasion, clearly intended as a special gift for a dear friend.[97] In "The Fiftieth Birthday of Agassiz," he perceptively stressed the textual basis of Agassiz's science—the notion, no doubt appealing to a writer, that Nature requires competent readers capable of deciphering

95 Fanny's opinion of Agassiz, at least at the time, was slightly more reserved: "We dine with Papa, next week, to meet the Swiss geologist Agassiz, who has finished his lectures here but remains to dissect Father Neptune's subjects, of whom he has a fearful amount of knowledge. Tadpoles and eels are his bosom friends, and a mere glance at their brains tells him their whole history" (to Thomas G. Appleton, 31 January 1847; *ML* 125).

96 "*Parcus deorum cultor, et infrequens*"; Horace, *Carmina* 1: 34.

97 The Houghton manuscript, which was transferred from Harvard's Museum of Comparative Zoology, has a note attached to it: "My Dear Agassiz Behold! Yours truly H.W.L. Nov. 12 1860." The original location of the manuscript seems to indicate that this was in Agassiz's possession; Longfellow probably copied the poem for his friend's personal use.

the signs and clues it has left for us. Here, then, is, in a poetic nutshell, the reason why Agassiz fascinated the likes of Emerson, Thoreau, and Lowell:

> It was fifty years ago
> In the pleasant month of May,
> In the beautiful Pays de Vaud,
> A child in its cradle lay.

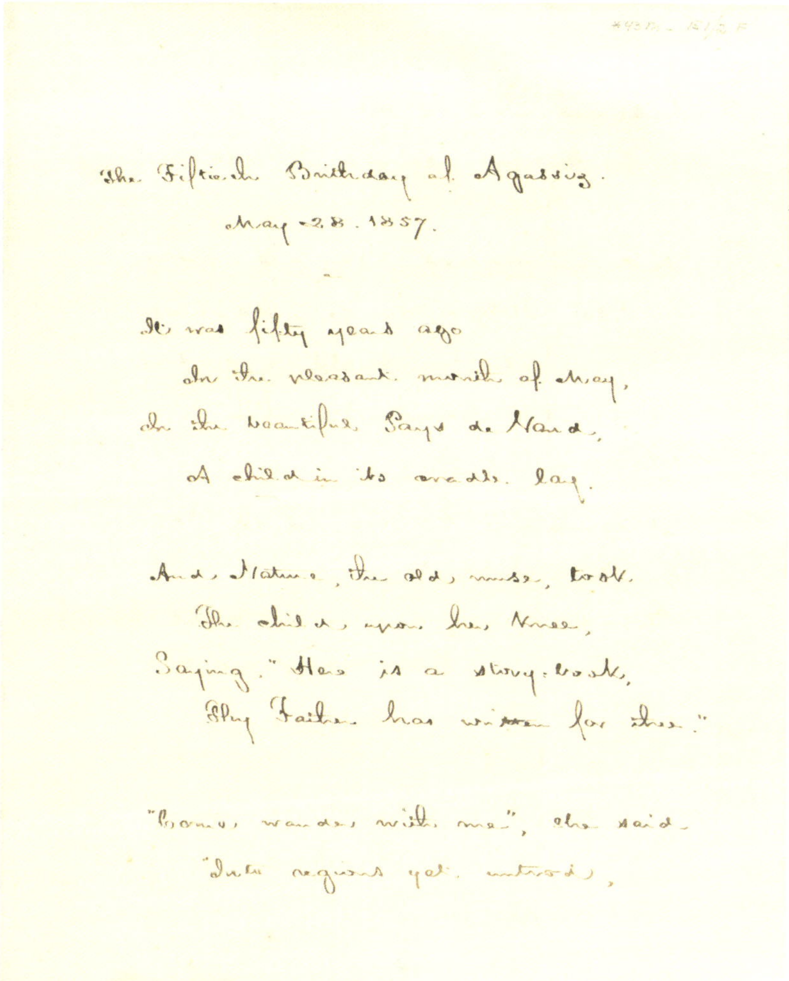

The Fiftieth Birthday of Agassiz.
May 28. 1857.

It was fifty years ago
In the pleasant month of May,
In the beautiful Pays de Vaud,
A child in its cradle lay.

And Nature, the old nurse, took
The child upon her knee,
Saying: "Here is a story-book
Thy Father has written for thee."

"Come, wander with me", she said,
"Into regions yet untrod,

Figure 30. Longfellow, "The Fiftieth Birthday of Agassiz" (originally written in 1857; this autograph in 1860), Longfellow, Miscellaneous Papers, Houghton, MS Am 1370

And Nature, the old nurse, took
  The child upon her knee,
Saying, "Here is a story-book,
  Thy Father has written for thee."

"Come wander with me," she said,
  "Into regions yet untrod,
And read what is still unread
  In the manuscripts of God."

(Longfellow, Miscellaneous Papers, Houghton, MS Am 1370, FIGURE 30)

In some ways, Agassiz was the closest friend both Longfellow and Fanny ever had in Cambridge after Sumner had moved to Washington. Their association went beyond dinner invitations, meetings of the Saturday Club, to which Agassiz had gotten Longfellow admitted, and shared summer sojourns on Nahant, where Agassiz kept a cottage, too (attached was the nation's first seaside laboratory). Longfellow and his wife greatly cherished the ease and European grace that Agassiz had brought into their lives. What a welcome change this was from the obsession of most Bostonians with their privacy, from the lack of "regular, nourishing" contacts with others. "There is no promenade, no Corso where one can meet and exchange a few refreshing words," wrote Fanny Longfellow, "no gallery to lounge in but the dreary Atheneum, where I rarely meet a soul I know." Hardly any of their friends could be relied on for "social purposes," added Fanny, except Agassiz. "Henry pines under this life" (*ML* 221). And so, needless to say, did she.

Agassiz was a great favorite with the Longfellow children who loved his "delightful and contagious laugh." Ernest Longfellow later called him "the most charming man of all my father's friends."[98] Longfellow loved to stop by Agassiz's museum to take a look at the wonderful viviparous fish from California or show up at his friend's lab on Nahant to admire a beautiful medusa, "just taken from the sea, a new species not yet described in books" (18 July 1857). It helped that Agassiz didn't just dissect fish but also liked to eat them: "The fish stories at dinner yesterday produced strange effects," Longfellow reported to him on 19 June 1861. The first thing he had done this morning was order some halibut from town. Then he had heard a fishmonger in Cambridge cry out "Fresh mackerel," and couldn't resist buying that either. And what should he find when he came home—more fish, "a beautiful turbot! A *splendid* turbot," which his good friend Agassiz had sent him for dinner. Fish aplenty. Life was good (*Letters* 4: 239).

Their friendship survived the disagreements they had, although there were some bumps in the road. In May 1850, Longfellow dragged his Ojibway friend Kah-ge-ga-gah-bow (also known as George Copway) to Agassiz's lecture on "The Races of Man."

98 Ernest Wadsworth Longfellow, *Random Memories* 25-26.

One wonders what Kah-ge-ga-gah-bow made of Agassiz's evocation of Caucasian superiority. Later that night, writing in his diary, all Longfellow had to say about Agassiz's talk was: "He thinks there were several Adams and Eves, and several gardens of Eden" (13 June 1850).[99] The brevity of the remark, coupled with the patent absurdity of the idea of multiple "gardens of Eden," speaks volumes. That said, Longfellow's radically different view of slavery had no lasting impact on his affection for Agassiz. "If my thoughts were arrows or if I could shoot my quills at you," Longfellow, overflowing with emotion, wrote to Agassiz when he was in Brazil, "I should before now have stuck you so full of them, that the Brazilians would not have known you from St. Sebastian." In the same letter he unabashedly asked Agassiz to bring home with him "2000 (two thousand) Bahia cigars, first quality" (17 April 1866; *Letters* 5: 48).

Moncure Conway (1832-1907), who later became famous as a minister and radical abolitionist, remembered how Agassiz, always the salesman, tried to warm Longfellow to the idea of a poem "on the great revelations of science concerning the earth." As he described the hypothetical work and the themes it would treat—"the successive periods of primeval rock, vast forests of fern, strange, huge creatures"—Agassiz, as it were, began to write the poem himself. Realizing what was happening, he paused: "There ought to be an epic written about it," he cried excitedly. No doubt, said Longfellow dryly, "there ought to be, and might be; but he was not the man to do it" (*Life* 3: 396).

Agassiz's letters, scribbled hastily and not always legibly, in often erratic spelling, on small sheets of paper, are usually extremely businesslike, focused on favors he needed (fish to be procured, observations to be made, books to be sent) and money that had to be collected. Thus, the beginning of the following letter, written shortly before Agassiz embarked on what became his last spectacular trip, a deep-sea dredging expedition around the Cape Horn, is doubly remarkable. Embedded into the most mundane of communications—Agassiz had been busy working in the natural history museum he had founded in Cambridge and wanted to warn his friend that he would be on Nahant later than planned—is nothing short of a declaration of love for the man who was so unlike him and yet so likable:

> Cambridge, August 18th, 1871.
> My dear Longfellow,

99 Agassiz did claim that human races were "distinct primordial forms of the type of man," which also implied that they couldn't have "originated from a common stock." However, as Longfellow very well knew, Agassiz's goal in asserting that "Adam and Eve were neither the only nor the first human beings created" was not to multiply the Biblical account but to assail "the supposed authority of the Mosaic record" as a whole. See Agassiz, "Geographical Distribution of Animals," *The Christian Examiner and Religious Miscellany* 48 (1850): 181-204, as well as Agassiz, "Sketch of the Provinces of the Animal World and Their Relation to the Different Types of Man," in J. C. Nott and George R. Gliddon, *Types of Mankind: or, Ethnological Researches* (Philadelphia: Lippincott, 1854) [lviii]-lxxvi.

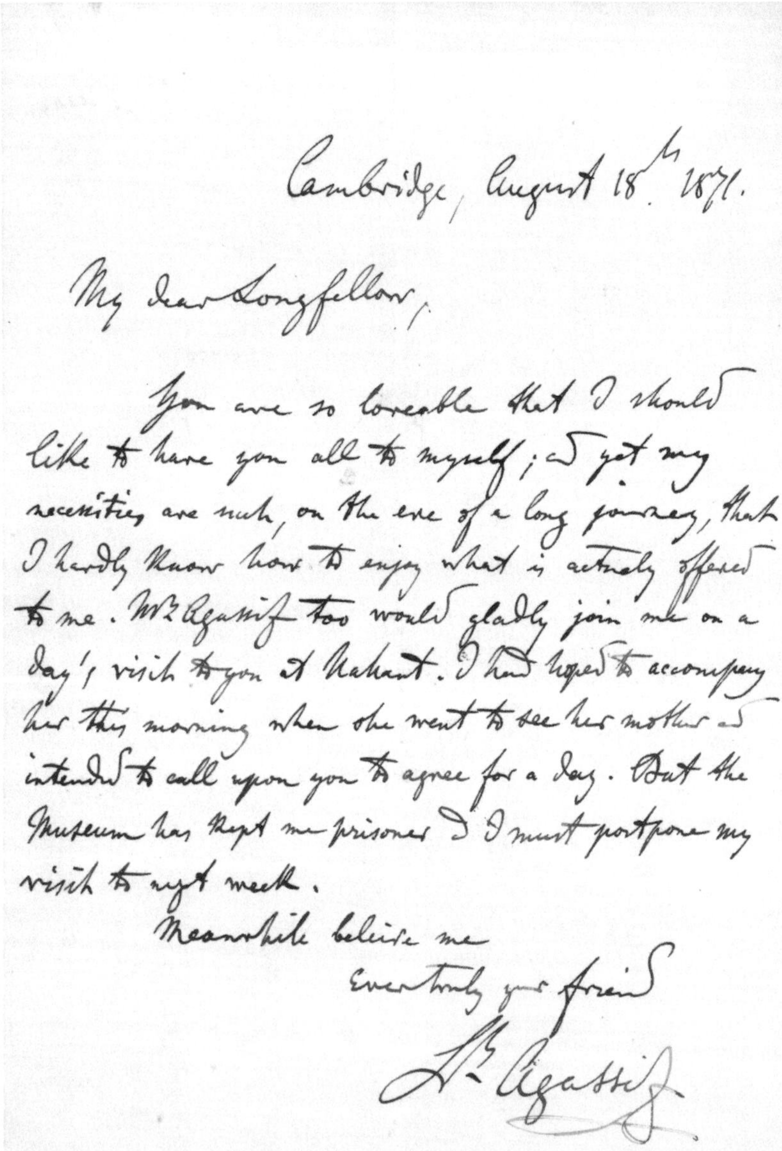

Cambridge, August 18th 1871.

My dear Longfellow,

You are so loveable that I should like to have you all to myself; and yet my necessities are such, on the eve of a long journey, that I hardly know how to enjoy what is actually offered to me. Mrs Agassiz too would gladly join me on a day's visit to you at Nahant. I had hoped to accompany her this morning when she went to see her mother and intended to call upon you to agree for a day. But the Museum has kept me prisoner and I must postpone my visit to next week.

Meanwhile believe me

Ever truly your friend

L. Agassiz

Figure 31. Louis Agassiz to Longfellow, 18 August 1871, Letters to Longfellow, Houghton, bMS Am 1340.2 (45)

You are so loveable that I should like to have you all to myself; and yet my necessitics are such, on the eve of a long journey, that I hardly know how to enjoy what is actualy [sic] offered to me. Mrs. Agassiz too would gladly join me on a day's visit to you at Nahant. I had hoped to accompany her this morning when she went to see her mother and intended to call upon you to agree for a day. But the Museum has kept me prisoner and I must postpone my visit to next week.

Meanwhile believe me

Ever truly your friend,

L^{s}. Agassiz

(Letters to Longfellow, Houghton, bMS Am 1340.2 [45], FIGURE 31)

Agassiz did not waver in his attempts to recruit the circumspect Longfellow for his cause. The Houghton collection contains one of the last notes Agassiz ever wrote, in early December 1873, requesting that Longfellow look over the proofs of a new essay, "Evolution and Permanence of Type." It became his parting shot in the long, unsuccessful battle he had been waging against Darwin:

> My dear Longfellow. May I trouble you with this proof? I have undertaken to write out my views upon the great question of the day I would like the advise [sic] of judicious friends. Write freely on the margin if you feel like it … I will call in the course of the day.
>
> Ever truly yours
>
> L^{s}. Agassiz[100]

Days later, the news spread like wildfire through Cambridge that the formidable Agassiz lay dying in his house on Quincy Street. Longfellow, stunned into speechlessness, cut out an article about Agassiz's illness from the *Advertiser*, pasted it on the back of a one-penny U.S. postal card, and mailed it to his friend Greene in Rhode Island.[101] He stopped by Agassiz's house every day but, since there didn't seem to be any good news, never dared go in. On what proved to be the last day of her father's life, Agassiz's daughter Pauline Agassiz Shaw sent Longfellow a letter regarding her father's condition. Agassiz was still showing "signs of recognition," she wrote, and he would answer questions, "though not very distinctly." He had been half-asleep all day, "only disturbed by increased heat in his head & great flushing of the face." Agassiz had never regained his ability to swallow and was now keeping his eyes closed most of the time: "his mind seems quite dormant, only occasionally roused by questions to make short answers—both in French & English according to the language by which he is

100 Agassiz Papers, Houghton, bMS Am 1340.2 (45).

101 Longfellow to George Washington Greene, 13 December 1873, *Letters* 5: 698.

addressed." Would Longfellow mind passing on this news to Charles Sumner, who had also inquired after Agassiz? "My letter may be confused—I am thinking so of father that I can hardly collect my thoughts."[102]

On 14 December 1873, Agassiz died. Three days later, on a snowless winter afternoon, Longfellow followed his casket to its final resting place in Mount Auburn Cemetery. We don't know what Longfellow thought of Agassiz's last essay, which came out posthumously in the January issue of *The Atlantic Monthly*. We do know, however, that Agassiz's death so devastated him that, when he told Greene about it, he took recourse to a language he dearly loved, Italian:

> Camb. 15. Dicembre 1873.
> Jernotte alle dieci mori il nostro caro Agassiz, o
> "quel che *morir* chiaman li sciocchi."
> "*C'est la fin*!" furono le ultime parole sue.
> (*Letters* 5: 699)[103]

A few months later, Longfellow wrote a sonnet remembering Agassiz, which, like the elegy for Sumner, became part of the sequence "Three Friends of Mine." (The third friend was Felton, who had died in 1862.) Later, Longfellow also included the Agassiz sonnet in his anthology *Poems of Places*, ostensibly so that he would have something to offer under the heading "Nahant, Mass." Like the Sumner poem, Longfellow's tribute to the dead Agassiz trembles with an overwhelming sense of personal loss ("Why art thou silent? Why shouldst thou be dead?"), to which the "familiar shore" of Nahant and the "waves of the distracted sea" serve only as convenient backdrops. But Longfellow goes on to show that a place—in this case the ocean—will always survive the people who inhabit it and who, like Agassiz, think they have completely understood it:

> The rocks, the sea-weed on the ocean floor,
> The willows in the meadow, and the free
> Wild winds of the Atlantic welcome me;
> Then why shouldst thou be dead, and come no more?

102 Pauline Agassiz Shaw to Longfellow, 14 December 1873, Letters to Longfellow, Houghton, bMS Am 1340.2 (5027).

103 "Last night at ten our dear Agassiz died, or / 'what fools call dying.' / 'This is the end!' were his last words." The quotation in l. 2 is from Petrarch's "Triumphus Mortis" I, l. 171. The question of whether or not Agassiz said anything before he died is a complicated one; assistants who claimed to have been present said he did, but those reports were always denied by Elizabeth Cary Agassiz. Her husband had died quietly, she said, and "merely stopped breathing"; see her letter to Henry Cary, 10 February [1896], Elizabeth Agassiz Papers, Schlesinger Library, A3, folder 32.

Ah, why shouldst thou be dead, when common men
Are busy with their trivial affairs,
Having and holding? Why, when thou hadst read
Nature's mysterious manuscript, and then
Wast ready to reveal the truth it bears,
Why art thou silent? Why shouldst thou be dead?
(3: 216-17)

The beach at Nahant was where Agassiz used to take his students "pour prendre la nature sur le fait." It was here that he believed he had come close to deciphering nature's secrets. Longfellow uses intransitively the two transitive verbs that characterize the ways in which ordinary humans—people unlike Agassiz, that is—pass the time, by "having" and "holding." But as a naturalist and museum director, Louis Agassiz had really been not much different; he, too, had, at all times and at all costs, wanted to "hold" and "have" it all. In Longfellow's poem, the speaker realizes that Agassiz's great promise hasn't come true. The wonderful would-be decipherer of nature discovers, in death, that nature, despite all that he has, during a busy life, had and held in his hands, silenced *him*.

Another member of the Saturday Club, James Russell Lowell (1819-1891), was also shaken by Agassiz's death. Immediately after he got the news (Lowell was in Italy at the time), he dashed off a long ode. In chatty lines dripping with sentiment, he lamented that the "mountain oak" had been uprooted and a man, "brimful of lusty blood" had been taken away from him and other writers before his time: "I cannot think he wished so soon to die." Like Longfellow, he viewed Agassiz as a *poète manqué*: "He had the poet's open eye / That takes a frank delight in all it sees."[104]

Part of the glue that held men like Agassiz, Longfellow, Lowell, and Sumner together was, it must be said, a shared enthusiasm for fine wine (see also Chapter 1, pages 31–32). Sumner, who ordered his wine directly from the source, didn't hesitate to use express mail to send Agassiz a particularly fine case of St. Georges.[105] In December 1864, as a Christmas present, Longfellow had a basket of six carefully selected wine bottles delivered to Agassiz's house on Quincy Street. He included a poem in French in which the different wine bottles, from Œil-de-Perdrix to Chartreux, can be overheard boasting about their connection with Agassiz as they noisily march up the steps to the Quincy Street house, loud enough to attract the attention of the Cambridge police:

104 "Agassiz," *The Complete Poetical Works of James Russell Lowell* (Boston: Houghton, Mifflin, and Co., 1903) 502, 509, 507.

105 Sumner to Agassiz, 20 October 1863, "Montesquieu in commending his wine to some of his English correspondents said that they would receive it 'first as he received it from the good God,' & I think I may say the same of this St. Georges," Louis Agassiz Papers, Houghton, bMS Am 1410 (622).

> Ils arrivent trois à trois,
> Montent l'escalier de bois
> Clopin-clopant! quel gendarme
> Peut permettre ce vacarme,
>   Bons amis,
> À la porte d'Agassiz!

The poem ends with the speaker telling the bottles—"idiots" ("ganaches") that they are—to shut up and leave the making of bad verse to the philosophers. The wonderfully onomatopoetic word "glouglous" ("gurglings") proves Longfellow's mastery of French:

> Chut, ganaches! taisez-vous!
> C'en est trop de vos glouglous;
> Epargnez aux Philosophes
> Vos abominables strophes!
>   Bons amis,
> Respectez mon Agassiz!
> ("Noël," 3: 153-54)

Verse as light as it is slight, but Agassiz, who had been homesick and depressed, was moved to tears, because Longfellow, whom he admired and loved, had given him a present that he could share with his mother back home—he could, he said, let her *read* the wine! And in a separate letter, Elizabeth Cary Agassiz thanked Longfellow for the "witty and graceful poem," every line of which expressed "loving sympathy": "I owe to you the happiest moments of my life."[106] In 1867, incidentally, Agassiz responded in kind, sending Longfellow "a Presentation Copy" of a "new Swiss poem in six Cantos" (*Letters* 5: 133). Longfellow's journal offers a translation of this cryptic sentence: "Agassiz sends six bottles of Swiss wine" (3 May 1867).

Good wine was more than a part of Cambridge *savoir vivre*. In Longfellow's Christmas poem, the talking bottles, chatty visitors from abroad, serve as a reminder that there is another world out there, not limited by the Puritan ethos that still pervaded Boston life and affected even those who, like the Transcendentalists, had spent their lives rebelling against it: "The Puritan doctrine is fading away," sighed the *bon vivant* Tom Appleton. "Alas! Their kitchen remains."[107]

106 Elizabeth Agassiz to Longfellow, Christmas 1864, Letters to Longfellow, Houghton, bMS Am 1340.2 (44).

107 See Louise Hall Tharp, *The Appletons of Beacon Hill* (Boston: Little, Brown and Co., 1973) 328.

In Agassiz, Longfellow and others delightedly discovered the "lusty laugh that the Puritans forgot"[108]— which is why he was willing to forget his misgivings about Agassiz's politics. One can only imagine how appalled Longfellow was when his excitable friend, the "amiable enthusiast" James Russell Lowell (23 October 1845), always eager to join a new cause, discovered temperance. Longfellow immediately feared for the safety of his wine cellar: "he is quite rabid now on temperance, and wants me to destroy all the wine I have" (15 April 1846).[109]

Luckily, Lowell's dedication to abstinence was short-lived. Henry and Fanny Longfellow learned to find his shifting allegiances and obsessions (Sylvester Graham's dietary ideas, beards, spiritualism) amusing rather than bothersome. There was much that separated the reticent Longfellow ("rather a silent man," as he characterized himself, 3 June 1861) from the Boston blue-blood Lowell, a busy essayist, satirist, and prolific writer of verse of the facile kind that Longfellow usually eschewed: poems about a candlestick, the Fourth of July, and the 100th anniversary of the Fight at Concord Bridge.

Poetry came to Lowell more easily than it did to Longfellow—in September 1848, for example, he was working on three volumes of poetry simultaneously: "This is playing upon Pan's reed truly," said an impressed Longfellow (5 September 1848). Lowell later embarked on a separate career as diplomat, representing his country first in Spain and then at the court of St. James, but Longfellow and he had found each other long before over their shared love for Italy. "Thou art my tropics and my Italy," Lowell wistfully addressed an unsuspecting American dandelion in one of his earlier poems, telling the humble weed that it unlocked memories of a "warmer clime" and a feeling of "summer-like … ravishment" in him.[110] In *A Fable for Critics* (1849), a tongue-in-cheek review of the state of contemporary literature and one of the volumes on which he was working when Longfellow dropped in on him in September 1848, Lowell spoofed Bronson Alcott ("While he talks he is great, but goes out like a taper, / If you shut him up closely with pen, ink, and paper"), William Cullen Bryant ("as dignified / As … an iceberg"), James Fenimore Cooper ("When a character's wanted, he goes to the task / As a cooper would do in composing a cask"), Ralph Waldo Emerson ("scarcely six converts he's got / To I don't [nor they either] exactly know what"), Nathaniel Hawthorne ("a Puritan Tieck"), and, last but not least, himself, this pathetic "Lowell, who's striving Parnassus to climb / With a whole bale of *isms* tied together with rhyme," a would-be poet who doesn't know the distinction "'twixt singing and preaching." Longfellow, however, he

108 Oliver Wendell Holmes, "At the Saturday Club," *The Poetical Works of Oliver Wendell Holmes*, 2 vols. (Cambridge: Houghton, Mifflin, and Co., 1892) 2: 267.

109 On 23 October 1845, Lowell stopped by Longfellow's house and proposed to write "a book in favor of fanaticism."

110 "To the Dandelion," *The Complete Poetical Works of James Russell Lowell* (Boston: Houghton, Mifflin, and Co., 1903) 111.

completely exempted from his irony. Certainly, he'd had problems with Longfellow's use of hexameter in *Evangeline,* which was, he thought, to the Greek original as Johann Strauss is to Beethoven or the "the coo of a pigeon" to the "roar of the sea." But if there was one thing one could not doubt about Longfellow, it had to be his gift for friendship, offered freely even in the face of malice. And malice was, at least in Lowell's opinion, what had driven Edgar Allan Poe, Longfellow's most vocal opponent. "Three fifths" of Poe were "genius" and two fifths "sheer fudge," he witheringly observed. Nothing could justify the"mud-balls" Poe and his colleague, writer and editor Cornelius Mathews, had been flinging at Longfellow:

> Does it make a man worse that his character's such
> As to make his friends love him (as you think) too much?
> Why, there is not a bard at this moment alive
> More willing than he that his fellows should thrive;
> While you are abusing him thus, even now
> He would help either one of you out of a slough;
> You may say that he's smooth and all that till you're hoarse,
> But remember that elegance also is force . . . .[111]

Such elegance abundantly manifested itself in a humorous exchange between Longfellow and Lowell that was provoked by the latter's absence, due to illness, from a meeting of the Saturday Club on 10 January 1866 and then again from a dinner at Craigie House on 12 January. Lowell sent his regrets in a poem in which he indicated he would try out the claret gargle ("Médoc'll do") Longfellow had once recommended as a cure for sore throat, "for my throat's so bad, / I'm not to be had, / Though Horace ask me to dinner."[112] Longfellow responded instantly "[a]l' illustrissimo Signor Professore Lowello" and, in a humorous poem titled "Prescrizione Nuova per il mal di gola," reiterated his advice on how to deal with his affliction. He took his cue from "Bacco di Toscana," a well-known poem by the seventeenth-century physician Francesco Redi (called "l' Aretino," because he was born in Arezzo), who was also a champion of Montepulciano wine. But, really, *any* red wine would do:

> Questo vino,
> L' Aretino
> Loda certo con ragione;
> Ma sta fresco

111 *Works of Lowell* 153-93, especially 184.

112 James Russell Lowell to Henry Wadsworth Longfellow, 12 January 1866, *Letters* 5: 19-20 n. 1.

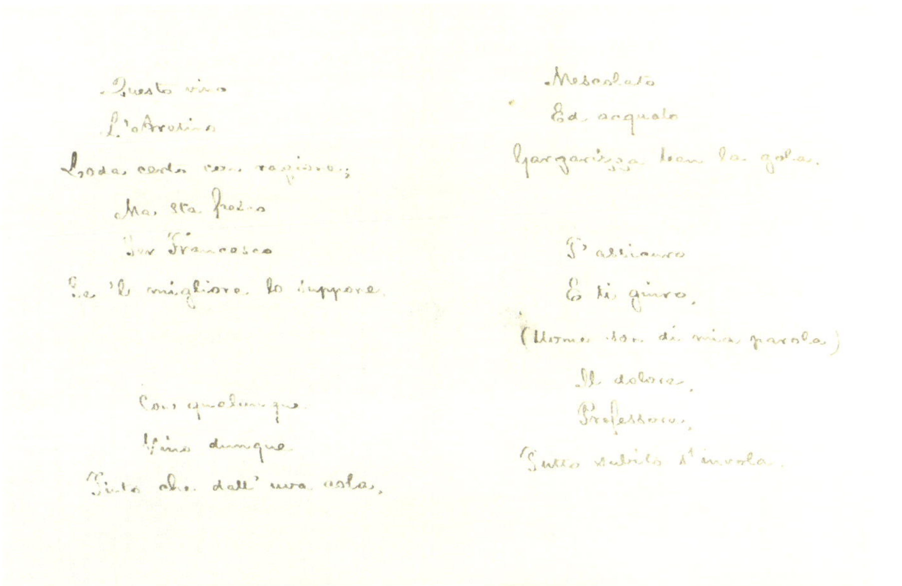
Questo vino
L'Aretino
Loda certo con ragione;
Ma sta fresco
Ser Francesco
Se 'l migliore lo suppone.

Con qualunque
Vino dunque
Tinto che dall' uva cola,

Mescolato
Ed acquato
Gargarizza ben la gola.

T' assicuro
E ti giuro,
(Uomo son di mia parola)
Il dolore,
Professore,
Tutto subito s'invola.

Figure 32. Longfellow, "Prescrizione Nuova per il mal di gola," 13 January 1866, Longfellow Papers, Houghton, MS Am 1340 (141)

Ser Francesco
Se 'l migliore lo suppone.[113]

Take the wine, mix it with water, rinse your "throttle" with it, and the beneficial effects of this treatment will be immediately evident:

T' assicuro
E ti giuro,
(Uomo son di mia parola)
Il dolore,
Professore,
Tutto subito s'invola.[114]
(Longfellow Papers, Houghton, Ms Am 1340 [141], FIGURE 32)

113 "Prescription for a Sore Throat. // […] / This same wine / The Aretine / Justly praises as he drinks it; / And yet but poor / His taste, I'm sure, / If the best of wines he thinks it" (translation in Samuel Longfellow, *Life*, 3: 443).

114 "I assure you / It will cure you / (Me a man of my word you'll own); / Your distress or / Pain, Professor, / All of a sudden will have flown" (*Life* 3: 443).

Figure 33. Annie Fields on the "piazza" of her house in Manchester-by-the-Sea. Mounted albumen photograph, unknown photographer, LONG 4686, LNHS

Longfellow was, as Annie Fields remembered, fond of Redi's poem and once suggested that she and her husband "Jamie" should use lines from it to label the wine-bottles he had sent them.[115] Her essay on Longfellow in *Authors and Friends*, a volume that also includes portraits of Ralph Waldo Emerson, Oliver Wendell Holmes, Harriet Beecher Stowe, Celia Thaxter, John Greenleaf Whittier, and Alfred, Lord Tennyson and Lady Tennyson, remains one of the best assessments of Longfellow's life and career. Fields's tone throughout the essay is one of admiration, even adulation, and, true to her technique in previous volumes, she has a tendency of letting her sources (often excerpts from her husband's diaries) speak too much for themselves. That said, Fields was the first to recognize the complexity of Longfellow's character: his love of art as a public spectacle (such as opera and theater) yet his reluctance to be made into such a spectacle himself, his dependence on company and the approbation of his readers yet his despair over being besieged by *too much* company (i.e., a steady stream of mail and long lines of adoring visitors), his horror of autobiography yet his irrepressible interest in the lives of others. Fields was a "proper Bostonian" if ever there was one: born on

115 Annie Fields, "Longfellow: 1807-1882," *Authors and Friends*, 6th ed. (1896; Boston: Houghton Mifflin, 1897) 3-64; see 57. The following quotations are all from this essay.

6 June 1834 in Boston into the famous Adams family, she had married the 37-year-old widower James Fields—"Sir James" to authors like Longfellow who admired him—in 1854. Fields's meteoric rise to a partnership in the publishing firm of Ticknor & Fields and to the editorship of *The Atlantic Monthly* put the couple at the center of the Boston literary elite and launched Annie's career as a hostess to writers both local and international, a life she continued with zeal after her husband's death, when she began to share her artifact-filled house with her new partner, the Maine writer Sarah Orne Jewett. From Emerson, Longfellow, and Dickens to George Washington Cable and Willa Cather, everyone with literary aspirations came to her literary salons. The Fields's townhouse at 148 Charles Street ("a little box of a house," in Ernest Longfellow's memory[116]) and her summer retreat in Manchester-by-the-Sea, known as "Thunderbolt Hill," became legendary.

Active in charity work, Annie Fields wrote prolifically, too. Longfellow liked her "Idyl of the Shakers," for example, and her short poem "Little Guinever" (*Letters* 5: 541; 583), and he told her that *The Return of Persephone*, a verse play Annie had written, had seemed "like a grotto, cool and refreshing" to him, as opposed to the "hot and feverish" quality of much modern poetry (*Letters* 6: 308). Fields was a learned poet, deeply versed in the classics, so when in a letter sent on 1 May 1878, she picked up his reference to "lovely Helen of Troy, / Still living and still beautiful" in "Kéramos" and applied it to Longfellow's new volume as a whole, her friend must have been gratified.[117]

But their friendship also expressed itself in other ways. Fields's Longfellow essay, for example, starts with a coded reference to their friendship, the lilacs in Fields's garden, which she had received from Longfellow himself: "Every year when the lilac buds begin to burst their sheaths and until the full-blown clusters have spent themselves in the early summer air, the remembrance of Longfellow—something of his presence—wakes with us in the morning and recurs with every fragrant breeze" (*Authors and Friends* 3). Longfellow had given those flowers to her—they were common, Fields admits, but beautiful—and from then on Fields's letters were filled with references to how these plants, "Cambridge visitors in Boston," were doing outside her house: "The lilacs are looking up and promising leaves in the future. Think of bestowing a garden-full [sic] of flowers all at once in this way." After James Fields's death in 1881, when the weather was unseasonably "chilly and damp," she wanted to send Longfellow "Jamie's" purple dressing-gown, the one her husband had "liked so much" and that she had had specifically made for him. "If the idea is sweet to you please let me send it to you."[118] We don't know if Longfellow accepted the gift; less than a year later, he would be dead, too.

116 Ernest Wadsworth Longfellow, *Random Memories* 36.

117 Annie Fields to Longfellow, Longfellow Family Papers, box 1, folder 29, LNHS.

118 Annie Fields, undated letter to Longfellow, and Annie Fields to Longfellow, 7 May 1881, Longfellow Family Papers, Box 1, folder 29, LNHS.

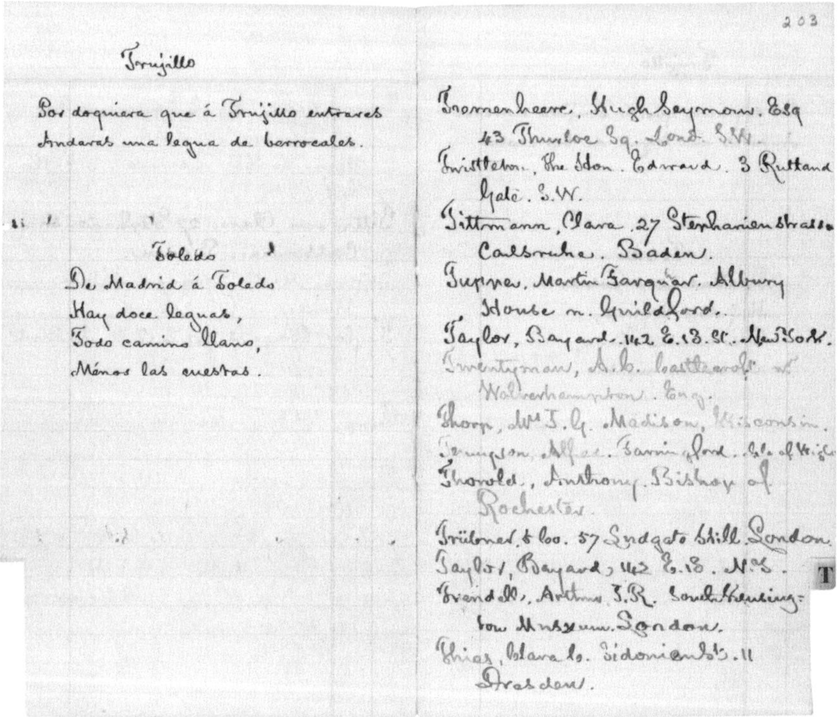

Trujillo

Por doquiera que á Trujillo entrares
Andarás una legua de berrocales.

Toledo

De Madrid á Toledo
Hay doce leguas,
Todo camino llano,
Ménos las cuestas.

203

Tremenheere, Hugh Seymour. Esq
43 Thurloe Sq. Lond. S.W.
Twistleton, the Hon. Edward. 3 Rutland Gate. S.W.
Tittmann, Clara. 27 Stephanienstrasse
Carlsruhe. Baden.
Tupper, Martin Farquhar. Albury
House n. Guildford.
Taylor, Bayard. 142 E. 18. St. New York.
Twentyman, A. C. Castlecroft n.
Wolverhampton. Eng.
Thorp, Mrs J. G. Madison, Wisconsin.
Tennyson, Alfred. Farringford. Isle of Wight
Thorold, Anthony. Bishop of
Rochester.
Trübner & Co. 57 Ludgate Hill London.
Taylor, Bayard, 142 E. 18. N.Y.
Trendell, Arthur J. R. South Kensington
Museum. London.
Thias, Clara C. Sidonienstr. 11
Dresden.

T

Figure 34. Longfellow, Address book, pp. 202-203 (1873-74), Longfellow Papers, Houghton, MS Am 1340 (34)

A beautiful albumen photograph of Fields (LONG 4686, LNHS, FIGURE 33) shows her mending a piece of cloth on the piazza of her house in Manchester-by-the-Sea, where Longfellow used to visit her, too (for the last time in 1879). Fields is wearing a light-colored dress with long sleeves; her dark hair is parted in the center and tied in a chignon. In the background, the heavy curtains shield photographer and sitter from the glare of the sun. Her feet rest on an embroidered footstool—an uncharacteristic image, with its associations of domestic tranquility, for a woman Longfellow knew possessed an intellect equal, if not superior, to his own.

One of Longfellow's surviving address books, dating from the 1870s, shows how wide he cast his net. Undistinguished fans like Clara Tittmann from Karlsruhe, Germany, would find themselves on the same page with literary celebrities like Alfred Lord Tennyson and strangers and hangers-on like Martin Farquhar Tupper. Oddly, Longfellow also used this address book (MS Am 1340 [34], FIGURE 34) to record Spanish proverbs he found in the book *L'Espagne par le Baron Chs. Davillier*, published in Paris 1874 (according to Longfellow's own note on the flyleaf). On page 220, for example, Longfellow included rhymed proverbs about places beginning with "T": Trujillo ("Por dorquiera que á Trujillo entrares / Andaras una legua de berrocales") and Toledo ("De Madrid á Toledo / Hay doce leguas, / Todo camino llano, / Ménos las cuestras").[119] On the facing page (page 203), we find a list of names beginning with "T":

> Tremenheere, Hugh Seymour, Esq 43 Thurloe Sq. Lond. S.W.
> Twistleton, The Hon. Edward. 3 Rutland Gate. S.W.
> Tittmann, Clara. 27 Stephanienstrasse. Carlsruhe. Baden.
> Tupper, Martin Farquhar. Albury House n. Guildford.
> Taylor, Bayard. 142 E. 13. St. New York.
> Twentyman, A. C. Castlecroft n[r]. Wolverhampton. Eng.
> Thorp, Mrs. J. G. Madison, Wisconsin.
> Tennyson, Alfred. Farmingford. Isle of Wight.
> Thorold, Anthony. Bishop of Rochester.
> Trübner. & Co. 57 Ludgate Hill. London.
> Taylor, Bayard 142 E. 13. N. Y.
> Trendall [sic], Arthur J. R. South Kensington Museum. London.
> Thies, Clara C. Sidonienst. 11 Dresden.

Hugh Seymour Tremenheere was the author of *The Political Experience of the Ancients* (1852); Edward Twistleton, an English barrister, had visited Boston in 1851, and bombarded Longfellow with questions about the public school system in America, "none of which do I feel to be very competent to answer" (*Letters* 3: 310); Martin Farquhar Tupper wrote a hugely popular series of moralizings in free verse called *Proverbial Philosophy* (1838-67), in which he would, among other things, recommend that a groom make sure his bride be "of wholesome stock"; Arthur Trendell was a delegate for Great Britain at the 1876 Philadelphia Exhibition. Nicholas Trübner, a London publisher and pioneer of "Oriental" Studies, had occasionally acted as a distributor of Ticknor & Fields books in England. Mrs. "J. G. Thorp" was the mother of Joseph Gilbert Thorp, Jr., who would later marry Longfellow's daughter Annie. I am not sure what Longfellow's connections with the Bishop of Rochester were or how he had come to know Arthur Charles Twentyman, a Justice of the Peace in Staffordshire, England, but here their names are, right next to that of the great traveler and translator Bayard Taylor, a frequent visitor in Longfellow's household, which is perhaps why he appears twice on the list.

"Time has sifted the Tennysons from the Tuppers," cheered Michael R. Turner, editor of an annotated anthology of *Victorian Parlor Poetry* in 1969, with audible

119 "From whatever side you approach Trujillo, / you are forced to traverse a league of rocky terrain" and "From Madrid to Toledo, / the distance is a dozen leagues / one smooth journey / if one doesn't count the hills"; see *L'Espagne par le Baron Charles Davillier, illustreés de 309 gravures dessinées sur bois par Gustave Doré* (Paris: Hachette, 1874) 495 and 547.

relief.[120] But in the pages of Longfellow's 1873 address book Tennyson and Tupper still happily coexist; as do the English and Spanish language; as do Madison, Wisconsin, Ludgate Hill in London, and Dresden, Germany, where on Sidonienstrasse 11 Clara Crowninshield Thies lived, who had accompanied Longfellow on his 1835-1836 trip to Scandinavia and Germany. (She had married the German art collector Louis Thies in 1843 and in 1866 moved to Dresden, Germany, where she died, ninety-seven years old, in 1907.[121])

One of the most obscure names on the list is probably Clara Tittmann. Her letter to Longfellow, sent from Karlsruhe on 24 February 1873, still survives. An immigrant to the United States, Tittmann had returned to Germany after her husband's death, only to find herself isolated there ("the reality was very cold to my feeling"), whereupon she went back to the New World again, feeling even more uncomfortable there. She promptly returned to Karlsruhe, where she now was, doubly disillusioned, a "poor steersman" on the "wide ocean of life," as she admitted. Through all these meanderings, her true home, the "bread of her existence," had been literature, more specifically, German and English poetry as well as "northern and Hindoo" legends. She was sending Longfellow her own version of a legend from the *Edda*, hoping that he would like it and be able to write a few appreciative lines to her brother, Julius Erasmus Hilgard (1825-91), one of the chief scientists associated with the United States Coast Survey, who had obviously stayed in the U.S. and done quite well there.[122] Was it because she wanted her brother to know that she, too, had accomplished something? Or because she wanted Longfellow to be able to save on overseas postage?

It is not clear if Longfellow did send the letter to Professor Hilgard, although, conscientious as he was in such matters, he probably did: a few noncommittal lines of praise, a general observation as to the use of such literary work, and a few words of thanks for having been permitted to read it. But why did he save Clara Tittmann's letter and, perhaps more poignantly, why did he enter the name of someone he had never met and to whose letter he apparently never directly replied into his address book, alongside those of people he knew well, such as Bayard Taylor and Clara Crowninshield Thies? Maybe he accepted Tittmann's own assessment of their relationship: Longfellow was, Tittmann told him at the beginning of her letter, perhaps the only one, her family included, with whom she felt "myself not a stranger."

120 *Victorian Parlour Poetry: An Annotated Anthology*, ed. Michael R. Turner (New York: Dover. 1992) viii.

121 See the introduction to *The Diary of Clara Crowninshield: A European Tour with Longfellow*, ed. Andrew Hilen (Seattle: University of Washington Press, 1956) xiii-xxxi.

122 Clara Tittmann to Longfellow, 24 February 1873, bMS Am 13402 (5568). Clara Hilgard "Tittman's [sic]" translation of the "Rishyasringa: A Tale of the *Mahabharata*," appeared in *Scribner's Monthly* 7.4 (February 1874): 385-90.

Chapter 5: The Public Poet

As the experience of hearing his name mentioned at a performance of the play *Hot Corn* in the Boston Museum proved once again, Longfellow could rarely go anywhere as a private citizen without being reminded that he was also a public person—public property, as it were. But he allowed this to happen only to a certain extent. Known for his reluctance to speak even in less formal settings, Longfellow consistently kept readers focused on his work rather than on his opinions. When he resigned from his professorship at Harvard in the spring of 1854, he vowed that he would never speak in public again (3 April 1854), a promise he kept religiously. For example, he declined to attend the James Fenimore Cooper Memorial meeting in New York in 1852. William Cullen Bryant, by contrast, showed up and held forth about "the Life and Genius of Cooper" (*Letters* 3: 334). When Bryant was to be the honoree, at a "Bryant Festival" held, on the occasion of the poet's 70th birthday, by the Century Association in 1864, Longfellow said he was "too unwell to be present" (*Letters* 4: 437). Ruses didn't help: in January 1860, Longfellow was getting dressed for a banquet and ball in honor of Franklin's birthday when he heard rumored that "I was expected to reply to a toast in compliment of the 'Poets of Cambridge.'" He wasn't taking any chances and sent the carriage away (18 January 1860).

During his last trip to Europe in 1868, Longfellow did feel compelled to speak on two or three occasions, responding to the members of the Carlisle Literary Society, for example,[123] or at a formal dinner in London, after William Gladstone, soon to be the new Prime Minister of England, had addressed him not only as a poet of "world-wide fame" but also as "a citizen of America" (apparently, Longfellow simply responded that he was "deeply grateful").[124] And in 1875 he let himself be talked into delivering a poem, "Morituri Salutamus," at the fiftieth reunion of his Bowdoin class. To his relief, he discovered that he would be reading from the pulpit: "Let me cover myself as much as possible; I wish it might be entirely."[125]

Longfellow was emphatically not a professional lecturer like Emerson—he spoke with his pen rather than his tongue, he told the citizens of Carlisle. As he saw it, the poetry he published was his form of public service, produced in private but always

123 "It was the first speech I ever made in my life, and I mean it shall be the last," Longfellow told Robert Carl Winthrop about his appearance in Carlisle. The speech was, Longfellow claimed with a mixture of hyperbole and self-irony, "only an inch long; but while impending, it cast a shadow over my life for three days" (*Letters* 5: 241-44).

124 See Samuel Longfellow, *Life* 3: 112-14.

125 Calhoun, *Longfellow* 241.

with the needs and expectations of a steadily growing public audience of readers in mind. From the marketing point of view, Longfellow's refusal to speak in public was extremely effective, too, since this ensured that nothing detracted from the impact of his poetry and that the seamless continuity between the private nature of his poetry and the public nature of the response it generated could be maintained.

Starting in the late 1850s, accounts and reproductions of Longfellow's study began to circulate in American and European newspapers and magazines. It was a place where work was being done, people were given to understand, but it was also, more symbolically, the ground on which the battle—a peaceful, civilized one—for the literary future of the United States was being fought, where Longfellow's contemporaries, represented by the crayon portraits of Emerson, Sumner, and Hawthorne, confronted the literary past of Europe, metonymically represented by the fragments from Dante's coffin, Coleridge's inkstand, and Thomas Moore's wastepaper basket.

At the same time, Longfellow, with his famous 1859 poem "The Children's Hour," had quite publicly established that his study was also a rather private place, the focal point of family life, where his girls were welcome to enter and interrupt him with their antics (see Chapter 3, pages 60-62). *Evangeline* was written here, some of it in semi-darkness, with Longfellow sitting on a chair next to the fireplace and using a pencil to spare his sore eyes. Several of Longfellow's pencils have survived, if only as stubs: pictured here (FIGURE 35) are the remnants of pencils used for writing *Evangeline* (LONG 7225), poems such as "Resignation" and "To My Children" (LONG 7228), the translation of Dante's *Divine Comedy* (LONG 7232), *The New England Tragedies* (LONG 7233), and "The Building of the Ship" (LONG 7234; all of them at LNHS). Autographs he wrote at his desk by the south window, as many as 80 on one particular morning, Fanny reported, while Charley was playing with his canary, Edith searching for pencils, and Annie skipping and hopping around, asking for her box of paper-dolls (Fanny Longfellow to Thomas Appleton, 9 January 1857, LNHS). It was a "plain, pleasant room," in the words of William Dean Howells, dominated by a round table in the middle, "laden with books, papers, and proofs" as well as unanswered letters from readers—so many, in fact, that, in the words of another observer, "only a sharp-toothed mouse could get through them in a month's time."[126] With popularity came responsibility, and Longfellow once explained to his publisher Fields that, the piles of papers and books and children around him notwithstanding, he would always show up for work appropriately attired (see Introduction, pages 4-5).

A drawing made most probably by Longfellow's young son Ernest (Henry Wadsworth Longfellow in his study, ca. 1851, LONG 19837, LNHS, FIGURE 36) shows Longfellow, sideburns and all, standing beside his upright writing desk (which had been placed on a round table, also faithfully portrayed). Longfellow's hand is reaching

126 Richard Henry Stoddard, *Poets' Homes: Pen and Pencil Sketches* (1879; Freeport: Books for Libraries, 1972) 9.

Figure 35. Longfellow's pencil stubs, LONG 7225, 7228, 7232, 7233, 7234, LNHS.

for a chair. The plaster statuette of Goethe that Longfellow kept on his desk (the subject of many discussions between him and his friends[127]) proved a bit more than Erny, who was perhaps six years old, could handle. In an effort to portray Goethe's trademark posture—the poet liked to fold his hands behind his back so that he would keep his spine straight and not hunch—he ended up giving the German sage the appearance of a small, wrapped-up mummy.[128]

"A nasty song! Fie! a political song," a student named Brander sings in a scene from Goethe's *Faust* after one of his friends began to chant a couple of lines mocking the Holy Roman Empire. Longfellow's friend Bayard Taylor, who translated *Faust I* and *II* "in the original metres," comments that this line "has been frequently quoted by

127 See, for example, the Diary of Annie Fields, 14 December 1870: "The statuette of Goethe was on the table surrounded by flowers. The occasion was the completion of the translation of Faust by Mr. [Bayard] Taylor's hand .... Longfellow said that Goethe never liked the statue by Rauch from which the statuette was made but preferred a bust made in his youth by a Lewis, a copy of which Taylor has ... ."(The Annie Adams Fields Papers, Massachusetts Historical Society). The original statue was made by the Berlin sculptor Christian Friedrich Rauch (1777-1857), who must have been disappointed when Goethe told him that it made him look "too fat" (*zu dick*); see Edna Arnhold, *Goethes Berliner Beziehungen* (Gotha: Klotz, 1925) 241.

128 On Goethe's posture, see G. H. Lewes, *The Life and Works of Goethe*, 2 vols. (Boston: Ticknor and Fields, 1865) 2: 450. Longfellow liked Lewes's "judicious" book; see Journal, 16 December 1855.

Figure 36. Ernest Wadsworth Longfellow, Henry Wadsworth Longfellow in his study, ca. 1851, LONG 19837, LNHS

Goethe's literary enemies as an evidence that he would exclude all political aspiration from literature."[129] Like Goethe, Longfellow always refused to produce an explicitly nationalist poem, one that would, as Goethe defined the purpose of such writing in a conversation with Frédéric Jacob Soret, "express the voice of a single nation." Instead, Longfellow cultivated an attitude "where one stands," to quote Goethe again, "to some extent *above* the nations, and sympathizes with the weal or woe of a neighbor people as with that of one's own."[130]

129 *Faust: A Tragedy by Johann Wolfgang von Goethe*, trans. Bayard Taylor (1870; Boston: Houghton, Mifflin, and Co., 1898) 85, 271.

130 In 1861—arguably an important time in the nation's history—George William Curtis urged him to write a "National Song": "I am afraid the 'Go ho! Let us make a National Song' will not succeed." Added Longfellow, "It [the National Song] will be likely to spring up in some other way" (21 May 1861). The Goethe quotations are from Taylor's notes to *Faust*, 272.

If one applies this definition, Longfellow *did* write a number of poems that had a significant political dimension—poems that were precisely meant to support the woes of people other than the Cambridge elite: from *Poems on Slavery* (1842) to "Enceladus" (1859), a "lament for the woes of Italy" (see Chapter 7, pages 164-65), to "The Revenge of Rain-in-the Face" (1875), a poem that sympathizes with those who killed General Custer: "our broken faith / Wrought all this ruin" (3: 113).

Longfellow, from the beginning of his career, was vigorous in his condemnation not just of slavery but of racial inequality in general. He wasn't free of racial prejudice himself; his opportunities to interact with the black community in Portland had been rather limited. When he first arrived in Cambridge, an African-American servant who worked in the boarding house where he lived would greet him in the morning with the cry of "Arise, Mr. Longfellow." As a "Negro," observed Longfellow, he had "a patent from Nature for all possible elegances of expression" (15 May 1837; *Letters* 2: 26). While stereotypical, Longfellow's assessment is a far cry from Emerson's shuddering observation, made while he was a Harvard student, that "in comparison with the highest orders of men, the Africans will stand so low as to make the difference between themselves & the sagacious beasts inconceivable."[131] Craigie House, where Longfellow rented two rooms in 1837, had a direct link to the history of slavery, since the original owners, the Vassall family, had made their fortune from the plantations in the West Indies and kept slaves both in Cambridge and abroad. On 22 March 1855, when old Mrs. Vassall ("born a slave in this house in 1769") and the Cambridge abolitionist and former slave Lunsford Lane visited Longfellow, life at Castle Craigie ground to a halt. They stayed so long that James Fields, who had been waiting to hear Longfellow read from his new *Hiawatha* manuscript, decided to leave (22 March 1855).

Old Mrs. Vassall might have felt emboldened to pay Longfellow a visit by the widely-noticed and well-received collection *Poems on Slavery* Longfellow had published in December 1842 after he came back from Europe. His health severely affected by his luckless pursuit of Fanny Appleton, Longfellow had asked for and been granted a six-month leave of absence from Harvard to "take the waters" in a German spa. Physically, he got better soon, but his stay abroad also reminded him how little he had achieved since coming back from his last European trip six years earlier. His sonnet "Mezzo Cammin," written on 25 August 1842, was replete with visions of failure and impending doom. At the end, the speaker even thought he heard "the cataract of Death far thundering from the heights" (1: 260). It had taken the combined efforts of Charles Sumner and Ferdinand Freiligrath, a radical German poet he had befriended while in Germany, to shake him out of narcissistic self-involvement. "Write some stirring words that shall move the whole land," Sumner commanded in a letter sent from the States.[132]

131 November 8-14, 1822; *Emerson in His Journals*, ed. Joel Porte (Cambridge, MA: Belknap, 1982) 20-21.

132 See Calhoun, *Longfellow* 155.

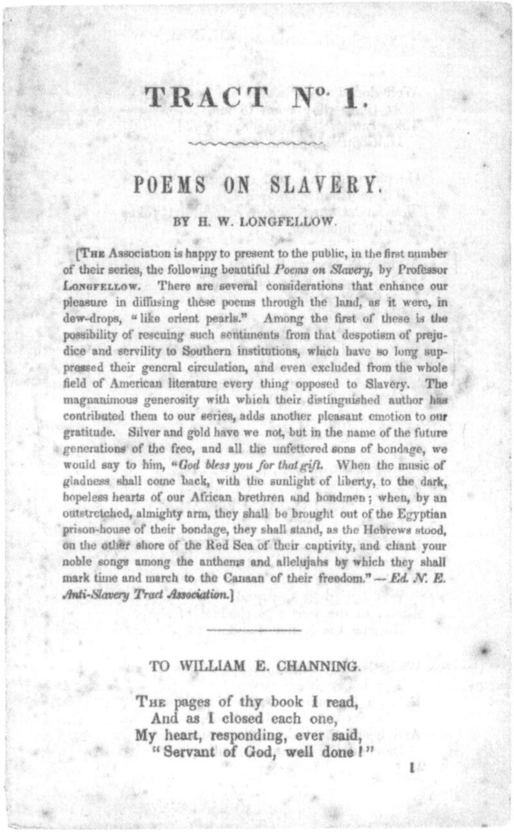

TRACT No. 1.

POEMS ON SLAVERY.

BY H. W. LONGFELLOW.

[The Association is happy to present to the public, in the first number of their series, the following beautiful *Poems on Slavery*, by Professor Longfellow. There are several considerations that enhance our pleasure in diffusing these poems through the land, as it were, in dew-drops, "like orient pearls." Among the first of these is the possibility of rescuing such sentiments from that despotism of prejudice and servility to Southern institutions, which have so long suppressed their general circulation, and even excluded from the whole field of American literature every thing opposed to Slavery. The magnanimous generosity with which their distinguished author has contributed them to our series, adds another pleasant emotion to our gratitude. Silver and gold have we not, but in the name of the future generations of the free, and all the unfettered sons of bondage, we would say to him, "*God bless you for that gift.* When the music of gladness shall come back, with the sunlight of liberty, to the dark, hopeless hearts of our African brethren and bondmen; when, by an outstretched, almighty arm, they shall be brought out of the Egyptian prison-house of their bondage, they shall stand, as the Hebrews stood, on the other shore of the Red Sea of their captivity, and chant your noble songs among the anthems and allelujahs by which they shall mark time and march to the Canaan of their freedom." — *Ed. N. E. Anti-Slavery Tract Association.*]

TO WILLIAM E. CHANNING.

The pages of thy book I read,
And as I closed each one,
My heart, responding, ever said,
"Servant of God, well done!"

1

Figure 37. First page of Longfellow, *Poems on Slavery*, New England Anti-Slavery Tract Association, 1843, Houghton *AC85.L8605.842pd (A)

Longfellow produced seven anti-slavery poems on the ship that took him back. Along with a previously written poem, "The Warning," Longfellow's poetic diatribe against slavery was first published in December 1842 by John Owen in Cambridge. When Boston-born Poe later ridiculed Longfellow's readers as those "negrophilic ladies of the North,"[133] he was thinking specifically of this objectionable little volume. Thin as it was, it established Longfellow's national reputation as an anti-slavery man. Seven of the poems ("The Good Part, That Shall Not Be Taken Away" was omitted) were reprinted in 1843 by the New England Anti-Slavery Tract Association, as an eight-page pamphlet without a title and with a short preface which imagines the freed slaves chanting the poems of their dear Henry Longfellow:

133 Edgar Allan Poe, *Essays and Criticism*, ed. G. R. Thompson (New York: Library of America, 1984) 762.

Tract No. 1: The Association is happy to present to the public, in the first number of their series, the following beautiful *Poems on Slavery*, by Professor LONGFELLOW. There are several considerations that enhance our pleasure in diffusing these poems through the land, as it were, in dew-drops, "like orient pearls." Among the first of these is the possibility of rescuing such sentiments from that despotism of prejudice and servility to Southern institutions, which have so long suppressed their general circulation, and even excluded from the whole field of American literature every thing opposed to Slavery. The magnanimous generosity with which their distinguished author has contributed them to our series, adds another pleasant emotion to our gratitude. Silver and gold have we not, but in the name of the future generations of the free, and all the unfettered sons of bondage, we would say to him, "*God bless you for that gift*. When the music of gladness shall come back, with the sunlight of liberty, to the dark, hopeless hearts of our African brethren and bondmen; when, by an outstretched, almighty arm, they shall be brought out of the Egyptian prison-house of their bondage, they shall stand, as the Hebrews stood, on the other shore of the Red Sea of their captivity, and chant your noble songs among the anthems and allelujahs by which they shall mark time and march to the Canaan of their freedom."
(*Poems on Slavery*; Houghton *AC85.L8605.842pd [A], FIGURE 37)[134]

Longfellow sent a copy of this little tract, "which you may be pleased to see," to his father in 1844, asking him to show it also to "General Fessenden." Samuel Fessenden was a member of the Maine militia as well as of the antislavery party in Maine (and the father of William Pitt Fessenden, to whom Longfellow's sister Elizabeth was engaged when she died of tuberculosis in 1829).[135] At least as far as the substance of his poems was concerned, Longfellow could still hope to score points with his father and his Portland peers.

Just how much Longfellow himself really prized these poems has been a subject of some debate, especially in view of the fact that he didn't raise his voice in protest when his Philadelphia publisher, Carey & Hart, fearing sales in the South would be curtailed, left them out of the 1845 edition of his *Poems*.[136] (A cheap, 50-cent edition of his poetry published by Harper & Brothers in New York the following year *did* contain

134 See the description in Luther S. Livingston, *A Bibliography of the First Editions in Book Form of the Writings of Henry Wadsworth Longfellow* (1908; New York: Franklin, 1968), 31-32.

135 Longfellow to Stephen Longfellow, 5 March 1844, *Letters* 3: 28. In 1847 the Liberty party, which was receiving large votes, nominated Samuel Fessenden for governor and for congress.

136 Longfellow to Carey & Hart, 3 April 1845 (*Letters* 3: 63; see n. 4).

them.)[137] Longfellow himself said, in an often-quoted letter to Isaac Appleton Jewett, that his poems were "so mild that even a Slaveholder might read them without losing his appetite for breakfast." But we need to remember here, too, that Jewett was working as a lawyer in New Orleans, and that Longfellow's description could also have been a perceptive comment on Jewett's obvious confusedness. In a letter to Longfellow written on 9 January 1843, Jewett had praised *Poems on Slavery* to the skies, since it dealt so many blows to one of the "old ... lies" of this age but had then gone on to reminisce about "one of those gorgeous nights one can only find in the Midi" when he enjoyed hearing the slaves sing on a friend's plantation. He also invited Longfellow to come along with him to the New Orleans slave market and watch the slaves dance.[138]

Walt Whitman, in the 1855 version of "The Sleepers," assumes the voice, the identity, the burden of pain, anger, and humiliation carried by the oppressed slave.[139] Longfellow, by contrast, speaks *for* the slave in his poems, from a safe distance, it seems, safe enough for Isaac Appleton Jewett, who apparently missed at least part of the message. But one doesn't have to read between the lines to realize that, in Longfellow's eyes at least, the disenfranchised slaves, chanting psalms at midnight, crouching in the rank grass of the swamp, or dying in the sand, might be the real Chosen People. Longfellow takes this reversal of conventional typological thinking a step further when, in "The Warning" (1: 111-12), the darkest and most powerful poem of the series, he suggests that the white Americans, depriving the Samson-like slave of his liberty, might in fact be the biblical Philistines. The fate of the slave and the survival of the nation, built on such lofty but apparently hypocritical principles, are inextricably connected:

> There is a poor, blind Samson in this land,
> Shorn of his strength and bound in bonds of steel,
> Who may, in some grim revel, raise his hand,
> And shake the pillars of this Commonweal,
> Till the vast Temple of our liberties
> A shapeless mass of wreck and rubbish lies.

Emerson, who, by his own admission, had suffered no "personal inconvenience" from slavery, needed the Fugitive Slave Law and the Nebraska Bill to "unglue" his eyes and condemn slavery, albeit in lofty terms ("Liberty ... [is] the oppressed Lady whom

137 When abolitionists chastised him for not insisting that Carey & Hart retain *Poems on Slavery*, Longfellow became uncharacteristically apoplectic, calling them "a nest of vipers" and declared: "They shall never have me under their control" (4 March 1846).

138 Longfellow to Isaac Appleton Jewett, 23 May 1843, *Letters* 2: 537-38; Isaac Appleton Jewett to Longfellow, 9 January 1843, Letters to Longfellow, Houghton, bMS Am 1340.2 (3028).

139 "I have been wronged .... I am oppressed .... I hate him that oppresses me," *Walt Whitman's Leaves of Grass: The First (1855) Edition*, ed. Malcolm Cowley (New York: Viking, 1955) 111.

true knights on their oath and honor must serve"), and Thoreau, for all the disgust he felt for slavery, was still able to find solace in the eternal laws of nature, which, as he reminded his readers, knows no "Missouri Compromise."[140] Longfellow's condemnation comes at a much earlier point and is, at least in "The Warning," less carefully framed. Slavery was, he said to George Lunt, "an unrighteous institution, based on the false maxim that Might makes Right." "God speed the time" needed to bring about an end to this injustice (4 January 1843; *Letters* 2: 494). He met with Ellen Craft, who had escaped from slavery dressed as a man, and encouraged her "to be proud of her act" (12 February 1850). And he condemned the presence of the slave-hunters in Boston as a "disgrace … to a Republic of the Nineteenth Century" (26 October 1850), cheering Sumner for his uncompromising stance on slavery especially in the face of mounting threats of violence against his person ("It is a great thing in one's life to stand so long and unflinching in the range of the enemy's artillery," 2 June 1854; *Letters* 3: 436). "Hung be the Heavens with black," he exclaimed, resorting to a quotation from the first part of Shakespeare's *Henry VI* (I.i.1-7), when Anthony Burns was arrested in Boston and surrendered to his master. "Dirty work for a country that is so loud about freedom as us" (26 May and 2 June 1854).

Uncle Tom's Cabin, Longfellow thought, was a "book of power" (9 May 1852). He and Fanny read themselves into despair over it, feeling their "blood boil" as they were turning the pages (22 May 1852).[141] His horror knew no bounds when, at a jeweler's shop, he came across an iron slave collar, "with an iron tongue as large as a spoon, to go into the mouth." It brought home to Longfellow the full reality of slavery, not only the disgrace of it, but the physical pain and torture that was involved: "Every drop of blood in me quivered."[142] Wherever he went, "disgusting reptiles" were creeping out from under the "dreadful stone of Slavery" (to Sumner, 30 April 1864, *Letters* 4: 409). And while others, like his friend Louis Agassiz, were recommending that one should leave all the ex-slaves to toil in the humid climate of the South and reserve the cultivated

140 Ralph Waldo Emerson, "Seventh of March Speech on the Fugitive Slave Law" (1854), *Transcendentalism: A Reader* (Oxford: Oxford University Press, 2000) 587 and 600; Henry David Thoreau, "Slavery in Massachusetts" (1854), *Transcendentalism* 614.

141 Longfellow made no secret of his admiration for Stowe, whose success—a "literary coup-de-main"—he viewed without envy: "At one step she has reached the top of the stair-case up which the rest of us climb on our knees year after year" (24 February 1853).

142 Longfellow to Frances Farrar, 8 May 1862; *Letters* 4: 284. Slave collars made of iron were used to identify and discipline slaves who were considered risks of becoming runaways. The implement described by Longfellow seems to have had the added purpose of silencing the wearer and preventing her or him from eating. See the description of the iron muzzle, one of the torture machines discovered by Olaudah Equiano during his stay in Virginia; Equiano, *The Interesting Narrative and Other Writings*, ed. Vincent Carretta (1789; New York: Penguin, 1989) 63.

North for whites only,[143] emancipation for Longfellow had only one goal, namely to put "the black man … upon the same footing as the white."[144]

From a modern perspective, the problem with all these impressive statements on behalf of African-Americans would be that Longfellow articulated them only in letters, his journal, and in conversation—not in public speeches, as Emerson did, nor in essays, as Thoreau did, whose "Resistance to Civil Government" Longfellow in fact admired ("extremely good"; 29 June 1849). There would have been opportunities aplenty for Longfellow to become more visible as a spokesman for the cause of abolition. Encouraged by Longfellow's *Poems on Slavery* ("From my heart I thank thee for them"), John Greenleaf Whittier, for example, took a chance and asked his colleague to run for Congress for the moderate abolitionist party, an offer Longfellow categorically declined: "I am not a member of any society, and fight under no single banner…. I should be found but a weak and unworthy champion in the public debate" (6 September 1844, *Letters* 3: 44-45). When Susan Porter of the Rochester Ladies Anti-Slavery Society asked for a contribution for *Autographs for Freedom*, he also passed, even though Frederick Douglass had supported the request, in a note he had scribbled on the letter, declaring that he should be "*most* grateful, as one of the oppressed, if you will favor the Society with an article." Longfellow's response was uncharacteristically cold: "as I have already published 'Poems on Slavery,' … I think no one, who cares about the matter will be at any loss to discover my opinion on that subject" (*Letters* 3: 348; 8 June 1852). Ironically, when *Autographs* was published a year later, it did contain a reference to Longfellow's "Psalm of Life" right in the title of the very first article, "Up and Doing," Senator William Seward's appeal to citizens, which he termed the "public conscience," not to trust the Constitution but to take matters into their own hands, at the local level: "Reform your own manners and customs and rise above the prejudice of caste." The volume contained poems by Whittier and Harriet Beecher Stowe and even a short note by Charles Sumner, which expressed a sentiment with which Longfellow would have hardly disagreed: "Ours is a noble cause; nobler even than that of our fathers, inasmuch as it is more exalted to struggle for the freedom of *others* than for our own."[145] A follow-up volume published the next year included a (somewhat cryptic) poem by Ralph Waldo Emerson, "On Freedom."

Longfellow's refusal to participate in this project seems at first puzzling, and his responses to the requests made by Whittier and others would appear to be needlessly coy or, to put it less charitably, arrogant. But what really was at stake here was again Longfellow's desire to be appreciated and known for his poetry rather than for his

143 See Louis Agassiz's letters to Samuel Gridley Howe, 9, 10, 11 August 1863, Agassiz Papers, Houghton, bMS Am 1419 (150-54), as well as Christoph Irmscher, *The Poetics of Natural History: From John Bartram to William James* (New Brunswick: Rutgers, 1999) 268-71.

144 Longfellow to Charles Sumner, 20 April 1864; *Letters* 4: 406.

145 *Autographs for Freedom* (Boston: Jewett, 1853) 2, 77.

views, though the latter might very well be implicit in the former. A writer, to him, was not a sage, with access to higher levels of insight, but a provider of texts that would help readers find themselves there, in delighted recognition that they "felt so likewise" (see the introduction to this book).

Those who would want to accuse Longfellow of political indifference will find their story considerably complicated by his account books, which prove that, even as he refrained from making public speeches against slavery, he gave money to support the abolitionist cause, individual slaves, and African churches. His interest in the latter was sparked in the summer of 1848 by a visit to an "Abyssinian" church in Pittsfield, Massachusetts, where a black preacher named Hunt gave a lively recreation of Genesis 6-9, describing in vivid detail how the people around Noah had a hard time believing him even when the rain he had predicted came: "They only jeered and jested. I think I can see them now going into their rum-holes and saying 'This is Noah's rain!' with a kind of a laugh. And another coming in to another place all wet, with his clothes all wet, saying, 'This is Noah's rain!'" The lesson was, of course, to do what God commands and not care about the opinions of other people.[146] Longfellow was impressed. As his "Book of Donations" (MS Am 1340 [155]), covering the period from January 1875 to March 1882, reveals, Longfellow continued to give money to African-American churches virtually until the day he died (see the references to "colored" churches and schools in the account book). In March 1882, the last month of his life, he gave $3.00 to a "Negro Church" (about $57.00 in current money)—not much, given that George Washington Greene received $50.00 from him the same month, but still considerable, if we take into account that this was only the last installment in a long series of donations recorded in this book, beginning with $5.00 for a "Colored Church at the South" in July 1875 (churches abroad, in Canada and Haiti, also received donations).

A Goethe motto Longfellow wrote on the flyleaf of his "Book of Donations" shows that he cared about what he was doing: "He who does not help / us at the right time, does / not help us at all."[147] His desire to help was genuine, not a matter of keeping up appearances. Perhaps in that vein, Longfellow, in an unpublished note, was criticizing also his own reluctance to be drawn publicly into the abolitionist cause. It didn't seem right, Longfellow wrote, not to give money to political and charitable causes just because

146 "The Negro's Sermon," transcribed by Henry Wadsworth Longfellow, in Unpublished Prose Fragments, MS Am 1340 (145). See Longfellow's Journal, 13 August 1848: "in the afternoon to the Negro Church, where we heard Mr. Hunt, a bald headed old man, preach a very good sermon on Noah, which I have reported elsewhere in full."

147 A free translation of a remark made by Natalie, who is explaining her educational principles to Wilhem Meister, in book 8 of Goethe's novel *Wilhelm Meisters Lehrjahre*: "Wer nicht im Augenblick hilft, scheint mir nie zu helfen . . . ." (Goethe, *Werke*, Hamburger Ausgabe in 14 Bänden, ed. Erich Trunz [Hamburg: Wegner, 1948 ff.] 7: 527).

one didn't want to be considered a fanatic: "How often do we excuse our own want of active charity by giving the name of fanaticism to the more ardent zeal of others."[148]

Shown here (Longfellow Papers, Houghton, MS Am 1340 [152], FIGURE 38) is a page-spread (pp. 178-79) from an earlier account book. The two pages cover, in reverse order, the years 1855 (when *The Song of Hiawatha* appeared) to 1856.

1856	
[April] Mr. Pounce, Negro-man	3.00
Mr. Somebody, a Pole	3.00
Alcott's Farm	50.00
To Theol. Library	25.00
May. Church in Kansas	10.00
[. . .]	
[June] 5. Father Hanson	10.00
[...]	
" 13. Anti Slavery Tract Soc. 5.00	
" " . To free a slave	5.00
" 15. Church in Washn.	15.00
[...]	
[from facing page: "Money given. 1855"]	
[...]	
March 13. Mr. Lang. col. church	5.00
[...]	
[March 24] For "Ida May" slave	6.00
March 30. Fugitive Slave	5.00

While many of Longfellow's beneficiaries have remained anonymous, "Father" Josiah Henson, mentioned as the recipient of donations in Longfellow's account books until the mid-1870s, was widely known as the model for Harriet Beecher Stowe's Uncle Tom. Born a slave in Charles County, Maryland, Henson, who experienced a religious conversion in 1828 and started preaching then, diligently saved money to buy his freedom. When he learned that his price had risen and that his master was planning to cheat him out of the money he had already paid, he escaped to Canada, where he eventually started a "manual-labor school" for black children. Capitalizing on the fame Stowe's book had brought him, Henson lectured and preached widely, even in England. His autobiography, *The Life of Josiah Henson*, was first published in 1849 and went through several editions. Longfellow met Henson in the summer of 1846, when the preacher called at Craigie House to get the famous poet to sponsor his school. Which apparently Longfellow did, and over a longer period of time: in March 1875,

148 Unpublished Prose Fragments, Longfellow Papers, Houghton, MS Am 1340 (145), folder 6.

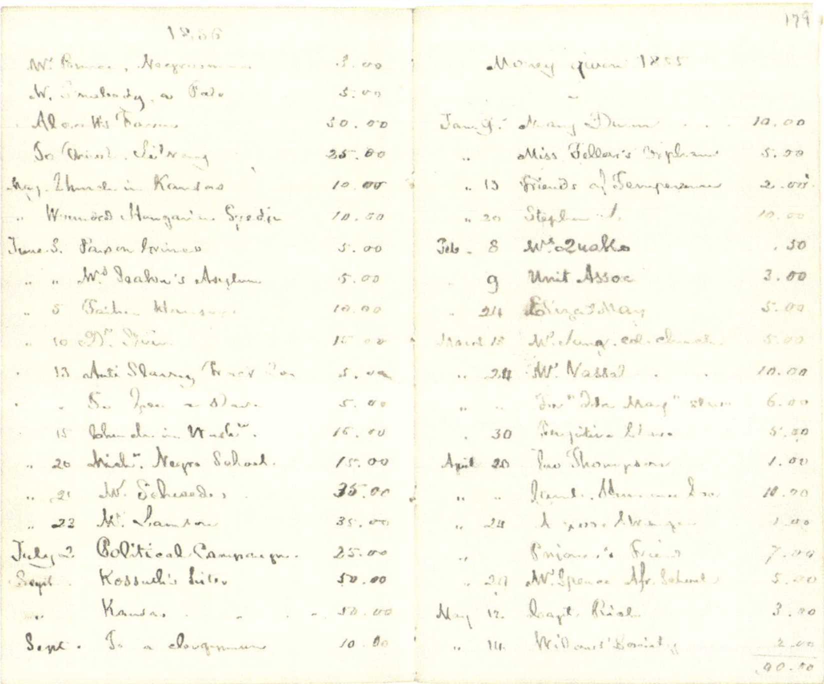

Figure 38. Longfellow, personal account book, pp. 178-79 (1855-1856), Longfellow Papers, Houghton, MS Am 1340 (152)

for example, "Father Henson" received $20.00 out of a total of $122.00 in donations for that month. Longfellow's journal description of Henson might seem unacceptably stereotypical today ("It seemed as if some Egyptian statue had come to life; and sat speaking in the twilight"), but it is in fact remarkable for the astuteness with which he notices the injuries inflicted on this "mild man" by the slaveholders: "His right arm was crooked and stiff. It had been broken by a strange blow with a stake from a fence" (26 June 1846). Longfellow's observations are so accurate that one must assume he had heard Henson himself tell the story of how as a young man he was so savagely beaten with a six-foot fence post that he ended up with a broken arm and broken shoulder-blades. Since no doctor was called to set the fracture, Henson healed only poorly and afterwards couldn't lift his arms properly.[149]

"Ida May," to whom Longfellow referred on 24 March 1855, was the title of a vastly popular novel by Mary Hayden Green Pike (1824-1898) from Eastport, Maine, who published her book in 1854 under the pseudonym "Mary Langdon." It is not clear if Longfellow knew that the protagonist of "Langdon's" novel was a white Pennsylvania girl

149 *The Life of Josiah Henson, formerly a Slave, Now an Inhabitant of Canada, as Narrated by Himself* (1849; Bedford, MA: Applewood, n.d.) 24-25.

who was kidnapped and sold into slavery. After trials that seem mild when compared with most slave narratives, she is eventually recognized for who she is and adopted. Later, as the new owner of her former fellow slaves, she proceeds to lead them to freedom. Filled with racial stereotypes about the "demi-civilized" negroes in whom emotion takes the place of intellect, the novel, as its subtitle indicates ("A Story of Things Actual and Possible") nevertheless dares white readers to imagine slavery as an experience reserved not only for African-Americans—a message that would have appealed to Longfellow.[150]

If Longfellow was aware of the narratives produced by and about slaves, it is also true that black authors were well aware of him. For example, James Watkins, whose flight from slavery in Maryland had led him all the way to England, ends his *Struggles for Freedom* with Longfellow's "The Slave's Dream." A more creative use of Longfellow occurs in *The Narrative of Thomas Smallwood, Colored Man*. The author, who had also escaped from Maryland but this time to Canada, simply takes a few lines from Longfellow's wistful fantasy "The Indian Hunter" and replaces "hunter" with "slave," the "beech" with a "cotton tree," "mourning" with the more ominous "murmuring," and "on the hills" with "south"—and thus, none too subtly but swiftly and successfully, he twists the poem to suit his own, more optimistic story: "A footstep was heard in the rustling brake, / Where the *cotton tree* shadow'd the misty lake, / And a *murmuring* voice, and a plunge from shore,— / And the slave was seen *in the south* no more."[151] Longfellow had become public property indeed.

His poetry was also omnipresent in African-American newspapers of the time. Several papers reprinted his *Poems on Slavery* juxtaposed with newspaper articles that proved that Longfellow's lines were based on reality and not the poet's imagination. On 16 February 1855, for example, readers of *Frederick Douglass' Paper* would have found a short newspaper excerpt preceding "The Quadroon Girl," to show, as the editor declared, that Longfellow's "story is by no means a mere fancy sketch, but a fearful tale of very frequent occurrence." A similar note had accompanied "The Slave in the Dismal Swamp" on 27 January 1854. On 30 July 1857, *The National Era* in Washington, D.C. cited another newspaper, *The New Orleans Picayune*, to reinforce what their readers already knew and appreciated, namely that Longfellow's abolitionist sympathies had made his works "a distasteful addition to a Southern Library, by mingling with the pure gold the basest alloy." After Longfellow died, *The Christian Recorder*, in its issue of 30 March 1882, declared that his "influence was always given on the side of Liberty."

Throughout his career, Longfellow was interested in making his works available to those who couldn't normally afford to buy them. The tract edition of *Poems on Slavery*

150 Mary Langdon (i.e., Mary Hayden Green Pike), *Ida May: A Story of Things Actual and Possible* (Boston: Phillips, Sampson, and Co., 1854) 81, 99.

151 *Struggles for Freedom; or The Life of James Watkins, Formerly a Slave in Maryland, U. S.* (Manchester: Printed for James Watkins, 1860) 89-90; *A Narrative of Thomas Smallwood, Colored Man* (Toronto: Printed for the Author, 1851) vi.

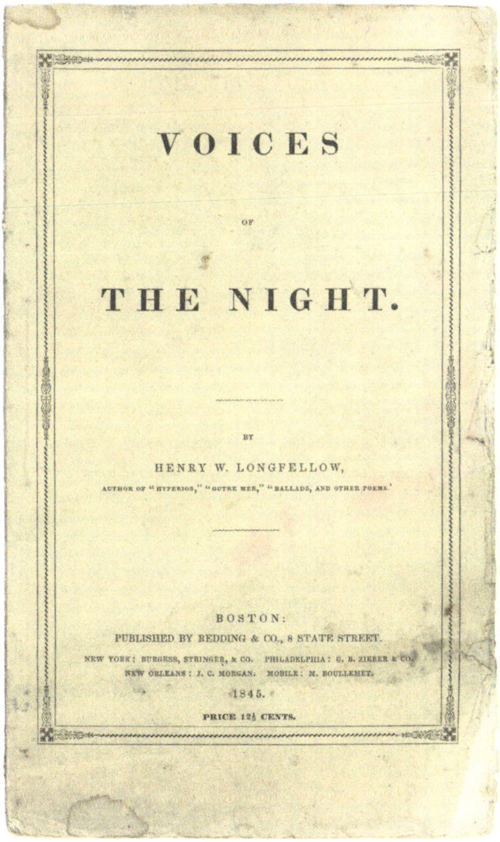
VOICES

OF

THE NIGHT.

BY

HENRY W. LONGFELLOW,

AUTHOR OF "HYPERION," "OUTRE MER," "BALLADS, AND OTHER POEMS."

BOSTON:

PUBLISHED BY REDDING & CO., 8 STATE STREET.

NEW YORK: BURGESS, STRINGER, & CO. PHILADELPHIA: G. B. ZIEBER & CO.

NEW ORLEANS: J. C. MORGAN. MOBILE: M. BOULLEMET.

1845.

PRICE 12½ CENTS.

Figure 39. Cover of Longfellow, *Voices of the Night* (Boston: Redding, 1845), Houghton *2001G-29

is one example; another, particularly intriguing one is the "shilling" edition of *Voices of the Night* (Houghton *2001G-29, FIGURES 39 and 40), published by Robert Redding in Boston in 1845. Houghton's copy features the rare original wrappers. Longfellow himself professed to be amused by the appearance of double columns (they looked like, he wrote in his diary on 15 January 1849, "travellers in a stage-coach" who had to sit "with their knees bent under them"), but he also knew that this format helped to make his books more affordable. Interestingly, Edgar Allan Poe, who had made fun of the fine appearance of an illustrated edition of Longfellow's poetry published by Carey & Hart, also disapproved of the shilling version of *Voices of the Night*, arguing that "the dignity of poetical letters should be maintained."[152]

If Redding's *Voices of the Night* is an example of the "cheap" Longfellow, the 1868 reincarnation of *Hyperion* represents the "expensive," collectible Longfellow. Houghton

152 See Irmscher, *Longfellow Redux* 56-57.

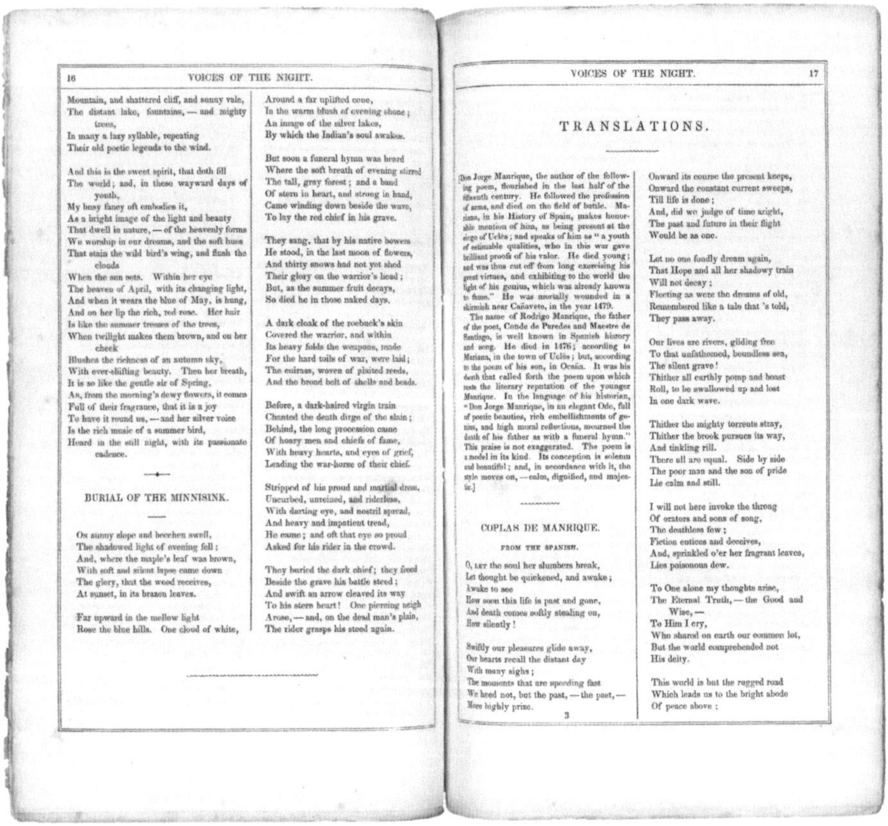
16 VOICES OF THE NIGHT.

Mountain, and shattered cliff, and sunny vale,
The distant lake, fountains, — and mighty trees,
In many a lazy syllable, repeating
Their old poetic legends to the wind.

And this is the sweet spirit, that doth fill
The world; and, in these wayward days of youth,
My busy fancy oft embodies it,
As a bright image of the light and beauty
That dwell in nature, — of the heavenly forms
We worship in our dreams, and the soft hues
That stain the wild bird's wing, and flush the clouds
When the sun sets. Within her eye
The heaven of April, with its changing light,
And when it wears the blue of May, is hung,
And on her lip the rich, red rose. Her hair
Is like the summer tresses of the trees,
When twilight makes them brown, and on her cheek
Blushes the richness of an autumn sky,
With ever-shifting beauty. Then her breath,
It is so like the gentle air of Spring,
As, from the morning's dewy flowers, it comes
Full of their fragrance, that it is a joy
To have it round us, — and her silver voice
Is the rich music of a summer bird,
Heard in the still night, with its passionate cadence.

BURIAL OF THE MINNISINK.

On sunny slope and beechen swell,
The shadowed light of evening fell;
And, where the maple's leaf was brown,
With soft and silent lapse came down
The glory, that the wood receives,
At sunset, in its brazen leaves.

Far upward in the mellow light
Rose the blue hills. One cloud of white,
Around a far uplifted cone,
In the warm blush of evening shone;
An image of the silver lakes,
By which the Indian's soul awakes.

But soon a funeral hymn was heard
Where the soft breath of evening stirred
The tall, gray forest; and a band
Of stern in heart, and strong in hand,
Came winding down beside the wave,
To lay the red chief in his grave.

They sang, that by his native bowers
He stood, in the last moon of flowers,
And thirty snows had not yet shed
Their glory on the warrior's head;
But, as the summer fruit decays,
So died he in those naked days.

A dark cloak of the roebuck's skin
Covered the warrior, and within
Its heavy folds the weapons, made
For the hard toils of war, were laid;
The cuirass, woven of plaited reeds,
And the broad belt of shells and beads.

Before, a dark-haired virgin train
Chanted the death dirge of the slain;
Behind, the long procession came
Of hoary men and chiefs of fame,
With heavy hearts, and eyes of grief,
Leading the war-horse of their chief.

Stripped of his proud and martial dress,
Uncurbed, unreined, and riderless,
With darting eye, and nostril spread,
And heavy and impatient tread,
He came; and oft that eye so proud
Asked for his rider in the crowd.

They buried the dark chief; they freed
Beside the grave his battle steed;
And swift an arrow cleaved its way
To his stern heart! One piercing neigh
Arose, — and, on the dead man's plain,
The rider grasps his steed again.

VOICES OF THE NIGHT. 17

TRANSLATIONS.

[Don Jorge Manrique, the author of the following poem, flourished in the last half of the fifteenth century. He followed the profession of arms, and died on the field of battle. Mariana, in his History of Spain, makes honorable mention of him, as being present at the siege of Uclés; and speaks of him as "a youth of estimable qualities, who in this war gave brilliant proofs of his valor. He died young; and was thus cut off from long exercising his great virtues, and exhibiting to the world the light of his genius, which was already known to fame." He was mortally wounded in a skirmish near Cañavete, in the year 1479.

The name of Rodrigo Manrique, the father of the poet, Conde de Paredes and Maestre de Santiago, is well known in Spanish history and song. He died in 1476; according to Mariana, in the town of Uclés; but, according to the poem of his son, in Ocaña. It was his death that called forth the poem upon which rests the literary reputation of the younger Manrique. In the language of his historian, "Don Jorge Manrique, in an elegant Ode, full of poetic beauties, rich embellishments of genius, and high moral reflections, mourned the death of his father as with a funeral hymn." This praise is not exaggerated. The poem is a model in its kind. Its conception is solemn and beautiful; and, in accordance with it, the style moves on, — calm, dignified, and majestic.]

COPLAS DE MANRIQUE.

FROM THE SPANISH.

O, let the soul her slumbers break,
Let thought be quickened, and awake;
Awake to see
How soon this life is past and gone,
And death comes softly stealing on,
How silently!

Swiftly our pleasures glide away,
Our hearts recall the distant day
With many sighs;
The moments that are speeding fast
We heed not, but the past, — the past, —
More highly prize.

3

Onward its course the present keeps,
Onward the constant current sweeps,
Till life is done;
And, did we judge of time aright,
The past and future in their flight
Would be as one.

Let no one fondly dream again,
That Hope and all her shadowy train
Will not decay;
Fleeting as were the dreams of old,
Remembered like a tale that 's told,
They pass away.

Our lives are rivers, gliding free
To that unfathomed, boundless sea,
The silent grave!
Thither all earthly pomp and boast
Roll, to be swallowed up and lost
In one dark wave.

Thither the mighty torrents stray,
Thither the brook pursues its way,
And tinkling rill.
There all are equal. Side by side
The poor man and the son of pride
Lie calm and still.

I will not here invoke the throng
Of orators and sons of song,
The deathless few;
Fiction entices and deceives,
And, sprinkled o'er her fragrant leaves,
Lies poisonous dew.

To One alone my thoughts arise,
The Eternal Truth, — the Good and Wise, —
To Him I cry,
Who shared on earth our common lot,
But the world comprehended not
His deity.

This world is but the rugged road
Which leads us to the bright abode
Of peace above;

Figure 40. Pages 16-17, Longfellow, *Voices of the Night* (Boston: Redding, 1845), Houghton *2001G-29

Library has an elaborately gilt-decorated leather copy of the novel published by Ticknor & Fields in 1868, a re-issue of the 1865 British edition of *Hyperion* (Houghton *2001G-19, FIGURE 41), illustrated by photographer Francis Frith (1822-1890). It sold for $25.00.[153] When *Hyperion* was first published, Longfellow claimed to be pleased by its less than enthusiastic reception: "I have been rending asunder some of the Boston cobwebs of prejudice and narrow-minded criticism by publishing a strange kind of a book, which I have the audacity to call a *Romance*" (to George Washington Greene, 1 October 1839, *Letters* 2: 177). Frith was a pioneer of travel photography; his well-deserved fame rests chiefly on the images that resulted from his three major trips to Egypt, Nubia, Palestine, and Syria between 1856 and 1859. Like other landscape photographers, he traveled with a wagon that he had turned into a photographic darkroom where he would process his wet-plate collodion prints. As lavish evocations of the German

153 See the advertisement in *The American Literary Gazette*, 15 October 1868, p. 304: "Attractive New Works, to Be Published This Autumn by Ticknor & Fields." *Hyperion* is listed under "November."

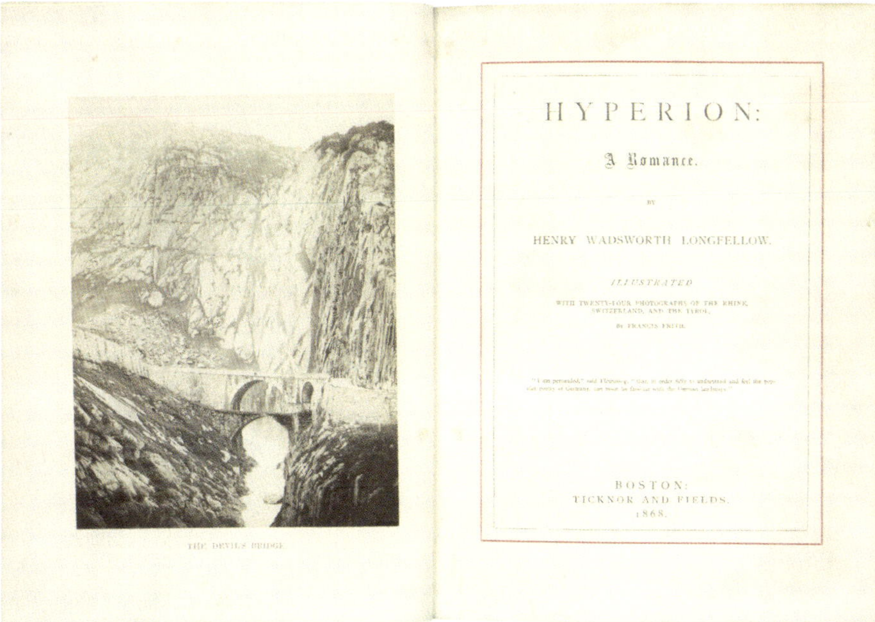

Figure 41. Frontispiece and title page of Longfellow, *Hyperion: A Romance* (Boston: Ticknor and Fields, 1868), featuring "The Devil's Bridge," a wet-plate collodion print by Frances Frith, Houghton *2001G-19

landscape, Frith's photographs (produced while he was retracing Longfellow's footsteps in 1864) seem intended to turn Longfellow's iconoclastic debut novel into a coffee table book for the discerning tourist. But it is easy to forget how innovative this conjunction of photography, fiction, and place really was: Frith's illustrated edition of *Hyperion* was, in fact, the first American literary volume published with original photographs.[154] The frontispiece ("The Devil's Bridge") shows Frith's brand of pictorial photography at its best. In Book III, chapter 2, of *Hyperion*, Longfellow's gloomy Flemming reaches the St. Gotthard Pass and crosses the legendary "Teufelsbrücke": "A mighty cataract howls beneath it, like an evil spirit, and fills the air with mist; and the mountain wind claps its hands and shrieks through the narrow pass, Ha! ha!" (8: 172).

From landscapes that he had seen himself, Longfellow, after he stopped traveling, turned to those he only imagined. Readers have pointed out that the "murmuring pines" featured at the beginning of Longfellow's most famous poem, *Evangeline: A Tale of Acadie* (1847), are to be found on the grounds of Bowdoin College rather than anywhere near the village of Grand-Pré. But authenticity wasn't Longfellow's goal anyway. Dulled

154 See Carol Armstrong, "Photographed and Described: Traveling in the Footsteps of Francis Frith," *Scenes in a Library: Reading the Photograph in the Book, 1843-1875* (Cambridge, MA: MIT Press, 1998) 332-42. Frith & Company, one of the most successful photographic establishments of the 19th century (they were instrumental in popularizing the picture postcard), ceased trading in 1971.

by familiarity, we usually don't recognize *Evangeline* today for the challenge it issued to the reading sensibilities of the American public: an English poem written in classical hexameters (for the most part) about the displacement of a Francophone community, featuring not a male protagonist (Gabriel has got to be one of the dullest characters in the history of the epic) but a female one. The "hybridity" of the finished product is reflected also in its genesis. Longfellow "owned" his poetry only in the sense that the profits from sales were his. Everything else—the content, the form, the details he used—was common property, which is why it seemed natural to him to seek the advice of others, especially when he was working on a longer poem.

That his Dante translation was honed and refined in regular meetings with the members of the Dante Club (see Chapter 7) is well known. Far less familiar is the fact that there was ample precedent for such a collaborative process in Longfellow's career. Inspired by the story the Reverend Conolly had conveyed to him, Longfellow started working on *Evangeline* in earnest on 28 November 1845. Fanny Longfellow and Sumner were "doubtful of the measure" he had chosen, the classical hexameter. But *that* part of the poem remained non-negotiable. Everything else was, however, fair game as Longfellow sent out the proof sheets for his new poems to friends.

The surviving sheets for *Evangeline*, a sample of which is shown here (Houghton f*AC85.L8605.847eaa, FIGURE 42), are heavily annotated throughout by Charles Folsom, Charles Sumner, and Cornelius Felton, as well as by Longfellow himself, usually in response to the remarks left by his readers. Their suggestions of improvement (not all of which Longfellow heeded) cover everything from missing or superfluous commas to the question, raised by both Felton and Sumner, as to whether or not the alligator mentioned in the second book of *Evangeline* "roars" (Longfellow decided it did and kept the phrase). On the first set of revisions (p. 14), Charles Folsom, drawing on his experience as a proofreader for the University Press in Cambridge, queried a line describing Evangeline's cheeks as "bright as the poppy, whose blossom / Blushed in the corn by her side" (p. 14). He was wondering if one could indeed so easily transplant this Old World image. "You know," he told Longfellow, "that the poppy is *only* a garden plant, not only not being indigenous, but having hardly got into fields at all except a little of late in West-chester County Pennsylvania & in Virginia. I doubt if it was ever seen in cornfields in New England or the British Dominions. I am very learned in this matter at this moment having just seen some sheets of Dr. [Asa] Gray's New Flora of the Northern States. The beautiful *corn-poppy* (which is red) was, I fear, all left behind in Normandy." Unstoppable by now, Folsom continued to write his comment in the top margin of the same page: "Your wide observation of foreign climes should put you on your guard in using images drawn from nature. Your brother of 'The yellow violet' & 'The Blue Gentian'[155] sung faithfully what he saw, before he travelled [i.e., before he let his imagination roam], & so have you been faithful to your *scene* hitherto, wherever you have laid it." Longfellow dropped the poppy metaphor.

155 A reference to William Cullen Bryant's poems "The Fringed Gentian" and "The Yellow Violet."

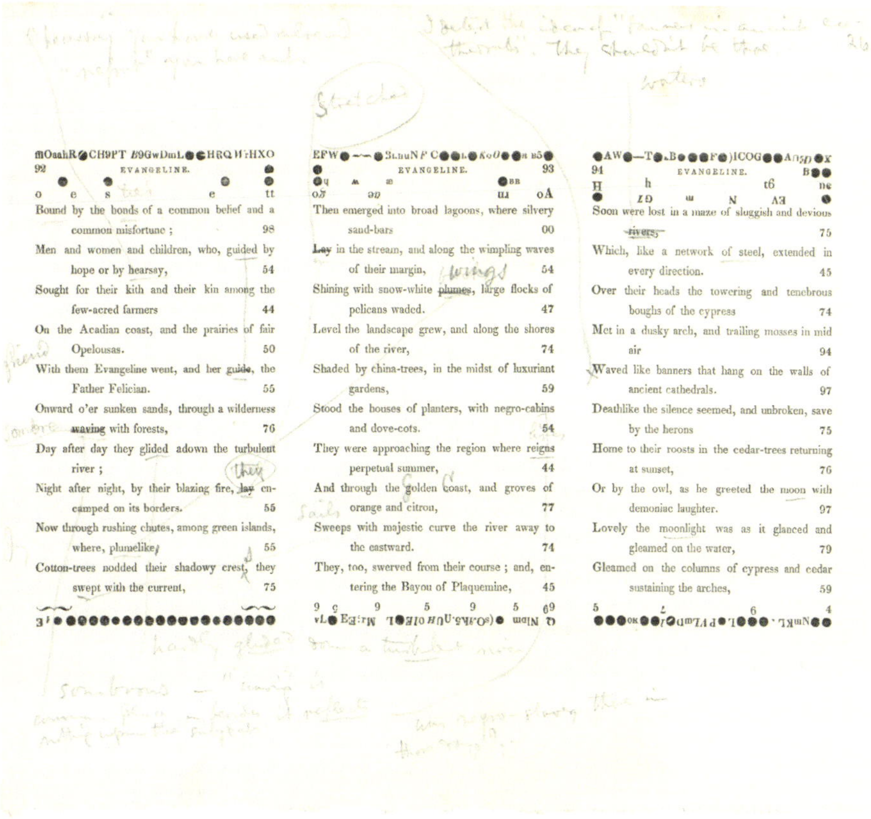

Figure 42. Proofsheets, 2nd set, 2nd revision, for Longfellow, *Evangeline*, with notes by Charles Sumner, 1847, Houghton f*AC85.L8605.847eaa

Longfellow had relied on Folsom's expertise many times before,[156] but this editing opportunity seemed more exciting than supervising the printing of a textbook. A letter from Folsom to Longfellow, written in March 1847, shows how pleased he was about the trust Longfellow had placed in him. Above all, Folsom promised not to be a pedant—after all, the King of Rome, Numa Pompilius, did not surround himself with dreary attorneys: "If you think any casual advantage which might result from my glancing over your proof-sheets would compensate the pleasure you would bestow, I shall be happy to let my dreams take their hue from your pages, if I can find them awaiting me in the evening at my house .... You may well discard pedants. We do not read that Numa was ever closeted with musty jurisconsults." [157]

156 See *Letters* 1: 363-70, 372, 415.

157 Charles Folsom to Longfellow, 7-9 March 1847, bMS Am 1340 (2023). When Folsom's suggestions for improvement came back, however, Longfellow, grateful as he was, couldn't help but feel that his friend

Shown here is a sheet from the second set of proofs (the second revision), on which Charles Sumner proposes that the "wilderness waving with forests" become a "wilderness *sombrous* with forests," because "waving is common place" and "reflects nothing upon the subject" (Longfellow obliged and replaced "waving" with "somber") and that the "maze of sluggish and devious rivers" be turned into a maze of "waters." Again Longfellow complied. Always more literal-minded than his poet-friend, Sumner points out that Evangeline's boat could hardly be "gliding" down "a *turbulent* river," and he strongly objects to the farmers from Grand-Pré being represented as entering an "ancient cathedral" when they come to the Bayou de Plaquemine (they were farmers, after all, and "shouldn't be there," Sumner said). He also suggests that "perpetual summer" doesn't "reign" in the region Evangeline enters—it simply "lives." Obviously, Longfellow was less interested in factual accuracy than in poetic effect—and a boat that "glides" down a stream in turmoil does seem more magical than one that is tossed around. Sumner's query, "was negro-slavery there in those days?" (regarding the "negro-cabins" Longfellow mentions), could have been easily answered by a reference to the Code Noir, regulating the behavior of slaves, that was passed in 1724 in New Orleans. Longfellow retained the reference. It should be noted here that Sumner loved the finished product, writing Longfellow in December 1847 that he had achieved "True Glory" and that he had "really moved the water—as with an angelic wing."[158]

Move the water Longfellow did also with his next bestseller, *The Song of Hiawatha*, praised by many but maligned by even more when it was first published in 1855, the same year as Whitman's *Leaves of Grass*. Longfellow began working on a poem about the Ojibway trickster-hero Manabozho in late June 1854, just a few weeks after 200 guards had marched the re-captured slave Anthony Burns through streets lined with shocked onlookers, beneath windows darkly draped in mourning and flags hung upside down, to the ship that would return him to Virginia. Across State Street, a black coffin labeled "Liberty" was suspended from ropes. Longfellow's anger knew no limits, but as a poet he wanted to be a healer rather than a political agitator. Hence his fantasy about a native messianic hero, a pacifist like his creator Longfellow, who could bring warring tribes to lay down their weapons and, as a kind of cultural ambassador, work towards a better future for his people. When Longfellow was in the middle of writing the poem, he started going to the opera again, attending, compulsively, within one week in January, performances of *I Puritani*, *La Favorita*, *Lucrezia Borgia*, *Norma*, and *Don Giovanni*. Entries such as "Morning 'Hiawatha.' Evening 'Norma'" (22 January 1855) are fairly typical. No wonder, then, that there is something operatic, too, about Longfellow's poem, in the careful stage-setting, the stylized interactions of the characters, the repetitiveness of the phrases that are being used, the tragic, yet visually spectacular

---

had become exactly the kind of pedant he had promised not to be: "Folsom's criticisms are minute and curious" (18 May 1847).

158 Charles Sumner to Longfellow, December 1847, Letters to Longfellow, bMS Am 1340.2 (5394).

ending.[159] The forest-dwelling, Italian-speaking Gallic Druids of *Norma* might have done their part in helping Longfellow envision and successfully complete *his* medley.

When Emerson thanked Longfellow for "your good gift of Hiawatha," he praised the poem's "wholesomeness" and said it was "very pertinent to us to read." But he also immediately complained that Longfellow had dignified material that really wasn't worth the effort: Indians were, he told Longfellow, "really savage" and had "poor small sterile heads" and had overall very little "to give." [160] Embarrassing romantic fantasy or not, *Hiawatha* was the product of serious study on Longfellow's part, derived no doubt from the conviction that "the Indians" had a *lot* to give and that one must try to understand exactly what. That an Anglo poet was allowed to take liberties with the material *after* absorbing and appreciating it Longfellow apparently didn't question. *Hiawatha* is a cultural mishmash, a collage of different tribal traditions: Longfellow had in fact mixed a mythical story told by the Ojibway but shared by several tribes—that of Manabozho, "a personage of miraculous birth, who was sent among them to clear their rivers, forests, and fishing-grounds, and to teach them the arts of peace"—with other "curious Indian legends," notably that of the charismatic founder of the Iroquois nation, Hiawatha (2: 379). He retained the Iroquois name of the protagonist, because it sounded good, but chose Minnesota as the setting for his poem and used words mostly from the Minnesota Indian languages Ojibway and Dakota Sioux.

A cavalier appropriation of native material, to be sure, perhaps only partly justified by the public purpose Longfellow wanted his poem to serve (he needed a hero who was an adventurer as well as a political leader). Given the eclecticism of *Hiawatha* as a whole, it is interesting to see how much research Longfellow put into the details. A case in point is the little duodecimo notebook that served him as a makeshift dictionary of the Ojibway language. Shown here is the end of the "M" entries and the beginning of the "N" section ("Notes for Hiawatha: Indian words and names," Longfellow Papers, Houghton, MS Am 1340 [92], FIGURE 43). Longfellow's notes here are more comprehensive than the wordlist that he finally printed as part of the notes to *Hiawatha*; there, for example, words like "Ne-jee" (friend) and "Nadowásees" ("enemies") don't show up.[161] He also lists his sources. "Alg." and "Oneot." point to Henry Rowe Schoolcraft's *Algic Researches* (1839) and *Oneóta* (1845). "McKeny," the abbreviation used after the phrase "Mush-kee-wau. darkness," stands for Thomas Loraine McKenney's *Sketches of a Tour to the Lakes,*

159 A reviewer in *The National Era* noted that *Hiawatha* had been written with an eye for "costume and scenic effect," 27 March 1856, 51.

160 Ralph Waldo Emerson to Henry Wadsworth Longfellow, 25 October 1855, *The Selected Letters of Ralph Waldo Emerson*, ed. Joel Myerson (New York: Columbia University Press, 1997) 386.

161 Throughout this section I have relied on the help of Stewart King, an Elder of the Wasauksing First Nation at Parry Sound, Ontario, who has decoded Longfellow's words for me, concluding that there is "substance" to his material (personal communication, 16 October 2006). In addition, Thomas Ford of Houghton Library has assisted me with several Ojibway words.

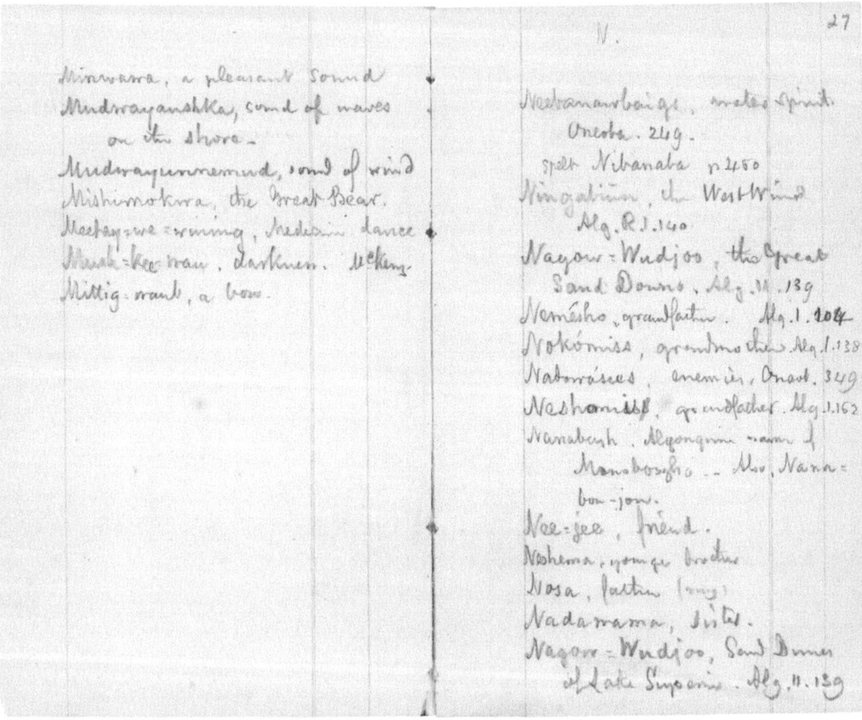
Minnewawa, a pleasant sound
Mudwayaushka, sound of waves
on the shore.
Mudwayaunnemund, sound of wind
Mishimokwa, the Great Bear.
Meetaywe, Medicine dance
Mush-kee-wau, darkness. McKeny.
Mittig-wauk, a bow.

27
N.
Nebanawbaigs, water spirit.
Oneota. 249.
spelt Nibanaba p 450
Ningabiun, the West Wind
Alg. R. I. 140.
Nagow-Wudjoo, the Great
Sand Dunes. Alg. II. 139
Nemésho, grandfather. Alg. I. 104
Nokómiss, grandmother Alg. I. 138
Nadowásees, enemies, Oneot. 349
Neshomiss, grandfather. Alg. I. 162
Nanabush. Algonquin name of
Manabozho.. Also, Nana-
bou-jou.
Nee-jee, friend.
Nosheema, younger brother
Nosa, father (my)
Nadawama, sister.
Nagow-Wudjoo, Sand Dunes
of Lake Superior. Alg. II. 139

Figure 43. Longfellow, "Notes for Hiawatha: Indian words and names," pp. 26-27, Longfellow Papers, Houghton, MS Am 1340 (92)

of the Character and Customs of the Chippeway Indians (1827), which, according to the charging books, Longfellow checked out from the Harvard College Library in October 1854, a month after he had borrowed *The Narrative of the Captivity and Adventures of John Tanner among the Indians* (1830) and Mary Eastman's *Dacotah, or Life and Legends among the Sioux* (1849), two other books mentioned in his notes to *Hiawatha.*[162] McKenney's book, part travel account, part ethnography, includes a "vocabulary of the Algic, or Chippeway language," based on the orthography established in Gallatin's *Table of the Indian Languages of the United States* (1826) and also used in Schoolcraft's volumes. Apparently, Longfellow discovered that McKenney's "Mush-kee-wan" was not correct; in the final version, he used "Guskewau" (2: 228) for "darkness," an approximation of the Ojibway verb *gashkii'waa* ("to be pitch-dark"). [163]

162 Kenneth Walter Cameron, *Longfellow's Reading in Libraries: The Charging Records of a Learned Poet* (Hartford, CT: Transcendental Books, 1973) 18.

163 For a site comparing Longfellow's words and the original Ojibway and Dakota words, see http://www.native-languages.org/hiawatha.htm.

Longfellow's wordlist gives us an inkling of the considerable ordering effort that went into making this poem. Schoolcraft, as he realized, wasn't a great help: "Three huge quartos," he wrote in his journal on 26 June 1854, "ill-digested, ill-arranged, and without any index. Verily book-making is an art like any other art, and one of the Fine Arts too, not so easily attained as many people imagine."

As a linguist, Longfellow cared about the sound of words, and there is evidence that the Ojibway language appealed to him even more than others. In at least one instance, Longfellow got new information about the pronunciation of a word ("opechee" or *opichi*) and changed a line in the first edition to reflect what he had learned. In a passage about the South Wind ("Shawondasee"), Longfellow had originally written: "He it was who sent the wood-birds, / Sent the Opechee, the robin," clearly thinking that the word's first syllable, as required by the trochaic tetrameters, had to be stressed. For subsequent editions, he revised the passage so that he could both retain his meter and have the reader pronounce the word properly: "He it was who sent the wood-birds, / Sént the róbin, thè Opéchee."[164]

One doesn't have to look very far for the source of Longfellow's newly-gained knowledge. In January 1856, when *Hiawatha* was "going at the rate of three hundred a day" (1 January 1856), James Tanner and his Ojibway wife visited Longfellow. James was the son of the former Indian captive and writer John Tanner, whose book Longfellow had also mined for *Hiawatha*.[165] As Longfellow described the event in his journal, Mrs. Tanner, "a gentle little woman, with a very soft, musical voice," performed a song for Longfellow: "it was in the minor key, very plaintive, and like the wind in the pines."

164 See editor Horace Scudder's note in the Riverside edition of Longfellow's *Complete Poetical Works* (Cambridge: Houghton, Mifflin, and Co., 1893) 665.

165 This was almost certainly the Reverend James Tanner, born in 1805, to John Tanner and his second wife, Theresa Lavallee. James Tanner, who worked as a missionary among the Salteaux Ojibway, married a woman called Marguerite Gunn or Govin (whose Salteaux name was "Poo-pee") in the Red River Settlement around 1834. He died under mysterious circumstance during the Red River Rebellion, led by Métis leader Louis Riel; there are some indications that he was killed by Canadian soldiers sent to Manitoba to quell the resistance. Tanner's wife died in 1915 in Kinosota, Manitoba, at age 104. The fact that Longfellow would have relied on James Tanner to help him make corrections to *Hiawatha* is not without irony given that Henry Rowe Schoolcraft had been his principal source when he set out to write the poem. Tanner's father John, kidnapped in Kentucky by the Shawnee when he was about 9 years old and later sold to an Ottawa woman, worked for Schoolcraft as an interpreter in Sault Ste. Marie for two years, until Schoolcraft dismissed him in 1830. Later, Tanner, whose Salteaux name was "the Falcon," was (probably wrongly) suspected in the murder of Schoolcraft's brother James. See George Woodcock, "John Tanner," *Dictionary of Canadian Biography*, vol. VII: *1836-1850* (Toronto: University of Toronto Press, 1988) 844-845; *The Falcon: A Narrative of the Captivity and Adventures of John Tanner* (1830; New York: Penguin, 1994); Peter Lorenz Neufeld, "John 'Falcon" Tanner's Death," *Manitoba Pageant* 20.3 (Spring 1975), available at http://www.mhs.mb.ca/docs/pageant/20/tannerdeath.shtml.

And Tanner informed him that "I have the accents all right in the Indian names in 'Hiawatha'; which was mostly by instinct, as the vocabularies for the most part do not indicate them" (3 January 1856).

Well, he got *almost* all the accents right. In a letter to Sumner about the same visit, written on 14 January 1856, Longfellow mentions the word *Opechee*; we may assume that it was then that the Tanners told him how to pronounce it properly (*Letters* 3: 523). Longfellow did like to think that he had a special affinity for the Ojibway language, so much so that, some occasional missteps aside, he knew what the words should sound like. Ojibway was, he informed Sumner, "more musical than the Italian" (a tremendous compliment coming from Longfellow): "Think then of the blockheads, who find no music in such words as *Oméme*, but prefer *pidgeon* [sic], which would frighten an Ojibway chief who saw it for the first time! No one—excepting always the blockheads—can hear the word *Opechee*, without hearing at the same time all the forest ring with the song of the birds! and it is not so with its English equivalent *robin*, which suggests the English landscape, groves and cottages, and gardens" (*Letters* 3: 523). Languages were equal yet different, and cultural diversity was a good thing.

The Song of Hiawatha was the apotheosis of the cultivated Indian, the glorification of the native who is both the producer and the product of literature. It is easy to scoff at Longfellow's drawing-room version of native life, uncontaminated by direct exposure to its realities, but we need to remember also how iconoclastic it was for a nineteenth-century white poet to assign cultural power to a Native American leader. Hiawatha's leadership manifests itself not only in reconciling warring tribes but also in bringing the gift of literacy to his own people. The central canto devoted to "Picture-Writing" shows that the tribal leader Hiawatha is also a teacher, a scholar, and a careful creator and interpreter of common cultural artifacts ("each figure had a meaning, / Each some word or thought suggested"; 2: 234) and in that, not unlike Longfellow himself. Longfellow nowhere promises—as Whitman famously did at just about the same time—that one would only need to "stop" with him for a while to "possess the origin of all poems." Instead, he wanted his "Indian" poem to be a fancier version of the "rude inscriptions" Hiawatha has taught his people to leave on their gravestones—a series of images left on the reader's mind: Hiawatha flanked by his two friends, the poet and the strong man; the nude Minnehaha, "unashamed and unaffrighted," dancing around the cornfield at night; the sun setting like a blood-red flamingo settling into her nest at nightfall.

As Longfellow's "Indian" trochees trickled into the minds of the American reading public, more parodies sprung up than anyone could count. Longfellow's own image became shared property, too. A particular aggressive believer in shared property was Julia Margaret Cameron, Tennyson's neighbor on the Isle of Wight. Hearing that Longfellow, on his well-publicized 1868 trip to England, was going to visit Tennyson, she came over to take advantage of the situation. "Longfellow, you will have to do whatever she tells you," Tennyson reportedly said. "I'll come back soon and see what is

Figure 44. Julia Margaret Cameron, *Henry Wadsworth Longfellow*, photogravure from *Alfred, Lord Tennyson and His Friends* (1893), Houghton *2001M-8, box 2. Notice the error in the caption: "W. H. Longfellow" instead of "H. W. Longfellow."

left of you" (FIGURE 44).[166] What was left of Longfellow was, in a sense, so much more than what had been there before. Longfellow's floating-haired, costumed likeness—he is wearing some kind of flowing dark cloak, similar to, though apparently a bit fancier than, the blanket-like one in which she wrapped Robert Browning for his portrait—is classic Cameron. Consider the attention to the effects of the light on the face, the dark background, the awkward posture, all of which illustrate Cameron's creative attempt to superimpose her own sense of what is important about Longfellow on whatever sense of identity her model might have had. It is remarkable how unkempt, Lear-like

166 See V. C. Scott O'Connor, "Mrs. Cameron, Her Friends, and Her Photographs," *Century Illustrated Magazine* 55.1 (November 1897) 3-8; see p. 8. Houghton's photogravure was published in *Alfred, Lord Tennyson and His Friends: A Series of 25 Portraits and Frontispiece in Photogravure, from the Negatives of Mrs. Julia Margaret Cameron and H. H. H. Cameron* (London: T. Fisher Unwin, 1893).

Longfellow, who was so fastidious about his appearance in real life, is made to look here. Cameron had a fascination with hair, and, in her book, white, unruly locks and a certain carelessness of appearance were the symptoms of a great intellect.[167] No slouch when it came to tooting her horn, Cameron, in a letter she sent Longfellow later on, declared the "Profile likeness very fine indeed & therefore worthy of you."[168]

This particular print, first published in 1893, is a photogravure—that is, an image produced from an engraving made after Cameron's original photograph. Photogravures combine the precision of the photograph with the art quality of the lithograph, a combination that draws attention to the painterly qualities of Cameron's work. The composition of the image, one of only a handful in which Cameron included a sitter's hand, is striking because it draws the viewer's attention in two different directions at once: the face, shown in profile, is turned to the left, while the hand points to the right. Longfellow's leonine, Olympian head is upright, rigid, even fierce, an image of control (since this is where the poetry originates), while his loose hand (the hand that would normally hold the pen) signals the place where we can always approach, even understand, him. The area of the heart, the place where the hand, lightly tucked into the folds of the cloak, has come to rest, is not incidental. This was the "Poet of the Heart," as readers everywhere knew him, a great writer, no doubt, firm in his purpose when it came to writing but ever so soft when it came to the interests and concerns of his readers, someone who is close to all of us. The Longfellow in Cameron's photo is private, absorbed in himself, but he has made the fact of his self-absorption public and therefore shareable.

167 See Mary Price, *The Photograph: A Strange, Confined Space* (Stanford: Stanford University Press, 1994) 111.

168 Julia Margaret Cameron to Longfellow, 26 July 1868, Longfellow Papers, Houghton, bMS Am 1340.2 (937).

Chapter 6: Longfellow's Readers

ACCORDING TO FELLOW poet John Greenleaf Whittier, it was Longfellow's celebrity that finally killed him: "My friend Longfellow," he wrote to Edward L. Pierce on 12 April 1882, "was driven to death by these incessant demands." Whittier knew about the price of popularity, too: ever since the publication of *Snow-Bound* (1866), fans had been showing up at his house, hoping to get a glimpse of the Quaker poet. He found it extremely hard to manage the correspondence, which seemed to increase by the day. For every letter he answered, "two more come by the next mail."[169]

Longfellow's popularity—and therefore also his correspondence—exceeded that of any serious American poet before or after him. Countless visitors—poets from Vermont and Germany, Cuban abolitionists, a Polish count, Italian beggars, a lady in black who thought he had already died and wanted to see his residence—came to Craigie House to get a glimpse of the "Poet of the Heart."[170] A few of them were celebrity-seekers who were only dimly aware of Longfellow's specific reputation or even the fact that it was *Longfellow* who lived here: "A traveler called today, and asked me if Shakespeare did not live somewhere about here! I told him I know no such person in the neighborhood" (18 October 1866). Others wanted money. But even harder to cope with were the people who sent letters to Longfellow, asking questions about his works, requesting autographs, telling him about their own lives, and sending along their own poems for critique and approval. Ernest Longfellow later remembered how his father would sit at the round table in the middle of his study dealing with mail from his fans: "He was very conscientious about answering his large correspondence himself, and refused to have a secretary till the last few years of his life, sacrificing a great deal of his valuable time to answering trivial demands upon his kindness."[171]

Except that Longfellow himself probably wouldn't have considered such requests "trivial." Sure enough, he frequently complained about the letters that poured in, imagining them hiding somewhere in the house, "sharpshooters" intent on ambushing

169 See J. G. Whittier to Edward L. Pierce, 12 April 1882, and Whittier to Rebecca Allinson, 12 February 1873, *The Letters of John Greenleaf Whittier,* 3 vols. (Cambridge, MA: Belknap, 1975) 3: 447-48 and 3: 289.

170 Eva L. Delano to Longfellow, 23 November 1881, Letters to Longfellow, Houghton, bMS Am 1340.2 (1523).

171 Ernest Wadsworth Longfellow, *Random Memories* 14.

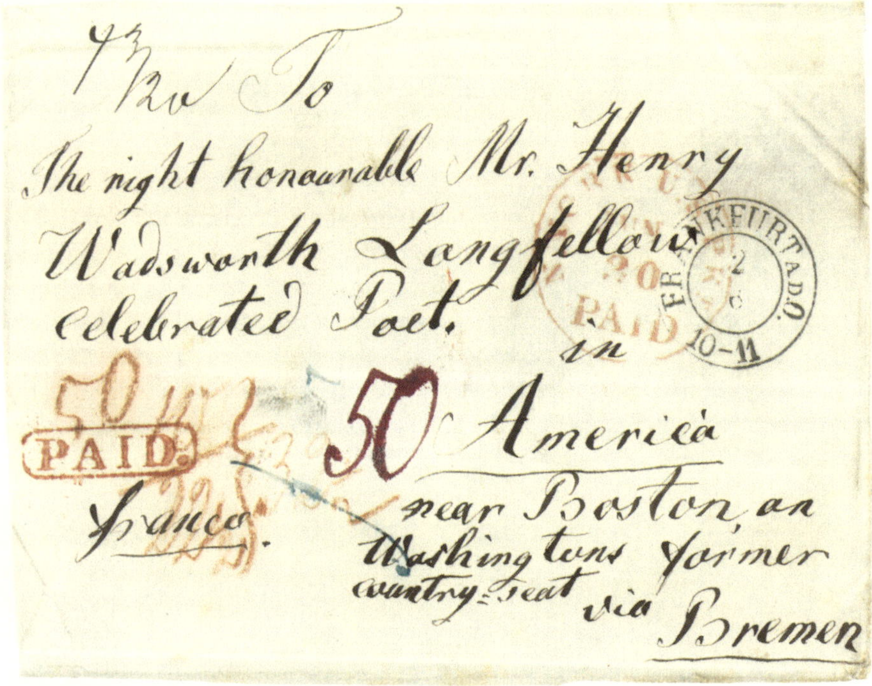

Figure 45. Clipping from an envelope addressed "To the right honourable Mr. Henry Wadsworth Longfellow celebrated Poet," from Longfellow's scrapbook, Longfellow Papers, Houghton, MS Am 1340 (198)

him and destroying the peace he needed for writing (9 May 1856). He would see himself wading, up to his armpits, through a "snow-drift" of unanswered mail,[172] and he did come to resent "the Perfect Stranger" who would write to him and claim his friendship "and always has 'an axe to grind'" (14 April 1862). He had a perfectly good reason to react the way he did: Houghton Library alone has letters from 6,228 correspondents, which fill seventy-three boxes, and this number doesn't even include the more than thirteen hundred requests for autographs also kept with Longfellow's correspondence (see the "Coda" to this book, pages 191-92). It is estimated that he must have received around twenty thousand letters altogether between 1821 and 1882. The very last entry in his journal, written on 31 January 1882, was about a request he had received that very morning, via postal card, from a "gentleman in Falls City, Nebraska," who also considered himself a "friend." He wasn't pleased with Milton's *Paradise Regained* and wanted Longfellow to write a new ending: "take up the poem where he left off, and continue it to the Millennium" (January 1882).

Longfellow was so famous that an envelope addressed only "To the right honourable Mr. Henry Wadsworth Longfellow celebrated Poet. in *America* near Boston, on

172 Longfellow to Alice Longfellow, 2 August 1875 (*Letters* 6: 55).

Washingtons [sic] former country-seat via *Bremen*" (Longfellow's scrapbook, Longfellow Papers, Houghton, MS Am 1340 [198], FIGURE 45) reached him with no problem. The post office required not much more than his name to deliver his mail to him, a distinction he shared, interestingly enough, with P. T. Barnum, the Great Showman.[173] Occasionally, Longfellow did consider the "uncivil" option of not answering his mail at all anymore (to George Washington Greene, 28 October 1881; *Letters* 6: 742). More typically, however, he sent back kind and cautious replies, especially when his correspondents had included samples of their own work: "I have read it with interest and pleasure," he wrote in December 1874 to the aspiring New York poet George Houghton, who had sent him his new and rather slim volume of verse, a pamphlet, really, called *Songs from Over the Sea*. He assured Houghton that he had always "been in favor of small volumes of poetry .... A large volume is oppressive, and fatigues the mind." Realizing that he needed to add some substance to his praise, he went on: "I particularly like your idea of singing on your way, and noting down gleams of landscape, and the thoughts that suggested themselves as you went along." Note that Longfellow talks about Houghton's *idea*, not the *execution*, a distinction that was likely lost on his correspondent.[174]

One of Longfellow's more famous correspondents, the actress Fanny Kemble, on 16 June 1851, tried to put her finger on what had made her experience of reading Longfellow so unique. Still reeling from her divorce she had turned to poetry for relief, and in Longfellow she found what she needed:

> My dear Sir—some little while ago I took up a volume of your poems and a load of most miserable suffering that had literally hardened my heart appeared to me to relax its pressure while I read it—for the first time for many months the iron grasp of sorrow seemed to relax and I experienced a moral relief which is indescribable but for which I blessed you most

173 "I had had letters from New Zealand, and other remote quarters of the globe ... and addressed simply to 'Mr. Barnum, America,' and the post-office officials ... regularly put these vaguely addressed letters in my New York box"; *Struggles and Triumphs: Or, Forty Years' Recollections of P. T. Barnum*, ed. Carl Bode (1869; Harmondsworth: Penguin, 1981) 379.

174 Longfellow to George Houghton, 29 December 1874, Houghton *2001M-8, box 1. Houghton's *Songs from Over the Sea* (New York: S. W. Green, 1874) contained an early poetic version of the dilemma more capably described in Robert Frost's later poem "The Road Not Taken." Houghton's "Switzerland" at least seems to have been based on an actual hiking experience: "Two different ways, and thou must choose, / And by the choosing gain or lose; / Then do not leave this out of sight; / The steepest path climbs first the mountain height!" (p. 11). One wonders, too, what Longfellow really thought of the following song offered in praise of daisies: "Beautiful daisies! / Swinging a censer whose breaths arise, / A pure adoration up to the skies" (p. 4). Longfellow's copy of *Songs from Over the Sea* is now in Houghton Library (AL 381.15*).

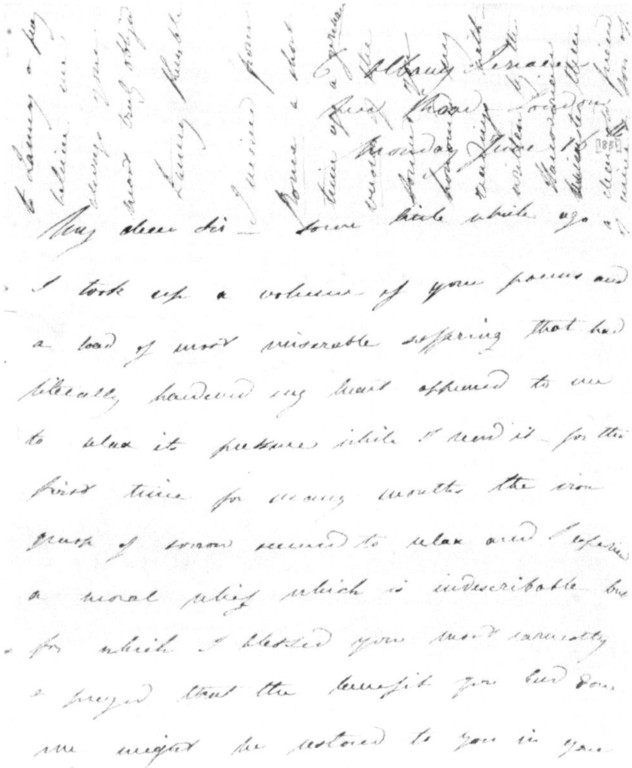

Very dear Sir — Some little while ago

I took up a volume of your poems and

a load of most miserable suffering that had

literally hardened my heart seemed to me

to relax its pressure while I read it — for the

first time for many months the iron

grasp of sorrow seemed to relax and I experienced

a moral relief which is indescribable but

for which I blessed you most earnestly

& preyed that the benefit you had done

me might be restored to you in your

Figure 46. Fanny Kemble to Longfellow, 16 June 1851, Letters to Longfellow, Houghton, bMS Am 1340.2 (3140)

> earnestly & preyed [sic] that the benefit you had done me might be restored to you in your need a thousandfold . . . .
> (Letters to Longfellow, Houghton, bMS Am 1340.2 [3140], FIGURE 46)

At the end of her letter, Kemble asked him to send a reassuring note to novelist William Makepeace Thackeray, who was nervous about a planned American tour.

Interestingly, Fanny Kemble saw her reading of Longfellow's poetry as part of an ongoing exchange of feelings that would also, at some point, possibly involve the poet himself. More precisely, the relief she had felt might, some day, be needed by *him*, too. The author, in this interpretation, is merely the medium through which sentiments shared by all circulate. In his reply, Longfellow responded appropriately, acknowledging that Kemble's experience—and, more precisely, the fact that "you should have been in such suffering, and that a song of mine should have strengthened and consoled you"—

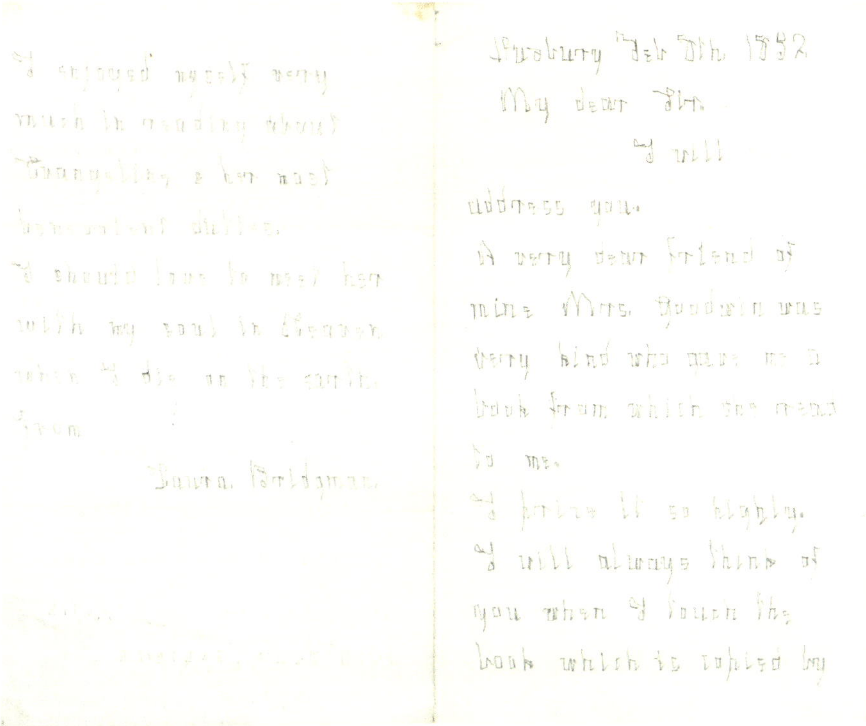
Sudbury Feb 8th 1852
My dear Sir.
I will
address you.
A very dear friend of
mine Mrs. Goodwin was
very kind who gave me a
book from which she read
to me.
I prize it so highly.
I will always think of
you when I touch the
book which is copied by

Laura Bridgman.

Figure 47. Laura Bridgman to Longfellow, 8 February 1852,
Letters to Longfellow, Houghton, bMS Am 1340.2 (723)

had made *him* weep, too. Regarding Thackeray, Longfellow declared that "he could not do better than to follow your example" (4 July 1851; *Letters* 3: 298). Apparently, Thackeray was not convinced. He postponed his visit.

A more unlikely reader of Longfellow's poetry made her presence known a year later—someone who had read Longfellow's poetry in a very literal, tangible way. Through his friend, the German poet Emmanuel Scherb, Longfellow received a letter from a young blind and deaf inmate of the Perkins Institution for the Blind, run by Longfellow's old associate and member of the Five of Clubs, Samuel Gridley Howe. The woman's name was Laura Bridgman. Bridgman had had Longfellow's *Evangeline*, his blockbuster poem about the displacement of the Acadians that was still selling at a pretty good clip in 1852, read to her or rather tapped out into her hand. "My dear Sir," she wrote in her letter dated 8 February 1852,

> I will address you.
> A very dear friend of mine Mrs. Goodwin was very kind who gave me a book from which she read to me.

> I prize it so highly.
> I will always think of you when I touch the book which is copied by you.
> I am so much interested in thinking of Evangeline who devoted all her time in doing so very much good to the sick & afflicted people during her life. I sympathize with her so far in her afflictions. I love her very dearly. She is so lovely & sweet. She is one of Christ's very dear Sisters.
> I enjoyed myself very much in reading about Evangeline & her most benevolent duties.
> I should love to meet her with my soul in Heaven when I die on the earth.
> from
> Laura Bridgman.
> (Letters to Longfellow, Houghton, bMS Am 1340.2 [723], FIGURE 47)

A remarkable letter, not only because of its style and tone, but also because Bridgman seems so convinced that Evangeline is a real person. As far as she was concerned, the *character* Longfellow had created was more important than the *author* (as Bridgman saw it, Longfellow had just "copied" the book that tells Evangeline's story).

Longfellow had initiated the exchange. Upon hearing from Scherb that Bridgman had been reading *Evangeline*, he immediately wrote a letter to her teacher, Mrs. Emma Goodwin, in which he presented himself as the grateful beneficiary of Laura's interest in his poem:

> Cambridge, Jan. 25, 1852
>
> Dear Madam,
>
> Mr. Scherb was here on Saturday, and he told me the story of your reading "Evangeline" to Laura Bridgman; a story which very much touched and gratified me. How and how much, I cannot easily express to you; but you can easily imagine it.
>
> As a slight acknowledgment of the pleasure this has given me, may I beg you to accept the accompanying copy of "Evangeline," which you will find beautifully illustrated.
>
> I remain
> With great regard
> Yours truly
> Henry W. Longfellow
> (Houghton *2001M-8, box 1)

The "beautifully illustrated" copy of his poem was obviously not intended for Bridgman but for Mrs. Goodwin; Longfellow had no real intention of engaging in a personal relationship with Bridgman. Interesting, then, that Bridgman, refusing to be content with her subordinate status, took the initiative and wrote back directly to him.

They had met before. And Longfellow was familiar with Bridgman's extraordinary story. Born in 1829 in Hanover, New Hampshire, Laura had suffered a devastating bout of scarlet fever when she was only two years old. Her illness rendered her deaf and blind and also damaged her sense of smell. Word about the severely impaired girl traveled fast in New England, thanks also to a newspaper account written by Reuben Mussey, professor of anatomy and surgery at Dartmouth College, who had examined the girl. Longfellow probably first heard of Bridgman in July 1837, when he traveled to New Hampshire in the company of Samuel Gridley Howe, George Hillard, Rufus Choate, and the Harvard student Samuel Eliot. The official reason for the trip was that Hillard had been asked to deliver a commencement address at Dartmouth College. But Howe, a man desperately in search of a cause, was much more excited about checking out Bridgman. Decades later, Samuel Eliot, the youngest member of the party, would remember how keen Howe was on gaining Bridgman for himself, how eagerly he had run over, on 25 July, to the "Bridgman house in quest of his prize." He returned, having convinced Laura's parents to relinquish their responsibilities to him and to send their daughter to Boston later that year.[175]

The journal that Longfellow kept during his trip to the White Mountains doesn't mention Bridgman;[176] it is likely, then, that Howe went to her parents' house by himself. But Longfellow definitely met Bridgman in the summer of 1841, when he and his friend Sumner took their friend Sam Ward's sister Julia to the Perkins Institution for a fateful first meeting with the dashing Howe (nicknamed "the Chevalier"). Julia married Howe a year later.[177] Their relationship, rarely tranquil, lasted 33 years, plagued by Howe's incapacity to make his wife—and not Laura Bridgman or his closest friend, Charles Sumner—the center of his affection and attention. Julia developed, as her daughters reported, an almost physical distaste for blind people.[178]

175 See Maud Howe and Florence Howe Hall, *Laura Bridgman: Dr. Howe's Famous Pupil and What He Taught Her* (Boston: Little, Brown, and Co., 1903) 39. Longfellow is misidentified here as his brother "Samuel" (see "Index," 392). See also Ernest Freeberg, *The Education of Laura Bridgman: First Blind and Deaf Person to Learn Language* (Cambridge, MA: Harvard University Press, 2001) 26-28 and Elisabeth Gitter, *The Imprisoned Guest: Laura Bridgman, the Original Deaf-Blind Girl* (New York: Farrar, Straus, and Giroux, 2001) 75-77.

176 Longfellow, "Journey to the Whites, July 1837," Longfellow Papers, Houghton, MS Am 1340 (193).

177 The encounter is summarized in Julia Ward Howe, "Reminiscences of Longfellow. (Second Paper)," *The Critic*, 22 April 1882, 115.

178 See the introduction to Julia Howe's *The Hermaphrodite*, a novel that, unpublished in Howe's lifetime, at least partly reflects on her marital problems (ed. Gary Williams, Lincoln: University of Nebraska Press, 2004), xx-xxi, as well as Laura Richards and Maud Howe Elliott, with Florence Howe Hall, *Julia Ward Howe, 1819-1910*, 2 vols. (Boston: Houghton Mifflin, 1915) 1: 105.

With minor interruptions, Bridgman lived at the Perkins Institution for the Blind until her death in 1889. Howe and his assistants taught her to write, read, and converse by using her fingers on the palms of her interlocutors' hands. The gain was also his, of course: Howe was widely celebrated for having found the key to unlock the secret of what makes humans human. Charles Dickens, who made a point of visiting Bridgman when he came to America in 1846, was so moved by the experience that in *American Notes* he called sight "a worker of hypocrisy."[179] Every day, Dickens claimed, we assume masks and attempt to represent ourselves in ways other than what we really are. Unconfined by such pressures, Bridgman seemed closer to the essence of humanity than most people. At the same time, because of her isolation, she was also more endangered than others. When Howe began working with her, Laura's "mind and spirit," as Howe put it, "were as cruelly cramped by her isolation as the foot of a Chinese girl is cramped by an iron shoe."[180] Enter her liberator Howe. To Dickens, who quoted liberally from Howe's notes on Bridgman, the success of the treatment was evident. When he saw Laura, her face was "radiant with intelligence and pleasure" (*American Notes* 46). He observed and carefully described her "square-hand writing," a technique Bridgman had perfected in which she placed a grooved guide made of cardboard underneath the sheet of paper, then used the grooves to guide her hand across the page. With her right hand she would draw the letter, covering it with her left forefinger as she went to draw the next letter. A finger's width separated words: "she kept her left hand always touching, and following up, her right, in which, of course, she held the pen. No line was indicated by any contrivance, but she wrote straight and freely" (*American Notes* 54-55). This procedure, of which the letter to Longfellow is a beautiful example, was called square-hand because the letters, produced within the grid formed by the grooves and the left forefinger, had an angular look.

In her letter, Bridgman thanks Longfellow but only in connection with the book that he has produced, which is a physical object for her, something to be felt and held. The more important relationship she has developed is an intangible one, the bond of sympathy that unites her with Evangeline, a girl who is afflicted herself (as Bridgman was) but is also—unlike Bridgman—a helper of the afflicted.

Longfellow's own response to Bridgman has not yet surfaced, only a cover letter he sent to Emma Goodwin on 16 February 1852:

> Cambridge, February 16, 1852
>
> Dear Mrs. Goodwin,
>
> I take the liberty of inclosing to you a letter to Laura Bridgman in answer to one from her, which Mr. Scherb has handed me.

179 Charles Dickens, *American Notes and Pictures from Italy*, ed. F. S. Schwarzbach and Leonée Ormond (London: Everyman, 1997) 40.

180 Samuel Gridley Howe, "Laura Bridgman," *American Journal of Education* 4 (December 1857): 383-400; see 389.

I have hardly ventured to tell Laura how beautiful her letter seems to me, and how very touching some of its phrases are; not knowing what your system is in regard to praise and blame.

Let me, therefore, to you, express more warmly my gratification at her note, and my delight in seeing what it was in "Evangeline" that she admired and sympathized with. I leave it with you, to interpret to her more fully than I have done, my feelings on this point. Certainly I have never received any commendation of that poem so valuable as this, or that goes so directly to the heart.

With much regard

Yours truly

Henry W. Longfellow

(Houghton *2001M-8, box 1)

Like Dickens, Howe, and others, Longfellow remained stuck in a conventional reading of Bridgman as the victim of a cruel fate. As if she were still a child and not a twenty-three-year-old woman, he addressed her mentor rather than Bridgman herself. Quite obviously, he didn't recognize how empowering her reading of *Evangeline* had become to Bridgman. What he did know was that they were both celebrities. Among his papers was a small envelope, dated January 1852 (i.e., before he had received Bridgman's letter), in which he had preserved her autograph, carefully labeled ("Autograph of Laura Bridgman [deaf, dumb, and blind]").

Both Longfellow and Bridgman were hot topics, as becomes clear in an article the *Boston Evening Transcript* ran on 18 February 1852, which was found with Longfellow's second letter to Mrs. Goodwin.[181] Longfellow, a devotee of scrap-booking, was an enthusiastic newspaper clipper, and he might have saved the article and sent it on to Mrs. Goodwin (which, in this case, would have meant that he mailed his letter two days after he wrote it). Or—which seems more likely—Mrs. Goodwin inserted the clipping into the envelope later.[182] Perhaps inevitably, the article trivializes the story. Bridgman apparently hated cats and would kick them on occasion. The *Transcript* article describes how she was cured of her aversion when her teacher pointed out to her that the saint-like Evangeline would "never have been rude" to an animal: Laura "looked the picture of humiliation, and has not been so vindictive against her enemy, the cat, since." The article ends with a tribute to Longfellow the poet and Howe the mentor: "How gratifying must it be to the heart of the Poet to have lighted for awhile with the sunny creatures of his imagination the dark night in which the spirit of the poor sense-locked girl is bound .... But if the poet has reason to consider the joy and

181 "Longfellow's Evangeline and Laura Bridgman," *The Boston Evening Transcript*, 18 February 1852.

182 Personal communication, 28 November 2006, from Victor Gulotta, Newton, who originally acquired the item.

Figure 48. Laura Bridgman, carte-de-visite, Houghton *2001M-8, box 1

the thanks of the young girl as one of the proudest triumphs of his muse, what must be the feelings of him, to whom Laura is indebted for all that she is …? Well, may he proudly stand by the side of his friend, the poet, claming part of the laurels ….” Note the condescending tone of the passage where Bridgman is concerned, a nineteenth-century Galatea to the proud Pygmalion of the Perkins Institution.

Far from being desperately "sense-locked," however, Bridgman, in the years that followed, increasingly began to take her life into her own hands. Under the surface swiftly polished by the efforts of Boston philanthropy, the tough New Hampshire farm girl reemerged.[183] Looking more and more birdlike as the years went by—as if intent on *not* becoming a pretty trophy Howe could display to visitors—Bridgman (who once bit Charles Sumner because he had squeezed her too hard) refused to assume an agreeable pose for photographs. She also ditched the green band that, like the other inmates of the Perkins Institution, she had kept wrapped around her eyelids for years and that Dickens noted she had also put on her doll (carte-de-visite, Houghton *2001M-8, box 1, FIGURE 48). In later photographs she can be seen wearing tinted glasses.

183 The phrase is Gitter's; see *Imprisoned Guest* 113.

Finally, Laura Bridgman also permanently rejected her mentor's flexible Unitarian beliefs. Her God was not one who had intended happiness to be the lot of humanity. Perhaps Evangeline, the afflicted helper of the afflicted, "one of Christ's poor sisters," also helped Bridgman make up her mind regarding her religious beliefs. With her formal baptism in 1862, by full immersion in a creek close to her parent's house, Bridgman went back to her parents' fundamentalist faith. She had turned, as Andrew Delbanco put it, "for comfort to the story of the suffering Christ who had died to expiate her sins—a bleeding God-man whom the Unitarians had tried to exile to the realm of idolatry and superstition."[184]

Bridgman communicated with Longfellow on at least one other occasion. In 1871, she sent him her poem titled "Holy Home." The version of the poem in Longfellow's possession, which was only recently discovered by the staff of the Longfellow House, is considerably different from the one reprinted in the memoir published by Howe's daughters:

> Holy home is illuminous,
> Like sun.
> Blind are we in part
> because we cannot imagine
> the beauty of holy home . . .
> but after the door of death
> Is opened . . .
> It is a glorious wonder
> to our eyes . . . .[185]

Note how Bridgman here interprets blindness as part of the general ignorance of humans when it comes to the life eternal, which would make her case only a particularly pronounced example of a fate shared by all: the "aching of heart, the restless unsatisfied longing, / All the dull, deep pain, and constant anguish of patience" that Longfellow's Evangeline experienced (2: 107-8).

Longfellow's poetry meant different things to different people in different places. He knew, for example, that he had devoted readers in India. Charles Eliot Norton, who had joined a Boston importing firm after his graduation from Harvard, had traveled all over India in 1849, finding Longfellow aficionados in the unlikeliest of places, as he reported (25 March 1850). A letter from Calcutta, written on 10 April 1862 by one Syud Hossein, corroborates Norton's story. "I don't know how to appologize [sic] for writing

184 Andrew Delbanco, "An Experiment in Darkness," *New York Review of Books*, 20 September 2001, 36-39; see p. 36.

185 "Bridgman Poem Comes to Light," *The Longfellow House Bulletin* 2.1 (June 1998) 6. See also Howe and Hall, *Bridgman* 289-90.

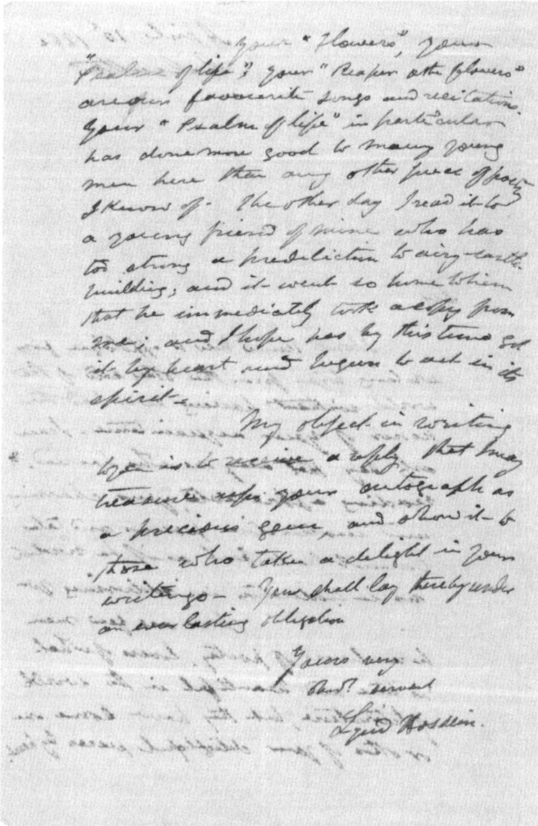

your "Flowers", your "Psalm of life", your "Reaper & the flowers" are our favourite songs and recitations. Your "Psalm of life" in particular has done more good to many young men here than any other piece of poetry I know of. The other day I read it to a young friend of mine who has too strong a predilection to airy-castle building; and it went so home to him that he immediately took a copy from you; and I hope has by this time got it by heart and begun to act in its spirit.

My object in writing to you is to receive a copy that may treasure up your autograph as a precious gem, and show it to those who take a delight in your writings. You shall lay truly under an everlasting obligation

Yours very truly
obed.t servant
Syud Hossein.

Figure 49. Syud Hossein to Longfellow, 10 April 1862, Letters to Longfellow, Houghton, bMS Am 1340.2 (2833)

to you from the other end of the world," Mr. Hossein begins his missive, "without having ever had the honor of your acquaintance." But then he continues, as most of Longfellow's American readers would, entirely unapologetically: "I can only say that any one who has read, & reading [sic] appreciated your charming and instructive poems and tales cannot but feel as if he needed no introduction in addressing you." Here in India, there were indeed other lovers of poetry like him, "lovers of what is true and beautiful in the world of literature," and they knew their Longfellow well: "Your 'Flowers', your 'Psalm of life', your 'Reaper and the flowers' are our favorite songs and recitations." And then like other readers paying tribute to Longfellow, Hossein goes on to describe his poetry not in terms of what it *is* but in terms of what it *does*. Poetry creates community, and an autograph from Longfellow, which Hossein unabashedly requests in the final paragraph of his letter, will further help cement those ties that unite the lovers of Longfellow in India:

> Your "Psalm of life" in particular has done more good to many young men here than any other verse of poetry I know of. The other day I read it to a young friend of mine who has too strong a predilection to airy castle-building; and it went so home to him that he immediately took a copy from me; and I hope has by this time got it by heart and begun to act in its spirit—
>
> My object in writing to you is to receive a reply that I may treasure & revere your autograph as a precious gem and show it to those who take a delight in your writings—You shall lay thereby under an ever lasting obligation
>
> Your very
> obdt. servant
> Syud Hossein
>
> (Letters to Longfellow, Houghton, bMS Am 1340.2 [2833], FIGURE 49)

While Mr. Hossein was recruiting young men as readers of Longfellow's poetry in India, the Danish writer Hans Christian Andersen was reading *Evangeline* in Copenhagen and dreaming about an American tour that would also take him to Cambridge. On 14 November 1851, Andersen's close friend Henriette ("Jette") Wulff, a more fearless traveler than he, wrote to him from the Virgin Islands to say how happy she was that Longfellow, "den nordamerikanske herlige Forfatter" ("the wonderful North American author"), had sent him his poems. She was reading Longfellow all the time, she said, loved his "poetic nature" ("poetiske Natur"), which is why she was so pleased to hear that Longfellow knew and "worshipped" her friend Andersen. Would Andersen mind sending him something of his, too? On 18 December 1851, Andersen confirmed that he had indeed received Longfellow's *Evangeline*.[186] When it rains it pours: the following year, Therese A. L. Robinson (a German writer married to an American philologist, whom Andersen had met in Weimar the year before) also gave him a volume of Longfellow's poems.[187] Andersen was hooked. In 1865, he wrote in his *dagbok* that Longfellow's poetry helped him cope when he felt melancholy.[188]

186 Letters 235 and 237, Hans Christian Andersen Database, Hans Christian Andersen Center of the University of Southern Denmark. The originals are in the Royal Library at Copenhagen. Thanks to Solveig Brunholm for providing me with these documents.

187 See Sven Hakon Rossel, "Going Places: Hans Christian Andersen, the Great European Traveler," *Hans Christian Andersen: Danish Writer and Citizen of the World*, ed. Rossel (Amsterdam: Rodopi, 1996) 1-121; see 80.

188 Vol. 2: 212 of Andersen's *Dagbøger*, quoted in Inge Kabell, "A Dane in Boston," *Angles* 9 (1986): 41-53; see 43.

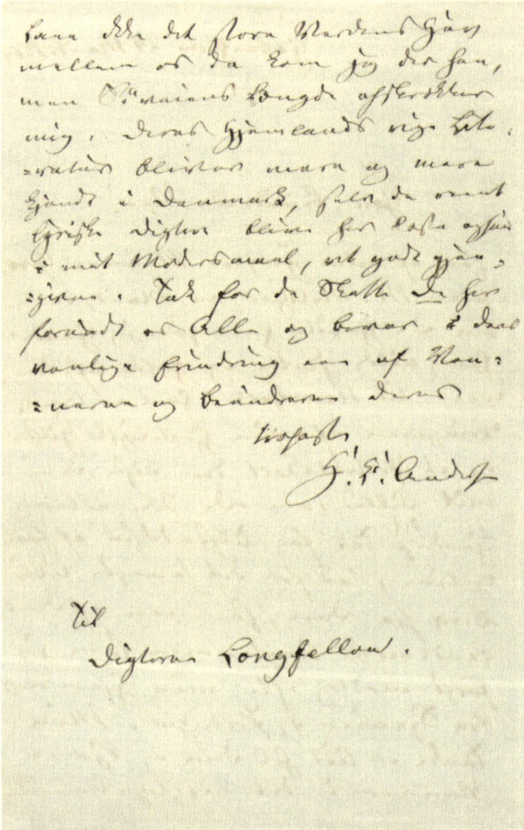
Til
Digteren Longfellow.

Figure 50. Hans Christian Andersen to Longfellow, 24 March 1868, Letters to Longfellow, Houghton, bMS Am 1340.2 (140)

Apparently, there was direct contact between the two men, both famous in their own countries, until 1866, when Longfellow provided a Harvard student, Charles G. Falls, with a letter of introduction to Andersen, explaining that he had written his note "trusting in the magnetism of literary sympathy." He said he did not want Falls to pass through Copenhagen without meeting him; besides, Falls was carrying with him, as a gift, the latest volume of Longfellow's poetry.[189] Two years later, Andersen reciprocated

189 Longfellow to Andersen, Letter 18687, H. C. Andersen Database. The letter is not included in Hilen's edition, although another letter for Falls, addressed to Jørgen Bølling, of the Royal Library of Copenhagen, who had given Longfellow Danish lessons in 1835, is (*Letters* 6: 35). Most likely, Longfellow had sent Andersen a copy of his *Tales of a Wayside Inn* (1863). We know Andersen owned the book because he sent it back to Denmark when he was in Holland in 1866 (Letter 12479, Andersen Database); see Estrid and Erik Dal, *Fra H. C. Andersens boghylde* (Copenhagen: Rosenkilde og Bagger, 1961) 50.

by sending over one of *his* friends, Moses Melchior, a wealthy businessman and head of the Copenhagen Wholesalers' Association, as well as a devoted fan of Andersen's work. In the letter Andersen wrote for him, he finally, with a delay of almost twenty years, thanked Longfellow directly for the gift of his *Evangeline*.

Kjøbenhavn 24 Marts 1868

Kjære, beundrede Ven!
Een af mine yngere Venner, Grosserer M. Melchior, en Mand, der om De kjendte ham som jeg kjender ham, vilde skatte og holde af, kommer til New York, han er Overbringeren af min hjerteligste Hilsen og et Portræt-Kort der viser Dem mit Billed, om De ikke allerede kjender det. Tak for Tilsendelsen af Evangeline, tak for det seneste lille Brev fra Dem, som een af Deres Landsmænd bragte, men som jeg først modtog efter min Hjemkomst fra Spanien og Portugal. Min Tanke er tidt hos Dem og kjære Venner i det mægtige Amerika. Laae ikke det store Verdens-Hav mellem os da kom jeg der hen men Søreisens Længde afskrækker mig. Deres Hjemlands rige Literatur bliver mere og mere kjendt i Danmark, selv de reent lyriske Digtere blive her læste ogsaa i mit Modersmaal, ret godt gjengivne. Tak for de Skatte De har forundt os Alle, og bevar i Deres venlige Erindring, een af Vennerne og Beundrerne, Deres

trofaste

H. C. Andersen

til

Digteren Longfellow

(Letters to Longfellow, Houghton, bMS Am 1340.2 [140], FIGURE 50)

Copenhagen, 24 March 1868

My dear admired friend,
One of my younger friends, wholesaler M. Melchior, a man whom, if you knew him as well as I do, you would esteem and love, will come to New York; he is the bearer of my most cordial greetings and of a portrait showing you my picture, in case you do not already know it. Thank you for sending *Evangeline*, thanks for the latest small letter from you delivered to me by one of your fellow-countrymen, but which I only received after my return from Spain and Portugal. My thoughts are often with you and my dear friends in mighty America. Were not the big ocean between us, then I would come

to you, but the length of the sea voyage discourages me. Your country's rich literature becomes more and more known in Denmark; even the purely lyrical poets are also read here in my language, fairly well rendered. Thank you for the treasures which you have given us all, and keep in your kind memory one of your friends and admirers,

Yours faithfully,

H. C. Andersen

to

the poet Longfellow[190]

Andersen's letter is remarkable not only as a sign of the Danish writer's admiration for Longfellow but also because of what it says about the Danish interest in American literature. By then, Longfellow, the "beundrede Ven" (admired friend), had been an Andersen fan for almost two decades. In September 1847, he had come across Mary Howitt's version of the *Wonder Stories*. On a rainy fall day, a "College Day," as Longfellow noted (which was, with him, shorthand for exhaustion and probably also the inability to work creatively), Fanny had decided to read Andersen to him. Longfellow liked Andersen's "charming 'Stories for Children'" enormously, though *not* Mary Howitt's translation, written "in her usual slipshod style" (10 September 1847). Perhaps he had realized, intuitively, that Howitt hadn't actually *translated* the stories from their original language but had in fact based her text on a German version. Longfellow's favorite story was, interestingly, "The Constant Tin Soldier." The gratuitous violence described there—at the end, the little boy, for no reason whatsoever, throws the soldier into the stove, where he melts down to his tin heart—found its way into "Little Merrythought," where Charley does something similar, though ultimately less disastrous, to the little wishbone-narrator.

The Longfellows continued their Andersen reading the next day: "Andersen's 'Story of My Life' has inspired me again for Danish literature. In fact, Autumn always brings back very freshly my autumnal sojourn in Copenhagen, which is very delightfully mingled with bracing air and yellow falling leaves" (11 September 1847). Andersen's book gave Longfellow occasion to reassert his own intimate connection with Danish culture and to remember a poem he had written two years earlier, "To an Old Danish

190 Translation and transription by Solveig Brunholm, Hans Christian Andersen Center of the University of Southern Denmark. Andersen notes the departure of Moses Melchior and his letter of introduction in his *Dagbog* (25 March 1868): "Tonight Moses Melchior leaves for St. Croix, maybe New York, his sister Jette accompanies him to England. He was given a letter to Jørgensen at St. Croix, a letter to Longfellow and to Marcus Spring in New-York" (*H. C. Andersen's Dagbøger*, 1825-1875, ed. Kåre Olsen og H. Topsøe-Jensen 12 vols. [Copenhagen: G. E. C. Gad, 1972-75] 8: 25. Translation by Solveig Brunholm). The letter discussed here has never been published.

Song-Book" (1: 249-251). Here he had captured some of the feelings that now came back to him, a mixture of nostalgia, sympathy and self-assertion. Longfellow addresses an old book—"soiled," "rain-molested," and stained with wine and the thumb-prints of careless readers—which he has brought with him from Denmark. The book preserves the voices of the past, of poets, peasants, students, and princes, but no one appreciates it anymore—except, of course, Longfellow himself: "Yet at least by one fireside / Art thou welcome." It is interesting how Longfellow the American poet represents himself here as the true heir of the Danish literary tradition. The old Danish book—Simon Poulsen's *Nyeste Samling af Selskabssange især for blandede Selskaber* (Copenhagen, 1793)—is still in Longfellow's library at the Longfellow National Historic Site.

"If not great rolling Ocean was between us and I was not 67 years old," Andersen again wrote, in somewhat shaky English, to Longfellow in July 1871, in a letter of introduction he had written for a young friend, the Danish journalist Robert Watt, "then I should arrive in your mighty country some pleasant summerday."[191] Longfellow probably didn't notice that the language Andersen used here was virtually identical to that in his earlier letter. He was hoping that he could convince Andersen to come for a visit, and he had Watt convey to him his idea that the Danish writer should simply learn to read three of his tales in English, come to America, give public readings, and make a fortune, as Dickens had done.[192] What he didn't know was that Andersen's dear friend, Henriette Wulff, had died in 1858, in a fire on board the *Austria*, less than 48 hours from New York. Scared to death by this event, Andersen was not seriously contemplating a voyage to the United States. But his admiration for Longfellow remained undiminished, as did Longfellow's admiration for him. He was the proud owner of Andersen's *Collected Works* as well as of a Royal Copenhagen wall plaque with a bas relief portrait of Andersen's face in profile.[193]

191 Andersen to Longfellow, Juli [sic] 1871, Longfellow Papers, Houghton, bMS Am 1340.2 (140). The letter also appears, cleaned up and edited, in Samuel Longfellow's *Life* 3: 180.

192 On 23 April 1872, Longfellow thanked Watt for his visit (Watt had made, he said, "a rainy day ... pleasant for us") as well as for the books he had brought, among them three of his own works as well as Adam Oehlenschläger's *Helge*, Ibsen's poems, and *Sangem om Hiawatha*, G. Bern's Danish translation of Longfellow's *Song of Hiawatha*. Watt's "Et Besøg hos Henry Longfellow" appeared in *For Romantik og Historie* 8 (May 1872): 470-481. For an English translation of the essay, see Inge Kabell, "A Dane in Boston" 41-51.

193 The plaque is on the west wall in the first floor side hall of Craigie House (LONG 5984). It was modeled by Christian Ehret, a figure-maker at the Royal Copenhagen Factory between 1869 and 1893, and was acquired during Longfellow's lifetime. Apart from the Hurd and Houghton edition of Andersen's *Works* (LONG 680-689), the first volume of which was inscribed by Andersen himself, and Howitt's translation of the *Wonder Stories*, Longfellow also owned Andersen's *To Be, or Not to Be?* trans. by "Mrs. Bushby" (London: Bentley, 1857; LONG 690), with owner's signature "Henry W. Longfellow, 1857" on the flyleaf and Andersen's autograph "From the Author" pasted in (perhaps an indication that Andersen wrote to him earlier than 1866), as well as *The Sand-Hills of Jutland* (Boston: Ticknor & Fields, 1860; LONG 748). The Craigie House

Andersen and Longfellow exchanged photographs and stayed in touch, if not directly then at least through Andersen's American editor, Horace Scudder, who became Longfellow's neighbor in Cambridge.[194] In 1874, at a dinner that included the American ambassador to Denmark, Andersen offered a toast in which he emphasized the close relations between Denmark and the United States. People from the North had visited and known North America before Columbus knew it, he explained. The Americans, in turn, had felt kinship with the North—and as the best example of that kinship he mentioned Longfellow's *Hiawatha*.[195] Longfellow and Andersen had much in common, though they wrote in different languages and in different genres. Both were celebrities at home and abroad (Andersen, in fact, had been a bestselling author in America before he ever received a penny[196]), and both had a special affection for children. While Longfellow drew cartoons, Andersen entertained his young friends and relatives with paper-cuts; over one thousand of them are still kept at the Royal Library in Copenhagen: "Det hele er Andersens poesi / I klipperi!" ("In Andersen's paper-cuts you see / His poetry").[197]

---

library also contains Alice Longfellow's copy of Andersen's *Wonderful Tales from Denmark*, translated by Charles Boner (New York: Francis, 1859; LONG 676).

194 See *The Andersen-Scudder Letters: Hans-Christian Andersen's Correspondence with Horace Elisha Scudder*, ed. Jean Hersholt and Waldemar Westergaard (Berkeley: University of California Press, 1949). Andersen writes to Scudder to ensure that Longfellow will get his copy of the Standard Edition of his *Works* (24 July 1868, p. 18) and admires the photograph Longfellow sent him through the American minister in Denmark (9 December 1869, p. 62), while Scudder assures him that all volumes published by Hurd & Houghton will in fact be sent to Longfellow (11 March 1870, p. 69). Longfellow and Scudder would read Andersen's letters and look at his photographs together (29 April 1874, p. 146). While Andersen never met Longfellow, he did run into Samuel Longfellow in Rome on 13 May 1861 when visiting the sculptor William Wetmore Story at the Palazzo Barberini (Robert Browning was also there, dressed up as the Pied Piper of Hamlin, reading his poems to the children. For a memorable description of this scene, see *The Diaries of Hans Christian Andersen*, ed. and trans. Patricia L. Conroy and Sven H. Rossel [Seattle: University of Washington Press, 1990] 279).

195 See Diana Crone Frank and Jeffrey Frank, "Hans Christian Andersen's American Dream," *The Scandinavian Review* 91.3 (Spring 2004): 70-79, as well as Andrew Hilen, *Longfellow and Scandinavia* (New Haven: Yale University Press, 1947) 73, and Rossel, "Going Places" 118. Hilen believes that Longfellow underestimated Andersen as a writer of fairy tales only and missed his "deep seriousness" (73). But this isn't accurate. In 1852, for example, he read Andersen's *Improvisatore*, which he admired, though he also complained that some of the details betrayed "the eye of the stranger," thus destroying the illusion that this was really the autobiography of an Italian (Journal, 21 October 1852). Of course, it would have been hard to trump Longfellow in terms of familiarity with things Italian.

196 See Elias Bredsdorff, *Hans Christian Andersen: The Story of His Life and Work 1805-75* (New York: Scribner's, 1975) 260.

197 See Jens Andersen's wonderful essay "Scissor Writing," accessible through the site of the Royal Library at Copenhagen, at http://www.kb.dk/elib/mss/hcaklip/intro-en.htm, as well as Johan de Mylius, *H.*

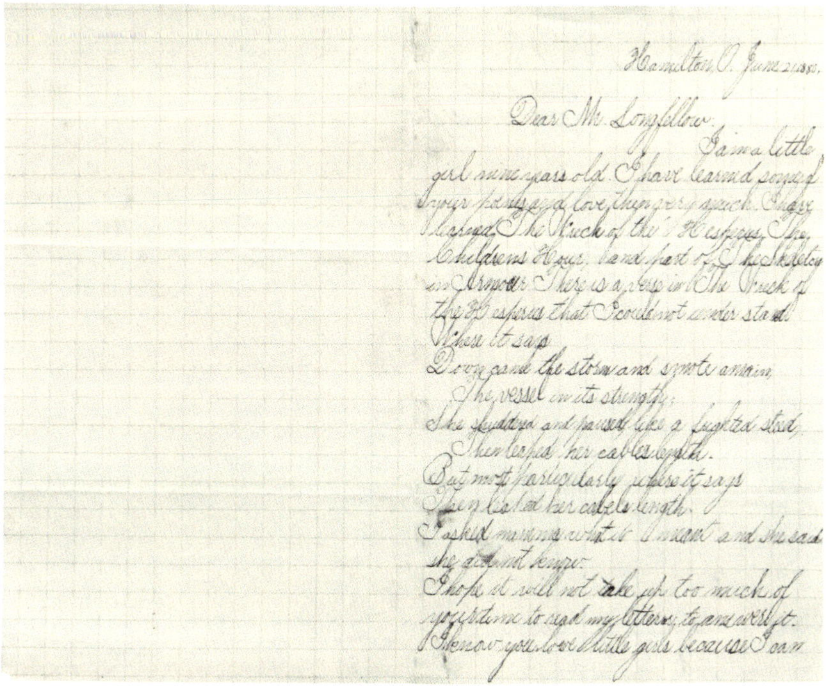

Hamilton O. June 21 1880.

Dear Mr. Longfellow:

I am a little girl nine years old. I have learned some of your poems and love them very much. I have learned The Wreck of the Hesperus, The Childrens Hour, and part of The Skeleton in Armour. There is a verse in The Wreck of the Hesperus that I could not under stand Where it says

Down came the storm and smote amain
The vessel in its strength;
She shuddered and paused like a frighted steed,
Then leaped her cables length.
But most particularly where it says
Then leaped her cabels length.
I asked mamma what it meant and she said she did not know.
I hope it will not take up too much of your time to read my letter, to answer it.
I know you love little girls because I am

Figure 51. Berta E. Shaffer to Longfellow, 21 June 1880,
Letters to Longfellow, Houghton, bMS Am 1340.2 (5010)

One of the youngest of Longfellow's correspondents was a girl from Ohio, Berta Shaffer, who, unimpressed by his fame, had a question about a line in one of his poems, which she posed to him in a letter dated 21 June 1880:

> Dear Mr. Longfellow:
>
> I am a little girl nine years old. I have learned some of your poems and love them very much. I have learned The Wreck of the Hesperus, The Children's Hour, and part of the Skeleton in Armour. There is a verse in The Wreck of the Hesperus that I could not under stand [sic] Where it says
>
> Down came the storm and smote amain [sic],
> The vessel in its strength;
> She shuddered and paused like a frighted steed,
> Then leaped her cable's length.
>
> But most particularly where it says
> Then leaped her cabel's [sic] length.

C. Andersen: Papirklip / Paper Cuts (Copenhagen: Komma & Clausen, 1992).

I asked mamma what it meant and she said she did not know.
I hope it will not take up too much of your time to read my letter to answer it. I know you love little girls because I can tell by reading your poems. As I am getting tired I will close.

Your little friend

Berta Shaffer

Direct to Berta E. Shaffer,
Care of George K. Shaffer.

Hamilton,
Ohio

(Letters to Longfellow, Houghton, bMS Am 1340.2 [5010], FIGURE 51)

Longfellow replied to his young admirer forthwith, on June 24, 1880, and entirely without condescension. He assured her that he, too, had thought about the problem that she had identified, while also admitting that he might have been pushing the envelope a bit.

Figure 52. Miniature moccasins, Dakota, given to Longfellow as a gift for his birthday, February 1882, by Mrs. M. C. Collins, missionary to the Dakotas, Oahe, Hughes County, LONG 7320-21, LNHS

Dear Miss Berta,

In answer to your question I would inform you that a "cable's length," is a sailor's phrase, and means the length of a ship's cable, or seven hundred feet and a little more!

You will say, that is a pretty long leap for a vessel to take; and I think so too. But then you must remember it was in a great storm, and in poetry you must not expect very exact measurements.

Even in prose we sometimes say "a thousand thanks," or "a thousand times," without meaning exactly that number.

And then poets, like children, occasionally exaggerate a little, and make things seem larger than they really are; as for instance when they say the waves "ran mountain high."

(*Letters* 6: 617)

Remarkably, Longfellow here explains that poetry is only a special form of everyday discourse, subject to the same imprecisions and obfuscations. The last sentence might appear to some as a bit of pandering on Longfellow's part, but this suspicion will be quickly dispelled by the quotation that he adds, the "mountain-high" waves, which was taken from Book XV of Samuel Butler's translation of *The Iliad*.

A sign of the popular esteem in which readers held him was the publication of *The Longfellow Birthday-Book*, arranged by Charlotte Fiske Bates (Boston: Houghton Mifflin, 1881). Bates (1838-1916), an aspiring Cambridge poet, had corresponded with Longfellow since 1866 and assisted him with the compilation of *Poems of Places* (see page 33). The birthday book is one of three published by Houghton Mifflin during that year (Emerson and Whittier got theirs too; in later years, Lowell, Browning, and Holmes would join the august company). In her short preface, Bates, waxing lyrical, apologizes for having truncated the excerpts so that they would fit the format of her calendar: "shortness of space has so often broken the graceful stem by which some blossom of thought was to be held." Presumably, she more than compensates for whatever damage she might have done to the integrity of her master's works with the fulsome quotation she has picked for 27 February, Longfellow's birthday: "Ah yes! We all / Love him from the bottom of our hearts" (words spoken about "Prince Henry" by the farmer Gottlieb in *The Golden Legend*; 5: 204). In Houghton Library's collection is a copy given by Longfellow, on his own birthday, to his daughter Edith (Houghton *AC85.L8605.D881ℓ), inscribed on the flyleaf: "To Edith, with her father's love. Feb. 27. 1881." The entries—birthdays of members and friends of the Dana family—appear to have been made by both Edith and her husband, Richard Henry Dana III.

Often Longfellow fans felt that a letter wasn't enough, and they would send him items that they hoped would interest him and that also, metonymically, symbolized their own emotional investment in his work—a fragment from an Acadian barn, for example, an Indian arrowhead or, in this case, a pair of miniature moccasins, made by a Dakota woman named "White Dog" (LONG 7320-21, LNHS, FIGURE 52). These off-white shoes, which have cardboard soles and are lined with white hand-sewn cotton, sport a diamond-shaped motif in orange, blue, and yellow. "Miss" Mary Collins (1846-1920), a missionary to the Dakota Indians from Oahe, Hughes County, in the Dakota Territory, had sent them to him in February 1882 as a birthday gift. "Are you not the friend of us all?" asked Miss Collins, rhetorically, in the letter that accompanied her present (LONG 27930, LNHS). Collins, who became fluent in Lakota, shared Longfellow's interest in intercultural understanding: after moving to the Standing Rock Reservation in 1885, she befriended and supported Sitting Bull (Tatanka Yotanka).[198]

198 Collins's papers are in the South Dakota State Archives, Pierre, SD.

Chapter 7: Longfellow as Translator, Longfellow in Translation

LONGFELLOW WAS NOT ONLY one of the most translated poets of the nineteenth century, he was also perhaps one of the most prolific and serious translators in the history of American poetry. A compulsive learner of languages, he spent a lifetime advocating the benefits of a multilingual education. As a poet and editor, he broadened the horizons of the general reader; as a Harvard professor, he forever changed the practice of foreign language teaching in higher education, insisting on the necessity of hiring native speakers as instructors as well as on the general necessity of maintaining functional Modern Languages departments. "By every language you learn, a new world is opened before you," he told his sisters, in a letter sent from Ariccia in Italy on 1 September 1828. "It is like being born again:—and new ideas break upon the mind with all the freshness and delight—with which we may suppose the first dawn of intellect to be accompanied" (*Letters* 1: 280).

Studying foreign languages in the countries where they were actually spoken, Longfellow also began to develop a strong interest in translation. Translation became one of the most visible ways of documenting and facilitating the traffic between cultures that he had made his life's mission. Longfellow later claimed (in a letter to his friend George Washington Greene, 22 June 1881) that the first poem he ever translated was "Let Me Go Warm," by Luis de Góngora, and that he did so in 1829 or 1830. But there is at least one earlier effort in one of his letters from Europe. On 28 March 1829, Longfellow included a stanza from Portuguese poet Cláudio Manoel da Costa's "The Lyre" in a letter to his sisters, adding that since he was feeling sad he'd tried to translate a sad ballad and failed miserably in the process (*Letters* 1: 304-5).

No wonder. Longfellow would later realize that the worst thing a translator could do is to make a foreign text sound as if it weren't foreign at all. Or, as he put it more elegantly in the notes he made while translating Dante: "The greatest of all fallacies in translation is to give, not what an author really says, but what you suppose he would have said, if he had been writing in your language."[199]

With fluency or near-fluency in nine languages and reading competence in at least eight others,[200] Longfellow's appetite as a translator knew few boundaries. His collected works contain translations from the Anglo-Saxon, Danish, French, German, Italian, Latin, Portuguese, Spanish, and Swedish. Among his papers at Houghton are

199 Longfellow, Divina Commedia Notes, Longfellow Papers, MS Am 1340 (110).

200 Information provided by Lauren Malcolm of the LNHS.

also a few "translations" of Persian poetry, essentially re-workings of prose translations by Alexander Chódzko, which is why Longfellow added a note that nothing in this portfolio (MS Am 1340 [142]) was to be published.

But no author dominated Longfellow's life as a translator more than Dante Alighieri. He got hooked on him during his Italian travels, studying the "gloomy pages" of the *Inferno* in Rome. When he visited Rimini in December 1828, Canto 5 of Dante's poem suddenly came alive for him. In his journal, he paid tribute to the famous thirteenth-century lover Francesca da Rimini, remembering the speech in which she tells Dante that her fall—her adulterous relationship with Paolo, her husband's own brother—was caused by their joint reading of a book, namely the tale of Launcelot and Guinevere. "C'est Francesca qui parle," wrote Longfellow, "et puis elle continue le récit, dans les paroles du poete [sic] 'come colui che piange e dice'" ("Francesca speaks here, and then continues to speak through the words of the poet 'come colui che piange' [as one who weeps]").[201] Over the years, Francesca, for Longfellow, turned into the archetype of the sentimental reader (and, by extension, his vision of what an ideal reader of a Longfellow poem should be like).[202] As far as he was concerned, Francesca offered proof that poetry *does* make things happen, both in terms of what befell her and in terms of what she, now an author in her own right, has now learned to do to others. When she is done, Dante swoons. "Io venni men così com' io morisse. / E caddi come corpo morte caddi." In Longfellow's later translation, "I swooned away as if I had been dying, / And fell, even as a dead body falls" (9: 47).

Longfellow's interest in Dante had been awakened. A week later, in a letter to George Washington Greene, whom he had just met, he somewhat melodramatically quoted Francesca's lines about the great sorrow caused by remembrance of happier times in the middle of misfortune ("nessun maggior dolore / Che ricordarsi del tempo felice / Nella miseria," *Inferno* 5, ll. 121-123) when he wanted to express how much he already missed him. Dante was never far from his mind during the following years; for his Italian grammar, published while he was teaching at Bowdoin College, he would again choose excerpts from *Inferno* 5 (see Chapter 8). And he began to study the *Divina Commedia* systematically in 1838 for a series of lectures he gave at Harvard in the late spring, when he was passing the hot days "upon a sopha," reading Dante and, presumably, thinking of Fanny Appleton (17 May 1838).

A page or two from his lecture of May 22 on the *Paradiso* will give us at least a glimpse of Longfellow the lecturer and his empathetic approach to reading the great works of the European tradition, which, as it rises to the level of poetry itself, also risks becoming as cryptic as the work that it seeks to elucidate. At its best, Longfellow's classroom prose begins to shine, like Dante's poetry. Here he is interested in what

201 Longfellow, Journal in Italy and Germany, 11 December 1828, Longfellow Papers, Houghton, MS Am 1340 (178), p. 53.

202 On Longfellow and Francesca da Rimini, see Irmscher, *Longfellow Redux* 272-73.

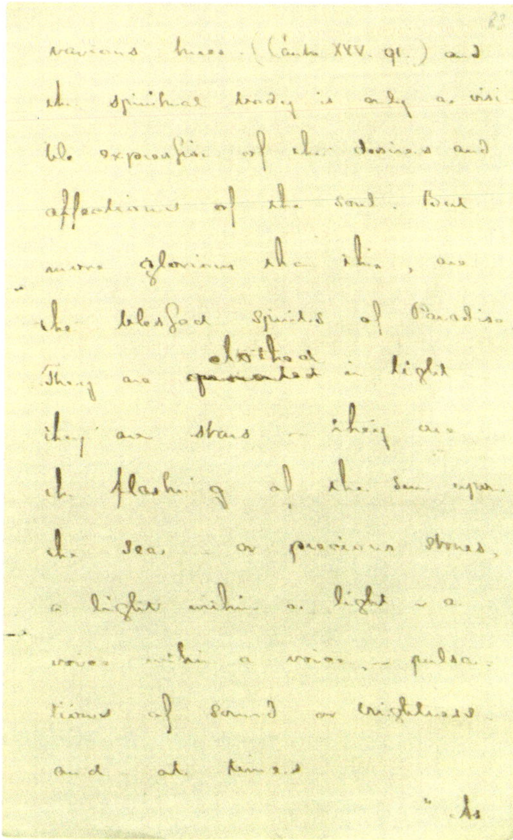

Figure 53. Longfellow, lecture on the "Divina Commedia," p. 53, Harvard College, 22 May 1838, Longfellow Papers, Houghton, MS Am 1340 (106)

happens to the body in the course of Dante's poem, the strange progression from bodies that bleed in the *Inferno* to souls that are flashes of light in the *Paradiso*. The clear focus of the passage allows Longfellow to differentiate the three parts of the *Divina Commedia* again, thus reminding the students of what they have learned so far:

> Observe, then, that while the Inferno is thronged, with souls, numerous as the falling leaves of Autumn; the way that leads to heaven is for the most part solitary—only here and there a little band of spirits, wending their way up the mount. Moreover the souls of the Inferno wear bodies as ~~of flesh~~ upon earth:—they are wounded and torn asunder, and bleed. In Purgatory the souls of men have spiritual bodies; that cast no shadow. The soul stamps itself upon the air, as the sun's ray through the misty atmosphere breaks into various hues. (Canto xxv.91) and the spiritual

> body is only a visible expression of the desires and affections of the soul. But more glorious than this, are the blessed spirits of Paradiso. They are ~~presented~~ clothed in light—they are stars—they are the flashing of the sun upon the sea—or precious stones, a light within a light—a voice within a voice,—pulsations of sound or brightness ....
> (Lecture on "Divina Commedia," Harvard College, "May 22, 1838, Midnight," p. 83; Longfellow Papers, Houghton, MS Am 1340 [106], FIGURE 53).

Longfellow's *Voices of the Night*, published the following year, contained a few selections from *Purgatorio*, titled "The Celestial Pilot," "The Terrestrial Paradise," and "Beatrice." But it was only in 1843 that Longfellow returned to that part of the *Commedia* in earnest, translating the first half of *Purgatorio*. He continued to teach Dante in college ("What a privilege it is to interpret thee to young hearts!" 6 May 1849), but didn't get around to finishing the *Purgatorio* before February 1853, when he completed Cantos 17 to 33, the long hiatus no doubt occasioned by the happy event of his marriage and the devastating death of his daughter Fanny.

Fanny Longfellow owned an engraving, by Luigi Calamatta, of a well-known painting by the Dutch artist Ary Scheffer (1795-1858), *Françoise de Rimini*, which Longfellow—in an amusing instance of early "show and tell"—took to show to his class at Harvard when he was teaching *Inferno* 5 (LONG 4674, LNHS, FIGURE 54).[203] It is tempting to visualize that moment—the undergraduate men, barely out of adolescence, staring raptly at Francesca's unclothed figure and tracing the outline of her left breast and buttock. Francesca's pose is so suggestive that the viewer forgets why exactly she is pressing herself so closely against Paolo's body (relentless winds are whirling both of them around). On the right, Dante and Virgil contemplate the scene. Scheffer's overt aim was to illustrate the nature of the lovers' sin (carnal lust) and thus the reason they have been placed in Hell, but his representation appears to stimulate the very kind of desire in the viewer that their tragic story had been intended to discourage. Scheffer painted several versions of this scene, which he first conceived in the early 1820s (a later incarnation, dating from 1851, is now in the Cleveland Museum of Art).[204]

Longfellow told one of his correspondents, George Park Fisher, that only "very little" had been done for Dante in this country." Thomas William Parsons had translated the *Inferno*, to be sure, but only ten cantos were published. Longfellow's own translation of the *Purgatorio* was unpublished and would probably remain so. "In the way of criticism

203 "Henry has gone to college to lecture on Dante, carrying with him my Francesca by Scheffer, to charm the young eyes of his hearers," undated letter by Fanny Longfellow to unknown recipient (*ML* 127). On 15 March 1847, Longfellow notes in his journal that he "delighted" his class with Scheffer's picture.

204 Leo Ewals, *Ary Scheffer: Sa Vie et son œuvre* (Nimegue: n. p., 1977) 60-61.

Figure 54. Engraving by Luigi Calamatta after Ary Scheffer, *Françoise de Rimini*, LONG 4674, LNHS

we are even worse off. An article or two in Reviews, I know not by whom, is all we have to offer in that way" (to George Park Fisher, 13 July 1853; *Letters* 3: 389-390). He had certainly done enough to change the status quo. The last lecture Longfellow gave as a college professor was about the last canto of the *Inferno*, "with a brief account of Purgatorio and Paradiso" (19 April 1854).

In his brother's biography, Samuel Longfellow mentions the edition of the *Divina Commedia* Longfellow used for teaching purposes, an "interleaved copy, … the blank pages of which he gradually filled with notes and with translations of noteworthy passages" (*Life* 1: 286). He is referring to *Divina Commedia, Opere poetiche di Dante Alighieri, con note di diversi per diligenza e studio di Antonio Buttura* (Paris: Lefevre, 1823), now in Houghton Library (*AC85.L8605.Zy823d). After inserting the blank sheets, Longfellow had the two-volume edition rebound in four separate volumes. The passage illustrated here (FIGURE 55) is the beginning of Francesca da Rimini's speech in Canto 5 (vol. 2, p. 280, in Buttura's edition). The notes on the facing page—references to the "Song of the Sun" (or "Solarlióð") from the *Edda*, Augustine's *Confessions*, a chapter from Goldsmith's *The Vicar of Wakefield*, and Jean-Jacques Ampère's *Viaggio Dantesco*—exemplify not only the multilingual breadth of Longfellow's reading but also give us an idea of how he assembled the notes that would accompany his translation.

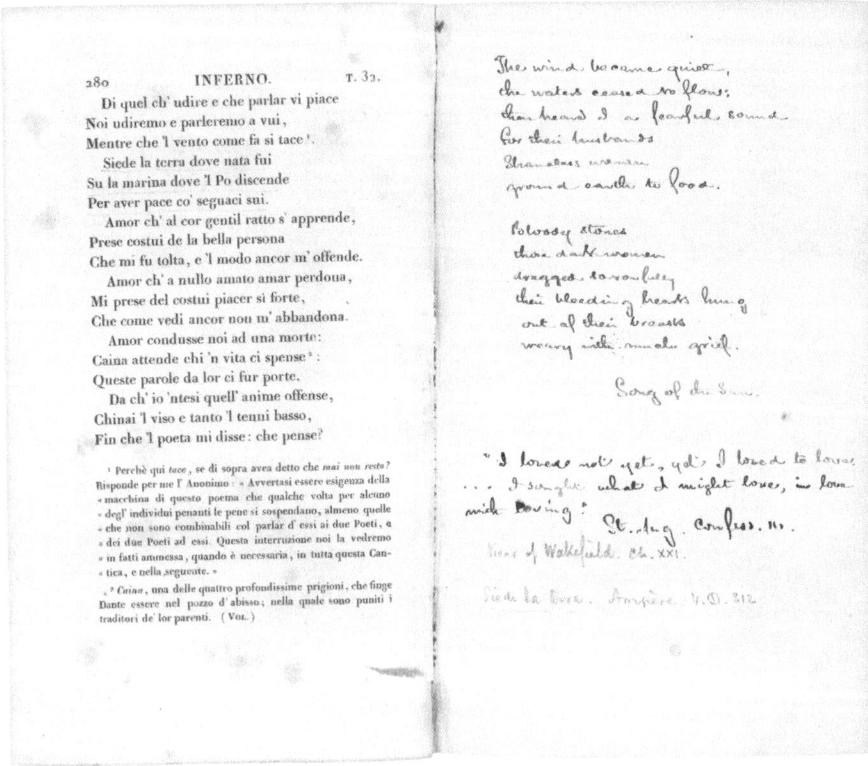

280 INFERNO. T. 32.

Di quel ch' udire e che parlar vi piace
Noi udiremo e parleremo a vui,
Mentre che 'l vento come fa si tace ¹.
Siede la terra dove nata fui
Su la marina dove 'l Po discende
Per aver pace co' seguaci sui.
Amor ch' al cor gentil ratto s' apprende,
Prese costui de la bella persona
Che mi fu tolta, e 'l modo ancor m' offende.
Amor ch' a nullo amato amar perdona,
Mi prese del costui piacer sì forte,
Che come vedi ancor non m' abbandona.
Amor condusse noi ad una morte:
Caina attende chi 'n vita ci spense ²:
Queste parole da lor ci fur porte.
Da ch' io 'ntesi quell' anime offense,
Chinai 'l viso e tanto 'l tenni basso,
Fin che 'l poeta mi disse: che pense?

¹ Perchè qui *tace*, se di sopra avea detto che *mai non resta?* Risponde per me l' Anonimo: « Avvertasi essere esigenza della « macchina di questo poema che qualche volta per alcuno « degl' individui penanti le pene si sospendano, almeno quelle « che non sono combinabili col parlar d' essi ai due Poeti, e « dei due Poeti ad essi. Questa interruzione noi la vedremo « in fatti ammessa, quando è necessaria, in tutta questa Can- « tica, e nella seguente. »

² *Caina*, una delle quattro profondissime prigioni, che finge Dante essere nel pozzo d' abisso; nella quale sono puniti i traditori de' lor parenti. (Vol.)

The wind became quiet,
the waters ceased to flow;
then heard I a fearful sound
for their husbands
Shameless women
ground earth to food.

Bloody stones
those dark women
dragged sorrowfully
their bleeding hearts hung
out of their breasts
weary with much grief.

Song of the Sun.

"I loved not yet, yet I loved to love ... I sought what I might love, in love with loving."
St. Aug. Confess. III.

Vicar of Wakefield. Ch. XXI.

Siede la terra. Ampère. V.D. 312

Figure 55. Dante, *Inferno*, Canto 5, p. 280 from vol. 2 of Longfellow's personal, interleaved copy of the *Divina Commedia* (Paris, 1823), Houghton *AC85.L8605.Zy823d

It was only after Fanny Longfellow's death in 1861 that Longfellow decided to take on the *Divina Commedia* as a whole, guided, perhaps, by the realization that Dante's quest for Beatrice offered a poignant model for Longfellow's own desire to be reunited with Fanny. And then there was, of course, another one of his identification figures, the compulsive reader *par excellence*, Dante's Francesca. For years, he would commemorate 10 May 1843, Fanny's and his "secret anniversary," by copying into his journal Francesca's outcry: "nessun maggior dolore / Che ricordarsi del tempo felice / Nella miseria" (see, for example, 10 May 1864 or 10 May 1867). Or, as he translated the passage in 1863, "There is no greater sorrow / Than to be mindful of the happy time / In misery...." (9: 47).

Perhaps not coincidentally, Longfellow began his translation with the *Paradiso*, translating Canto 20 to 33, as if he were in a rush, in a little more than a month, from 20 February to 31 March 1862 (Cantos 1 to 19 were completed the next year, from 1 February to 11 March 1863).[205] Longfellow's translation of the *Inferno* was finished in mid-April

205 See the note in the bound manuscript, Longfellow Papers, Houghton, MS Am 1340 (113), [p. 4].

1863, and he completed his revision of the *Purgatorio* a little less than a year later, on 17 March 1864. "I do not at all grow weary of my work," he wrote to Sumner while he was putting the finishing touches on the *Inferno*. "The great undulations of Dante's verse lift me and bear me onward in spite of myself" (*Letters* 4: 319). The notes to Dante's poem ("so tragic that he [Dante] called it a Comedy"[206]) weren't "undulating" quite so much for him, though. "I wish," he said to Greene, "somebody would pour a barrel of brandy into the grave of the Commentators, as the bridegroom in the old Icelandic tale did into the grave of his friend the toper, to moisten the dry bones" (*Letters* 4: 405-6). Then followed the proofreading and the constant trips to the printer, so many in fact that Longfellow's fat terrier Trap, "from going so often to the Printing-Office, thinks he has translated Dante" (to George Washington Greene, 18 January 1865, *Letters* 4: 459).

The manuscript of Longfellow's Dante translation, preserved at Houghton Library in three bound volumes (MS Am 1340 [111-113]), with its numerous pencil corrections, bears evidence of Longfellow's meticulousness as a translator. As he did with earlier works (see the genesis of *Evangeline*, discussed in Chapter 5), he prized the advice of his peers, particularly of those gathered in the Dante Club that met on Wednesday nights at Craigie House—meetings that were made famous by Matthew Pearl's debut novel, *The Dante Club* (2003). A loose group of Italophiles, the club included James T. Fields, George Washington Greene, Oliver Wendell Holmes, William Dean Howells, James Russell Lowell, and Charles Eliot Norton. During the Club meetings, Longfellow read from the page proofs he had received. The Houghton manuscripts record the conversations Longfellow was having with himself about his translation *before* the manuscript went to the printer (whose smudged fingerprints are all over the pages) and *before* he submitted it and himself to the judgment of his peers.

The level of the discussions at the Club meetings stunned Howells and Greene (of somewhat "lighter metal" than the others) into awe and silence.[207] Entries in Longfellow's journal show how focused and technical the exchanges between the members were. On 17 January 1866, for example, Lowell, Norton, and Fields were at the House to talk about *Paradiso* 11. Thomas Appleton had joined them, a landscape painter named Gray in tow: "Great discussion of the meaning of *in basso* in the third line," recalled Longfellow later that night. "Also about *ricerna* and what follows in line 23; and *dritto segno* in line 120." In a letter he wrote to the absent Greene a day later, Longfellow clarified that, among other things, he and his colleagues had debated whether the *in basso* in line 3 of *Paradiso* 11, about the senseless acrobatics of human reason that keeps one from achieving loftier goals (*che ti fanno in basso batter l'ali*), indicated *direction*, in the sense of a "motion downward," or *location*, as a "motion below" (*Letters* 5: 23). Longfellow's manuscript shows that he had originally preferred the latter interpretation: "How ~~very defective~~ inconclusive are the syllogisms / That

206 Longfellow to James Fields, 16 June 1865, *Letters* 4: 493.

207 Howells, *Literary Friends and Acquaintance* 163.

make thee beat thy pinions down below!" (Houghton, MS Am 1340 [113], p. 105).[208] But Greene, along with other members of the Club, also thought "downward" was right: the phrase gave a kind of disastrous fatality to the normal pursuits of humans from whom Dante, high in heaven with his Beatrice and "from all these things emancipate" (11: 55) has dissociated himself.[209] And this is how Longfellow revised the line for publication: "How inconclusive are the syllogisms / That make thee beat thy wings in downward flight" (11: 25).

Many crucial edits, then, were made long *after* the manuscript had first gone to the printers. Another good example is the extraordinarily successful translation of "la caligine del mondo" in *Purgatorio* 11 as "the smoke-stains of the world." Longfellow's manuscript version (MS Am 1340 [112], p. 107, dated "March 13.1864") still has "purging away the *darkness* of the world," and so does Longfellow's earlier translation of the same passage from 1843 (Houghton, MS Am 1340 [110], p. 2).

Pictured here (Houghton, MS Am 1340 [111], p. 53, FIGURE 56) is a page with the beginning of Francesca's famous speech in Canto 5 of the *Inferno*: "Sitteth the city, wherein I was born, / Upon the sea-shore where the Po descends / To be at peace with all in peace with all its followers." Or, as Longfellow would have read it in Italian in his edition with the interleaved pages: "Siede la terra dove nata fui / Su la marina dove 'l Po discende / Per aver pace co' seguaci sui" (Longfellow underlined the passage in his edition, see FIGURE 55). Longfellow's translation illustrates his desire to create an English text that would wherever possible remind his readers of the Italian original without slavishly imitating it—an approach that puzzled Longfellow's predecessor at Harvard, George Ticknor, who told Longfellow that he would "always read your translation with the original ringing in my ears," a backhanded compliment at best, since Ticknor also felt Longfellow had not provided what "an *absolutely English* reader covets."[210]

Longfellow has been accused of engaging in needless archaisms, but his decision to use the old-fashioned "Sitteth" rather than the more colloquial "Sits" helps him retain precisely the effect created by the Italian "Siede." Nevertheless Ticknor wasn't right when

208 This matches the translation suggested by Longfellow's popular British predecessor, Henry Francis Cary: "How vain and inconclusive arguments / Are those which make thee beat thy wings below" (*The Vision of Dante Alighieri, or Hell, Purgatory and Paradise translated by the Reverend H. F. Cary* [1805-14; London: Dent, 1908] 340).

209 Charles Eliot Norton—who might have been the one to suggest this revision to Longfellow—later also used "downward" in his own prose rendering of *Paradiso*: "O insensate care of mortals! How defective are those syllogisms which make thee downward beat thy wings!" (*The Divine Comedy of Dante Alighieri*, trans. Charles Eliot Norton, 3 vols. [1901; Boston: Houghton Mifflin, 1920] 3: 85). See also John Ciardi's modern translation of the passage, which clearly owes something to Longfellow's version: "how worthless is that exercise of reason / that makes you beat your wings into the ground!" (Dante, *The Paradiso: A Verse Rendering for the Modern Reader* [New York: New American Library, 1970] 128).

210 George Ticknor to Henry Wadsworth Longfellow, 1 June 1867; see *Life* 3: 90-91.

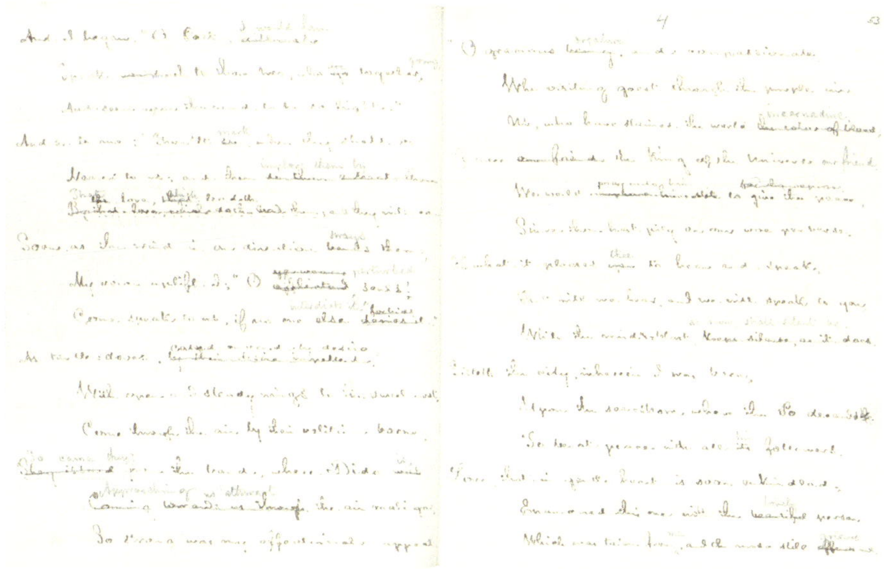

Figure 56. Longfellow, autograph translation of *The Inferno*, Canto 5, pp 52-53, Longfellow Papers, Houghton, MS Am 1340 (111)

he asserted that Longfellow was so enamored with the Italian original that he wouldn't stray away from it when necessary. The translation of "terra" as "city" is, strictly speaking, incorrect ("territory" would have been a more appropriate phrase). Nevertheless, it allows Longfellow to create a nice alliterative echo with "Sitteth," giving the passage in English the lilt it has in Italian, the music that it needs as an evocation of how the river Po flows into the ocean. The linguistic "infelicities" of Longfellow's Dante translation, denounced by Newton Arvin,[211] are not part of a general strategy, the result of a desire to sound deliberately odd and retrograde. Rather, they are carefully calibrated to achieve a specific effect. The manuscript shows that Longfellow, in line 98, had at first written "descendeth." But he then changed his mind and wrote "descends," certainly to preserve a more regular iambic meter. Dante's *terza rima* he had decided not to reproduce anyway: "something must be relinquished," he reasoned in his journal on 7 May 1864, "Shall it be the beautiful rhyme, that blossoms all along the lines, like honeysuckle in a hedge? I fear it must, in order to retain something more precious than rhyme, namely fidelity—truth—the life of the hedge itself." It is interesting how Longfellow defines "fidelity" here– not as the goal that motivates the translator of the original to choose certain words rather than others, but as a quality of the living thing itself.

Translating, for Longfellow, was an exercise in self-objectivation, a continuation, in a different field and with slightly different tools, of what he was trying to achieve in

211 Arvin, *Longfellow* 253.

his poetry, too. "It seizes people," he told George Washington Greene, "with irresistible power, and whirls them away, till they are beside themselves" (7 March 1879; *Letters* 6: 455). Process more than product, a translation is never really finished. Longfellow's certainly wasn't. In February 1865, ten advance copies of the first volume of Longfellow's *Divine Comedy* were privately printed in honor of the six hundredth anniversary of Dante's birth.[212] The special copy intended for Italy was received from the binder on 10 February 1865 and forwarded the next day to Senator Sumner in Washington, who was to hand it to the Italian minister. In Italy, George Perkins Marsh, the United States minister, formally presented it to the government. Longfellow's translation had become a bicultural event, another occasion on which private need (Longfellow's attempt to cope with Fanny's death) and the interest of the public met.

But such official approbation of his efforts didn't hinder him from continuing to tinker with *The Divine Comedy*. Volumes 2 and 3 were issued in 1866 and 1867 respectively. In the spring of 1867 the translation was revised and published in three quarto volumes, with notes and an index, but Longfellow continued to revise his text, making changes for subsequent printings. A good example of his continuing quest for perfection is his personal copy of the "European" edition of *The Divine Comedy*. The first volume, first printing of the Tauchnitz edition, the *Inferno*, is shown here —opened, again, to the beginning of Francesca da Rimini's account in *Inferno* 5 (pp. 30-31; Houghton *AC85.L8605.865dd v.1, FIGURE 57).

The Tauchnitz edition is identical to the American first edition, apart from the print quality and price. The differences between the published volumes and the manuscript (from which the private edition was printed) are significant. Line 99, for example, "to be at peace with all his followers" becomes "to *rest* in peace with all his *retinue*," a version that is arguably closer to the Italian original because it replicates Dante's internal rhyme in that line ("Per aver *pace* co' seg*uaci* sui"). And "Love, that in gentle heart is soon enkindled" turns into "Love, that on gentle heart doth swiftly seize" (l.100), a more overtly poetic line that also conveys more accurately the violence of the transformation Francesca experiences. But this particular copy also shows that Longfellow just couldn't refrain from making changes even *after* a revision of his translation had been printed: in line 135 he crossed out the bland "one," substituting for it a word he added in pencil in the margin, "man": "This *man*, who ne'er from me shall be divided, / Kissed me upon the mouth all palpitating."

Longfellow's Tauchnitz copy of the *Inferno* is interesting for bibliographical reasons, too. Christian Bernhard, Freiherr von Tauchnitz (1816-1895), the founder of the firm of Bernhard Tauchnitz, came from a family of printers and publishers and started his

212 Nine of the ten copies of this private edition have been accounted for; see *Longfellow House Bulletin* 5.2. (December 2001): 7, and Joan Nordell, "Search for the Ten Privately Printed Copies of Longfellow's Translation of the *Divine Comedy* '*In Commemorazione del Secentesimo Anniversario della Nascita di Dante Alighieri*,'" *Harvard Library Bulletin* 16.3 (Fall 2005): 5-36.

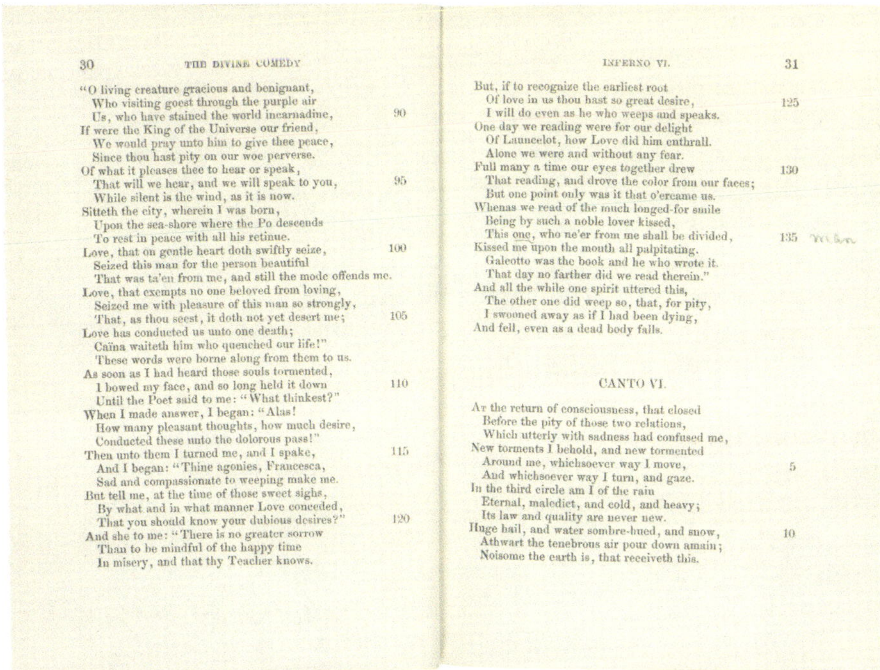
30 THE DIVINE COMEDY

"O living creature gracious and benignant,
Who visiting goest through the purple air
Us, who have stained the world incarnadine,
If were the King of the Universe our friend,
We would pray unto him to give thee peace,
Since thou hast pity on our woe perverse.
Of what it pleases thee to hear or speak,
That will we hear, and we will speak to you,
While silent is the wind, as it is now.
Sitteth the city, wherein I was born,
Upon the sea-shore where the Po descends
To rest in peace with all his retinue.
Love, that on gentle heart doth swiftly seize,
Seized this man for the person beautiful
That was ta'en from me, and still the mode offends me.
Love, that exempts no one beloved from loving,
Seized me with pleasure of this man so strongly,
That, as thou seest, it doth not yet desert me;
Love has conducted us unto one death;
Caïna waiteth him who quenched our life!"
These words were borne along from them to us.
As soon as I had heard those souls tormented,
I bowed my face, and so long held it down
Until the Poet said to me: "What thinkest?"
When I made answer, I began: "Alas!
How many pleasant thoughts, how much desire,
Conducted these unto the dolorous pass!"
Then unto them I turned me, and I spake,
And I began: "Thine agonies, Francesca,
Sad and compassionate to weeping make me.
But tell me, at the time of those sweet sighs,
By what and in what manner Love conceded,
That you should know your dubious desires?"
And she to me: "There is no greater sorrow
Than to be mindful of the happy time
In misery, and that thy Teacher knows.

INFERNO VI. 31

But, if to recognize the earliest root
Of love in us thou hast so great desire,
I will do even as he who weeps and speaks.
One day we reading were for our delight
Of Launcelot, how Love did him enthrall.
Alone we were and without any fear.
Full many a time our eyes together drew
That reading, and drove the color from our faces;
But one point only was it that o'ercame us.
Whenas we read of the much longed-for smile
Being by such a noble lover kissed,
This one, who ne'er from me shall be divided,
Kissed me upon the mouth all palpitating.
Galeotto was the book and he who wrote it.
That day no farther did we read therein."
And all the while one spirit uttered this,
The other one did weep so, that, for pity,
I swooned away as if I had been dying,
And fell, even as a dead body falls.

CANTO VI.

At the return of consciousness, that closed
Before the pity of those two relations,
Which utterly with sadness had confused me,
New torments I behold, and new tormented
Around me, whichsoever way I move,
And whichsoever way I turn, and gaze.
In the third circle am I of the rain
Eternal, maledict, and cold, and heavy;
Its law and quality are never new.
Huge hail, and water sombre-hued, and snow,
Athwart the tenebrous air pour down amain;
Noisome the earth is, that receiveth this.

Figure 57. Tauchnitz edition of Longfellow's *The Inferno*, trans. Longfellow, pp. 30-31, with Longfellow's own marginalia (Leipzig 1867), Houghton *AC85.L.8605.865dd v.1

own business in Leipzig in 1837. One of the mainstays of his company was the highly successful series of cheap reprints called "Collection of British Authors," which, despite its title, included works by both British and American authors (it was not until 1930 that the Tauchnitz company officially changed the designation to "Collection of British and American Authors"). Tauchnitz was the first European publisher to avail himself of the new international market that been created by the continent-wide system of railway lines in Europe, and he did so by courting the authors themselves, offering them strong financial incentives to secure their loyalty. As Longfellow noticed with satisfaction, Tauchnitz paid "handsome sum[s] for copyright" (to Johann Georg Kohl, 20 June 1860, *Letters* 4: 180). Longfellow received an advance payment of $200 for the first volume sometime in March and then, in June 1867, another payment of $100. In a letter of 10 August 1867, Longfellow acknowledged what would have been the third payment within four months—more than the £75.00 the bestselling British writer Bulwer-Lytton would get a few months later for his *Miscellaneous Prose Works*, poetic justice given that Bulwer-Lytton had given Longfellow the cold shoulder when the latter had stopped by for a visit in 1835.[213]

213 Calhoun, *Longfellow* 98. For the details on Longfellow's payments and the history of the Dante edition, see William B. Todd and Ann Bowden, *Tauchnitz International Editions in English, 1841-1955. A Bibliographical History* (1988; New Castle, DE: Oak Knoll Press. 2003) items 900 and 952.

Taking advantage of new developments in stereotyping (harder alloys, the use of mother plates for casting purposes, and so forth), Tauchnitz was able to publish its one-thousandth title (an edition of the New Testament in English) in 1869. By 1887, Tauchnitz had over a million stereotype plates and matrices at his disposal. Soon his market wasn't limited to Europe anymore: Tauchnitz editions reached the United States and Africa; they were sold in Tehran as well as in Peking. They were available on railway stalls and in hotels as well as from booksellers. Printing his books on white, fine paper, he undersold even the publishers of the original editions, pushing American editions out of the market, at least until 1891, when the Chace Act (also known as the International Copyright Act) made it effectively illegal to export foreign editions to the United States. An Allied raid destroyed the firm in 1943.

Perhaps because he was such an active translator himself, fellow translators felt emboldened to try their hands at Longfellow's work, too. Longfellow's well-publicized interest in their national poet Dante must have seemed like music to the ears of Angelo Messedaglia, an economist, member of the Italian House of Delegates, and firm believer in the goal of fidelity ("fedeltà") in literary translation. Interestingly, "fedeltà," for Messedaglia, did not rule out a certain poetic license (as opposed to "pedestrian" literalism). Here is his translation of the ending of Longfellow's "Enceladus," the poem he had chosen to open his volume, *Alcune Poesie di Enrico W. Longfellow*:[214]

> Vedi? In cielo divampa un rosso ardore:
>   Dei tetri occhi è il bagliore.
>   Odi? Fremono l'aure, irrompe il turbine
> Sull' Alpe e l'Apennin, la terra trema . . . .
>   —Sorgi! È giunta, o Titan, l'ora suprema.
> (Houghton *AC85.L8605.E1866m)

Even readers not familiar with the Italian language will notice that Messedaglia has replaced Longfellow's exclamation points with question marks. Here is the original:

> See, see! the red light shines!
>   'T is the glare of his awful eyes!
> And the storm-wind shouts through the pines
> Of Alps and of Apennines,
>   "Enceladus, arise!"
> (3: 66)

214 Messedaglia, *Alcune Poesie di Enrico W. Longfellow, traduzione dall' inglese di Angelo Messedaglia* (Padova: D. Prosperini, 1866) 2.

Longfellow wrote "Enceladus," one of his most overtly political poems, in February 1859 as a kind of "lament for the woes" of Italy, as he told Charles Sumner (the money *The Atlantic Monthly* paid him for publication went to the *Risorgimento* fighters). The central figure of the poem is the giant Enceladus, buried under Mount Etna for his insubordination against the Olympians and now rebelling, like Italy itself, against his chains. Messedaglia, Italian nationalist that he is, further radicalizes Longfellow's message. The last stanza, reprinted here, is a case in point. The concise exclamation that ends Longfellow's poem ("Enceladus, arise!") Messedaglia replaces with an unabashedly interpretive statement, in which the speaker tells the giant that his hour has finally come. The two questions ("Vedi?" "Odi?"—"Do you see?" "Do you hear?"), followed by an emphatic imperative ("Sorgi!"—"Arise!"), add more drama to a text that has now become an interactive poetic manifesto for the Italian republican movement.

Messedaglia's slim volume, which also includes "The Quadroon Girl" ("La Fanciulla Mesticcia") from *Poems on Slavery*, gives the Italian reader a rather specific version of Longfellow, as a campaigner, with the weapon of the word, against slavery and political imperialism, an American poet who is a natural ally in the cause of Italian independence. Messedaglia sent the copy now owned by Houghton to Longfellow, with the inscription: "All' Grande Poeta dell' America Omaggio del suo Traduttore A. Messedaglia" ("To the Great American Poet with the respects of his Translator, A. Messedaglia"), along with a letter in which he fulsomely praised Longfellow's Dante translation, which he said had only increased "the admiration and affection which I profess for you, an admiration and affection which will be in the heart of every Italian to whom the Divine Poet is sacred."[215] Longfellow admitted that he was flattered ("I shall be happy to know that it is well received in Italy"), but, after seeing the full extent of Messedaglia's creative re-translating, probably couldn't resist a little dig: "That work was for me entirely a labor of love and I strove, to use the legal term to tell 'the truth, the whole truth and nothing but the truth'" (15 February 1868, *Letters* 5: 212).

For Longfellow, some of the "foreignness" of the original had to be preserved in every translation. In a fragment, unpublished in his lifetime but included later in Samuel Longfellow's biography, he mused on the "color of words" and the reason why some degree of unfamiliarity could be a necessary prerequisite for any appreciation of beauty—why, indeed, a perception of, and an understanding for, *strangeness*, might lie at the heart of any form of cultural exchange:

> The difficulty of translation lies chiefly in the *color* of words. Is the Italian "Ruscelletto gorgoglioso" fully rendered by "Gurgling brooklet"? Or the Spanish "Pájaros vocingleros" by "Garrulous birds"?

215 "… l'ammirazione e la simpatia che Le professo, ammirazione e simpatia che saranno al certo nell'animo d'ogni Italiano per cui è sacro il nome del Divino Poeta"; Angelo Messedaglia to Henry Wadsworth Longfellow, 7 July 1867, Longfellow Papers, Houghton, bMS Am 1340.2 (3848).

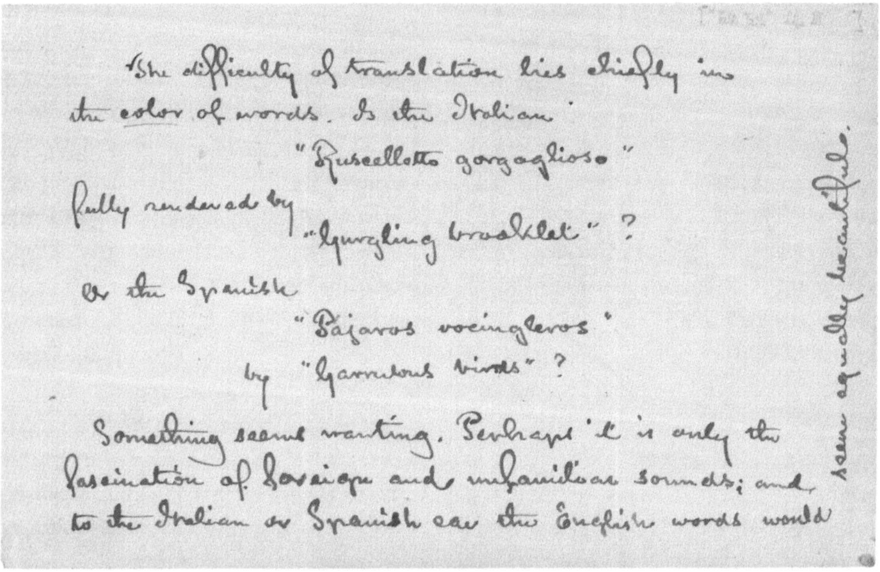
The difficulty of translation lies chiefly in
the color of words. Is the Italian
"Ruscelletto gorgoglioso"
fully rendered by
"Gurgling brooklet"?
Or the Spanish
"Pájaros vocingleros"
by "Garrulous birds"?
Something seems wanting. Perhaps it is only the
fascination of foreign and unfamiliar sounds; and
to the Italian or Spanish ear the English words would
seem equally beautiful.

Figure 58. Aphorism on translation, from Longfellow, Unpublished Prose Fragments, Longfellow Papers, Houghton, MS Am 1340 (145)

> Something seems wanting. Perhaps it is only the fascination of foreign and unfamiliar sounds; and to the Italian or Spanish ear the English words would seem equally beautiful.[216]
> (Longfellow Papers, Houghton, MS Am 1340 [145], folder 7 of 9, FIGURE 58)

Such strangeness was very much at play, and the color of words assumed an unforeseen literal meaning, when Longfellow, in October 1865, received a Chinese fan decorated with a translation of "A Psalm of Life" (LONG 23418, LNHS, FIGURE 59), in calligraphy. It was sent to him by a "Mandarin," as he stated without elaboration in a journal entry on 30 October 1865. It was truly a thing of beauty: the light-colored wooden slats, the end pieces carved with genre scenes, the thick paper, covered with flecks of gold and bordered with black at the top. Handscrolls, hanging scrolls, album leaves, and fans were all popular formats for both painting and calligraphy, so there is nothing unusual about the existence of the fan as such. But the fact that this was a translated poem made this artifact unique. In 1948, the eminent Chinese scholar Qian Zhongshu suggested that "A Psalm of Life," in his opinion "a bad and rather foolish poem," might have been the first English poem ever to have been translated into Chinese, a fact that distressed him a great deal: "what is temporary and mortal in

216 See also *Life* 3: 410-11.

Figure 59. Mandarin Fan, calligraphy by Dong Xun, ca. 1865, LONG 23418, LNHS

a nation's literature is more likely to be among the nation's first exports together with its riff-raff of adventurers and emigrants."[217] The process of translating this ephemeral product of American cultural imperialism was, as Qian described it, surprisingly complicated, involving at least initially the English envoy to China, Thomas Wade, who was reasonably fluent in Chinese and prepared a rough, unrhymed, and apparently rather inarticulate Chinese prose version of Longfellow's poem. The calligrapher Dong Xun, also spelled Tsung Hun (1807-1892), an official at the Zongli Ramen, the Chinese Foreign Ministry, then went ahead and transformed Wade's version into nine stanzas

217 Qian Zhongshu (C. S. Ch'ien), "An Early Chinese Version of Longfellow's 'Psalm of Life,'" *Philobiblion* 2.2 (March 1948): 10-17, reprinted in *A Collection of Qian Zhongshu's English Essays* (Beijing: Foreign Language Institute, 2005) 374-87, and Tsuen-hsuin Tsien, "First Chinese-American Exchange of Publications," *Harvard Journal of Asian Studies* 25 (1964/1965): 19-30. Qian Zhongshu's view was recently disputed by Zhou Zhenhe in "Longfellow or Milton? An Early Chinese Translation of a Poem in English," trans. Robert Neather, *Ex/Change* 14 (October 2005): 4-6. The problem mentioned by Professor Zhou—that the British traveler Robert Ferguson claims to have seen the fan in September 1864 (see *Life* 3: 43)—is easily solved: Ferguson, who had gone on to New Orleans, was back at Craigie House in December 1865 (see Longfellow to Sumner: "Mr. Ferguson has gone," 29 December 1865, *Letters* 4: 521). Ferguson probably saw the fan then and became confused about the date in retrospect.

of four seven-word lines each, in "impeccable" classical style, according to Quian.[218] Dong Xun signed the fan "Yangzhou Dong Xun" and dated it "the second month of spring, 1865" (Yangzhou was the name of the thriving commercial city in the south of China where he was born).[219]

Even Qian Zhongshu would have had to admit that Longfellow welcomed his "Chinese" poem back in style. He held a dinner in celebration of the fan, to which he invited the historian John Gorham Palfrey (the postmaster of Boston), the writer and lawyer Richard Henry Dana, Jr.,[220] and Charles Sumner—"the original Free-Soilers," in other words (30 October 1865). The link between these anti-slavery men and Chinese culture was supplied by a special guest, Ansom Burlingame, who came with his wife. Abraham Lincoln had appointed Burlingame as U. S. minister to China in 1861. A committed abolitionist at home, he now devoted his life to the smoothing of diplomatic relations between the two countries and would become the driving force behind the Burlingame Treaty in 1868, which guaranteed the autonomy of China. Catering for Longfellow's dinner was provided by Joshua Bowen Smith, the mixed-race businessman and member of the Boston Vigilance Committee, who was Sumner's friend and associate.[221] Dressed in foreign clothes, Longfellow's poem had traveled back to him and an America that had for too long been absorbed in its own internal problems—a reminder that translation, apart from serving to facilitate the traffic of ideas from one culture to another, also carries its purpose in itself, as an acknowledgment of the exciting diversity of the world at large. Incidentally, Dong Xun's "Psalm of Life" was called "Ch'ang-yu-shi," which simply means "Longfellow's Poem" or, more literally, "*Tall Friend's* Poem."[222]

218 Qian Zhongshu, "Early Chinese Version" 183.

219 Adriana Proser of the Asia Society in New York helped me understand both this artifact and the context in which it was produced.

220 Dana had a direct connection with China; see his *Journal of a Voyage Round the World, 1859-1860*, a record of the 14-month circumnavigation that took Dana to California, Hawaii, China, Japan, Malaya, Ceylon, India, Egypt, and Europe. See Richard Henry Dana, Jr., *Two Years Before the Mast and Other Voyages*, ed. Thomas L. Philbrick (New York: Library of America, 2005) 541-870; see especially 751-86 ("China, April-June 1860").

221 See the entry for Smith in the guide to the *African American Heritage Trail, Cambridge, Massachusetts* (Cambridge: Cambridge Historical Commission, 2000) n.p.

222 My emphasis. For another tribute to Longfellow rendered by a Chinese scholar, see Almira Hayward's article about Kun-hua-ko ("Professor Ko"), an instructor in Chinese at Harvard University, who died one month before Longfellow, on 14 February 1882. Among his poems was "To Henry W. Longfellow," printed here in an English version prepared from Ko's own prose translation: "Your fame has filled the Western world, / And not one country merely; / Your staff and shoes men seek to find. / But search in vain; for clearly / You walk among the thick white clouds . . . ." ("A Chinese Professor," *Our Continent*, 18 October 1882, 463-66).

Chapter 8:
"Weltliteratur"

In a late poem, "My Books," written on 27 December 1881, the "clouded and confused" speaker, clearly modeled on the aging Longfellow himself, looks at the books that surround him, "my ornaments and arms of other days" (3: 322). He compares himself to a medieval knight, gazing sadly at the weapons "he could no longer wield." But the fact is that the size of Longfellow's library at that point would have exceeded any collection of medieval weapons imaginable. The analogy between books and the two-handed sword and shield of a warrior, which seems strange anyway coming from one of the most peace-loving poets of the nineteenth century, contradicts other passages in Longfellow's work in which he celebrates the "love of learning, the sequestered nooks, / And all the sweet serenity of books" ("Morituri Salutamus"; 3: 211). Nevertheless, the sheer number of books (around fourteen thousand were collected by him and his family members) and their incredible diversity (over fifty languages are represented) do make the association with a knight-errant's travels or, as the poem puts it, "the lost delight / of tourney or adventure in the field" quite plausible. When Erny drew his father's portrait in December 1852, he quite naturally pictured him holding a book in his hand (left profile view of Longfellow reading a book, LONG 19944, LNHS, FIGURE 60).

When Longfellow writes about knights, Cervantes's Don Quixote, his favorite literary protagonist, is never far from his mind. Like Don Quixote, himself the owner of a considerable library, Longfellow devoured books, too. But he loved them not only for their content but also for their beauty, as physical objects. Many of them were given to him by friends or eager admirers, but the majority of his library reflects his collecting interests and, above all, his conviction that the American language and American culture can only be grasped in an international, global context. The languages represented in Longfellow's library at Craigie House include, apart from the usual suspects (French, German, Italian, and Spanish), Armenian, Celtic, Chinese, Cornish, Danish, Dutch, Finnish, Flemish, Greek, Greenlandic Eskimo, Hawaiian, Hindi, Japanese, Latin, Persian, Provençal, Romansch, Russian, and Welsh. The topics and genres of books range from foreign language dictionaries and grammar to poetry anthologies and children's books. Examples of significant volumes are folios printed by the Italian type designer Giambattista Bodoni (purchased in Rome during Longfellow's last European trip),[223] illustrated atlases of China, Africa, and Asia from the 1670s, Gustave Doré's illustrated works of Dante, and a 1496 Venetian edition of Plutarch,

223 Longfellow "bore them off in triumph." See his letter to his French translator Xavier Marmier, 31 December 1868, *Letters* 5: 271-72.

Figure 60. Ernest Wadsworth Longfellow, Henry Wadsworth Longfellow reading a book, signed E. for "Erny" in lower left corner and dated "Dec. 1852," LONG 19944, LNHS.

which Longfellow, incidentally, had acquired during a visit to Portland.[224] Longfellow's Scandinavian collection—unique for its time—boasts over 380 books in Swedish, Danish, and Icelandic. On exhibit in the historic rooms of the Brattle Street house are 4,388 volumes.

During the six years he taught at Bowdoin, Longfellow published no fewer than five textbooks, in an attempt to rectify the sorry state of foreign language instruction at his own institution as well as elsewhere. He doubted, at least privately, that the Bowdoin professors could speak the languages they were supposed to teach (*Letters* 1: 297). A particularly interesting example of Longfellow's educational efforts is his *Syllabus de la grammaire Italienne* (Boston: Gray et Bowen, 1832), which Houghton owns in its original state, with its reddish-purple muslin cover and a printed paper label on the spine (Houghton *2001G-479, FIGURE 61). The very existence of the book—an Italian grammar written in French, for use by American college students—is strange. But Bowdoin's curriculum required the completion of a course in French before undertaking the study of Italian. Longfellow's grammar, by combining both these languages into

224 See Longfellow to Greene, 27 September 1877, *Letters* 6: 303. Longfellow also adds here that this might be the first time he has bought a book "on account of its age"—an important reminder that Longfellow normally collected books for their content and not for ostentatious display.

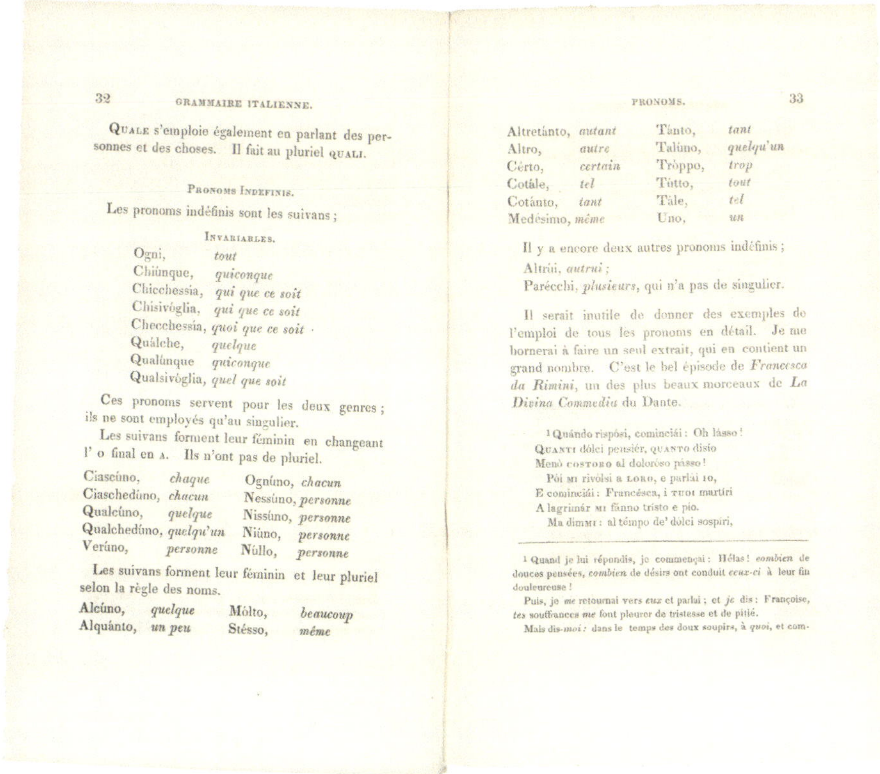

32 GRAMMAIRE ITALIENNE.

QUALE s'emploie également en parlant des personnes et des choses. Il fait au pluriel QUALI.

PRONOMS INDÉFINIS.

Les pronoms indéfinis sont les suivans ;

INVARIABLES.

Ogni,	*tout*
Chiúnque,	*quiconque*
Chicchessia,	*qui que ce soit*
Chisivóglia,	*qui que ce soit*
Checchessia,	*quoi que ce soit*
Quálche,	*quelque*
Qualúnque	*quiconque*
Qualsivóglia,	*quel que soit*

Ces pronoms servent pour les deux genres ; ils ne sont employés qu'au singulier.

Les suivans forment leur féminin en changeant l' o final en A. Ils n'ont pas de pluriel.

Ciascúno,	*chaque*	Ogníno,	*chacun*
Ciaschedúno,	*chacun*	Nessúno,	*personne*
Qualcúno,	*quelque*	Nissúno,	*personne*
Qualchedúno,	*quelqu'un*	Niúno,	*personne*
Verúno,	*personne*	Núllo,	*personne*

Les suivans forment leur féminin et leur pluriel selon la règle des noms.

Alcúno,	*quelque*	Mólto,	*beaucoup*
Alquánto,	*un peu*	Stésso,	*même*

PRONOMS. 33

Altretánto,	*autant*	Tánto,	*tant*
Altro,	*autre*	Talúno,	*quelqu'un*
Cérto,	*certain*	Tróppo,	*trop*
Cotále,	*tel*	Tútto,	*tout*
Cotánto,	*tant*	Tále,	*tel*
Medésimo,	*même*	Uno,	*un*

Il y a encore deux autres pronoms indéfinis ;

Altrúi, *autrui* ;

Parécchi, *plusieurs*, qui n'a pas de singulier.

Il serait inutile de donner des exemples de l'emploi de tous les pronoms en détail. Je me bornerai à faire un seul extrait, qui en contient un grand nombre. C'est le bel épisode de *Francesca da Rimini*, un des plus beaux morceaux de *La Divina Commedia* du Dante.

[1] Quándo rispósi, cominciái : Oh lásso !
QUANTI dólci pensiér, QUANTO disío
Menò COSTORO al doloróso pásso !
Pói MI rivólsi a LORO, e parlái IO,
E cominciái : Francésca, i TUOI martíri
A lagrimár MI fánno trísto e pío.
Ma dimmi : al témpo de' dólci sospíri,

[1] Quand je lui répondis, je commençai : Hélas ! *combien* de douces pensées, *combien* de désirs ont conduit *ceux-ci* à leur fin douloureuse !

Puis, je *me* retournai vers *eux* et parlai ; et *je* dis : Françoise, *tes* souffrances *me* font pleurer de tristesse et de pitié.

Mais dis-*moi* : dans le temps des doux soupirs, à *quoi*, et com-

Figure 61. Longfellow, *Syllabus de la grammaire Italienne* (Boston: Gray et Bowen, 1832), pp. 32-33; presentation copy, inscribed to Charles Folsom ("Charles Folsom Esq. / with the Respects of the / Author"), Houghton *2001G-479

one book, is an innovative attempt to help students master this requirement more smoothly. Having performed the initial leap of accepting one foreign language as a viable means of communication, his American students (at least "ceux qui possèdent la Langue Française") would be more inclined to perform another leap and embrace the Italian language, too, if only so that they could read Dante in the original. In the "avertissement" to the book, he emphasized that he had compiled his short grammar for those wishing to *read* rather than *speak* the language.

A good example of Longfellow's innovative approach is the section on Italian indefinite pronouns ("pronoms indéfinis"), the principles of which Longfellow cleverly illustrates not with one of the usual inane grammar exercises but with his favorite section from the *Inferno*, the Francesca da Rimini passage from the end of Canto 5 (from "Quando rispósi" to "E cáddi cóme córpo cáde"). The indefinite pronouns are capitalized so that they will be easier to identify for the student: "Il serait inutile de donner des exemples de l'emploi de tous les pronoms en détail. Je me bornerai à faire un seul extrait, qui en contient un grand nombre. C'est le bel épisode de *Francesca da Rimini*, un des plus beaux morceaux de *La Divina Commedia* du Dante" (p. 33). By that time, Francesca must have seemed like an old friend to Longfellow's students. In the section on "Degrés de comparaison," she already had to perform yeoman's service showing them how the comparative works in Italian: "Nessún MAGGIÓR dolóre / Che ricordarsi .... " ("There is no *greater* sorrow / Than to be mindful ..."). If we bear in mind that Longfellow had mixed French and Italian in his travel diaries before he started teaching at Bowdoin, it is hard not to assume that Longfellow might have been guided by less than pragmatic considerations in compiling his French-Italian textbook—that sheer linguistic exuberance and the joyful knowledge that all the languages of the world participate in a common project might have been motivating factors, too. The present copy, given to Charles Folsom, editor for the University Press in Cambridge that printed the volume, is of special significance. It was probably the first copy off the press and was sent to Folsom with an errata sheet; throughout, one can see Folsom's penciled editorial corrections.

After his grammar had paved the way, Longfellow persuaded Gray and Bowen (now, amusingly, called "Presso Gray e Bowen") to publish a book this time in Italian only, an anthology of Italian short stories, with selections ranging from Giovanni Boccaccio's "Fra Cipolla" to the "Fantasmi Notturni" by the eighteenth-century writer and philosopher Francesco Soave, *Saggi de' novellieri italiani d'ogni secolo: Tratti da' più celebri scrittori, con brevi notizie intorno alla vita di ciascheduno* (Houghton *AC85. L8605.832s [A]). Houghton's copy, a first edition, sports the original rose-colored cloth cover, with a paper spine label. Longfellow's eclectic anthology also contains (on pp. 48-49) Niccolò Machiavelli's misogynistic but entertaining "Favola: Belfagor arcidiavolo che prese moglie" (1469), a novella about a devil who is sent to the world to investigate if it is true that men are sent to Hell by their wives, gets married, finds out that the rumor is indeed true, and runs back to Hell as fast as he can ("Belphegor" is among the texts studied by the high-strung Roderick Usher in Poe's "The Fall of the House of Usher").

It seems fair to say that during his Bowdoin years, Longfellow was already gesturing toward the concept of comparative literature that he was to develop and endorse in his years as a Harvard instructor and, after his resignation from Harvard, as an editor of such ventures as the multivolume anthology, *Poems of Places* (1876-1879). At Harvard, he taught Dante, Molière, and, notably, Goethe, a writer whose encyclopedic interests in world literature—Goethe had in fact coined the very term ("Weltliteratur," in German)—resembled his own, though Longfellow also believed that his own practice as a writer was quite different. Goethe figured prominently in Longfellow's novel *Hyperion*, in long discussions between Longfellow's alter ego, Paul Flemming, and his friend, the Baron of Hohenfels, who both go and visit Goethe's birthplace in Frankfurt. Flemming makes fun of Goethe's admirers and the epithets they use for him ("The All-sided One!", "The Representative of Poetry on Earth!") and claims that he finds Goethe's "sensuality" offensive—just consider the *Roman Elegies* and "that monstrous book," *The Elective Affinities*. Goethe's works are populated by "sinful Magdalens and rampant Fausts," not by Apollos or Madonnas, argues Flemming, getting carried away. The Baron challenges him by calling Goethe "a glorious specimen of a Man," after which Flemming at least admits that there is some resemblance between him and Benjamin Franklin: both had a very practical tendency of mind, sharing an interest in science and maxims that would help one live one's life. Above all, Goethe's posture, as represented in a "full-length cast" he sees at the birthplace, impresses him: "by Heavens! he was nearly eighty years old when that was made." At the end of the end of the chapter, Flemming, ever the American tourist, wants to acquire a copy of the cast to ship it home (8: 137-145).

Much of Flemming's doubts here reflect Longfellow's own. He had been reading *Wilhelm Meister's Lehrjahre* ("the book is not good") and Goethe's autobiography ("the garrulity of old age … tedious") while in Heidelberg in late 1835 and early 1836.[225] *Werthers Leiden* downright repelled him: "This is not the company I love to keep" (29 December 1835). He grabbed a copy of Johann Peter Eckermann's *Conversations with Goethe* hot off the press, but what he read there didn't impress him much either. The author, "a jackal to this German lion," reminded him of Boswell, and that was not intended as a compliment (8 June 1836). Longfellow's negative assessment of Goethe didn't persist (on his writing desk at Craigie House he later conspicuously placed a statuette of Goethe—see Chapter 5), though some of the old ambivalence remained. In the lectures on Goethe that Longfellow delivered at Harvard in 1837, he approached the subject more systematically, arguing that some of the more "subjective" traits of Goethe (his egocentrism, his sensuality) were actually qualities the German writer himself had wanted to exorcize, hoping that a balanced personal life, achieved under the soothing influence of art, would translate into public benefit. This is how Longfellow understood the second part of *Faust:*

> In the character and life of Faust, Göthe has exhibited doubtless many traits of his own character, and many passages of his own life: It is his own figure thrown back upon the Past in gigantic shadow. There is a desperate desire to know, what man can never know; to be more than man; —the same disappointment and despair;—Then the lofty aspirations of the soul are quenched in sensuality;—then the World of Art unfolds itself ~~upon~~ before the weary spirit;—and finally Faust ends where Göthe ended, in homely, useful activity.
> ("Illustrations of Faust," Longfellow Papers, Houghton, MS Am 1340 [49], p. 97, FIGURE 62)

225 See the journal entries for 29 December 1835 and 5 March 1836.

Longfellow's reading is actually quite sophisticated, offering as it does a psychological reading of Goethe's verse drama as an exercise in self-therapy. Interestingly, art and the public good appear to be linked, a conjunction that must have appealed to Longfellow.

The lectures reveal Longfellow's considerable respect for Goethe. But they also show that some of his skepticism persisted: throughout Goethe's works one finds, he tells his Harvard students, "the same voice, only somewhat counterfitted [sic]; the same face partially concealed, under various masks." The objective poet—a poet like Longfellow, we may presume—describes "without exhibiting the peculiarities of the describer" and never speaks "in his own person." As the modernists would later say, he is interested in nothing but "the thing itself." For Longfellow, Goethe's egomania, his tendency to strut, became even more troubling in the light of a comment he made to Friedrich Jacob Soret in 1832, the last year of his life: "I have collected and turned into account all that I have seen, heard, observed .... Every one of my writings has been

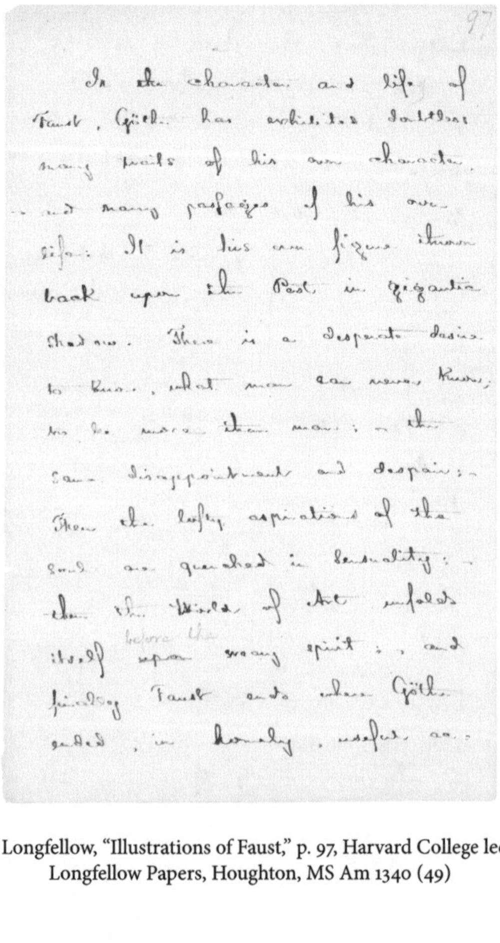
97

In the character and life of Faust, Göthe has exhibited doubtless many traits of his own character, and many passages of his own life: It is his own figure thrown back upon the Past in gigantic shadow. There is a desperate desire to know what man can never know; to be more than man; — the same disappointment and despair; — Then the lofty aspirations of the soul are quenched in sensuality; — then the world of Art unfolds itself before the weary spirit; and finally Faust ends where Göthe ended, in homely, useful ac-

Figure 62. Longfellow, "Illustrations of Faust," p. 97, Harvard College lecture, 1837. Longfellow Papers, Houghton, MS Am 1340 (49)

furnished by a thousand different persons, a thousand different things."[226] Longfellow would have agreed with the premise of this statement—that literature comes not from some mythical inner place but reflects what a writer has seen, heard, or read elsewhere. But rather than regard himself as a monstrous machine that picks up and "turns into account" the feelings, impressions and ideas that once belonged to other people, Longfellow would continue to see himself as the facilitator of such different voices, as the funnel through which they, still recognizable in their specificity, were allowed to make themselves heard.

Goethe reappears in Longfellow's journals during his second decade of teaching at Harvard, especially in June 1846, when Longfellow started reading the *Italienische Reise* (*Italian Journey*). Longfellow now finds himself responding very powerfully to Goethe's language, probably because it so much reminds him of his own emotional ties to Italy and his own passion for the Italian language. Remembering his reading experience and quoting and translating as he is going along, Longfellow writes in his journal at the end the day:

> Sat under the trees with Charley; and read Göthe's "Italiänische Reise" .... The traveller's heart dilates as he journeys southward into the sunshine. He is curious to see "whether the wrinkles that have formed and pressed themselves in his mind will come out again;" he rejoices as if he had been born and bred in Italy, "and was returning from a journey to Greenland or a whaling voyage;"—he is glad "that the beloved language is living, and the language of daily use."
> (11 June 1846)

Longfellow briefly contemplates writing a review of Goethe's book in which he would compare it with Dickens's *Letters from Italy* ("drollery," while Goethe's travelogue offers "wisdom") but discards the idea because of his poor eye-sight—perhaps a pretext, because Longfellow at this point in his life had pretty much given up writing criticism anyway. A more powerful effect of his Goethe reading is felt a few days later, when Longfellow, trying to quench his thirst for foreign travel, takes the omnibus to town and ends up on Boston's Haymarket. Despite Longfellow's misgivings about overt sensuality in literature, this passage is as evocative as anything in Goethe:

> where the mingled and delicious odors of the vegetables, and the sight thereof transported me straightway to France. There is no more powerful

226 Longfellow, "Goethe as an Author," 10th lecture, 22 June 1837, Longfellow Papers, Houghton, MS Am 1340 (45). Goethe's remarks to Soret are quoted in a source extensively mined by Longfellow: Sarah Austin, *Characteristics of Goethe; from the German of Falk, von Müller, & c., with Notes, Original and Translated, Illustrative of German Literature*, 3 vols. (London: E. Wilson, 1833) 3: 76-77.

medium of association than odors. On my way out, stood awhile on the bridge, looking at the water and saying to myself that this was a portion of the same sea that washes the shores of England and of Italy. I then got into the omnibus and there found some some [sic] Spanish people, men and girls; and heard the sweet tongue again, and saw the well-known Spanish beauty of face and form, and imagined myself in Andalusia. (16 June 1846)

A few weeks later, on 21 June, Longfellow dreams that Goethe is "alive and in Cambridge" and that he is taking him out to supper "at Willard's tavern." In Longfellow's dream, Goethe had "a beautiful face" but he also looked enormous, like one of the freaks from Barnum's museum, the "Belgian Giant," wearing "an immeasurable black coat." An intimidated Longfellow informs him that he thinks "Clärchen's Song" in Goethe's drama *Egmont* was his best poem, a rather strange compliment given that Goethe had produced so many more ambitious works. Goethe seemed amused: "The God smiled" (16 June 1846).[227]

Despite their shared excitement over Italian culture, Goethe remained somewhat threatening to Longfellow, a Barnum monstrosity, appealing as well as appalling. When his friend Rölker embarked on a translation of *Die Wahlverwandtschaften* or *The Elective Affinities* (Goethe's novel about a strange kind of adultery, one committed in the imagination only, but nevertheless with real-life consequences), Longfellow refused to support it, arguing that the novel would "smell very offensively in this climate, whatever it may do in Germany" (27 July 1851). The great challenge Goethe had issued to Longfellow concerned his vision of "Weltliteratur" or "grand cosmopolitan literature," as Sarah Austin, one of Longfellow's main sources in his Goethe lectures, had translated the phrase.[228] Longfellow's remark about Rölker's translation showed that he, on occasion, still had trouble with Goethe's vision of a community of writers from different nations, his hope that "the living and dying authors" of the world would "meet one another and resolve, on the basis of their own inclinations as well as of sound

227 The "Belgian Giant" is a reference to "Monsieur E. Bihin," one of Barnum's giants, who was born in 1807 in Belgium and made his American debut at the Bowery Theater on 23 March 1840 in *The Giant of Palestine*. See Alvin Goldfarb, "Gigantic and Minuscule Actors on the Nineteenth-Century American Stage," *Journal of Popular Culture* 10.2 (Fall 1976): 276-79.

228 Austin, *Characteristics* 3: 307. In Austin's miscellany, Longfellow would have also discovered that Goethe, "equally a master of Italian, French, and English," kept himself "*au courant* of all the important works that appeared in the three languages" (Austin 3: 70), that he "took the liveliest and most generous interest in the literature and art of other countries" (Austin 3: 309), and, finally, that he was firmly convinced that poetry, regardless of national origin, belonged to "*the whole race of man*" (Austin 2: 246). Goethe's statements on "Weltliteratur" are collected in *Werke*, Hamburger Ausgabe in 14 Bänden, ed. Erich Trunz (Hamburg: Wegner, 1948 ff.) 12: 361-64.

communal sense" to collaborate. Goethe believed that "face-to-face" encounters would be required to make "Weltliteratur" happen, but Longfellow, who would have noticed that lack of exposure to Persian culture had not prevented Goethe from compiling his *West-Eastern Divan*, had come up with a different idea.[229]

In 1845, Longfellow published his important anthology *The Poets and Poetry of Europe* with Carey & Hart in Philadelphia, a veritable brick of a book, eight-hundred pages strong. The book was intended, as Longfellow explained in the preface, "to bring together, into compact and convenient form, as large an amount as possible of those English translations which are scattered through many volumes, and are not easily accessible to the general reader" (*Poets and Poetry* v). Longfellow, with the help of his wife Fanny and his colleague, the classicist Felton, had collected poems from ten different languages and national traditions, ranging from the Anglo-Saxon to the Portuguese. Each section of the anthology presented poems in roughly chronological order, and each was preceded by a lengthy and wide-ranging introduction, written by Longfellow himself. Individual authors were introduced by short and often refreshingly unacademic headnotes (the note on Goethe mentions his interest in the weather in America) that tried to forge links between different writers or poems, often by mentioning who had translated whom (Adalbert von Chamisso had translated the poems of Béranger, Ippolito Pindemonte the plays of Racine, and so forth). Longfellow's volume abounds with intercultural comparisons. The Danish author Ludwig Holberg, we are told, is "to his country what Molière is to France, and Cervantes to Spain" (61). The Swedish poet Johan Erik Stagnelius is compared with the German Novalis (173), and Amable Tastu in France reminds the editors of the British poet Felicia Hemans (497).

The Poets and Poetry of Europe wasn't just about literature as a sort of collaborative exercise involving the efforts made by writers from different nations, it was itself the product of vigorous collaboration. Plagued by vision problems that, in the fall of 1843, prompted him to seek help from Dr. Samuel Elliott, a specialist in New York, Longfellow had relied on Fanny and Felton to do much of the reading and research for him.[230] Longfellow acknowledged Felton's co-authorship in the preface to, though not on the title page of, *Poets and Poetry*, whereas the extent of Fanny's contributions is evident only from the manuscript. In a letter to Longfellow's sister, Mary Greenleaf, written when Henry was "very busy with his work of translations from ten nations," Fanny explained that she enjoyed "greatly aiding him therein." In fact, "my eyes and

229 Johann Wolfgang von Goethe, "Die Zusammenkunft der Naturforscher in Berlin" (1828), *Sämtliche Werke: Gedenkausgabe*, 17 vols. (Zurich: Artemis, 1948-71) 14: 909-10.

230 Longfellow described his affliction as "partial blindness." He remained in that state until 1848 (see Edward Wagenknecht, *Longfellow: A Full-Length Portrait* [New York: Longmans, Green, 1955] 17-18), but what exactly was wrong with his eyes seems as impossible to ascertain now as it was in the (remarkably similar) case of Emily Dickinson's visual troubles.

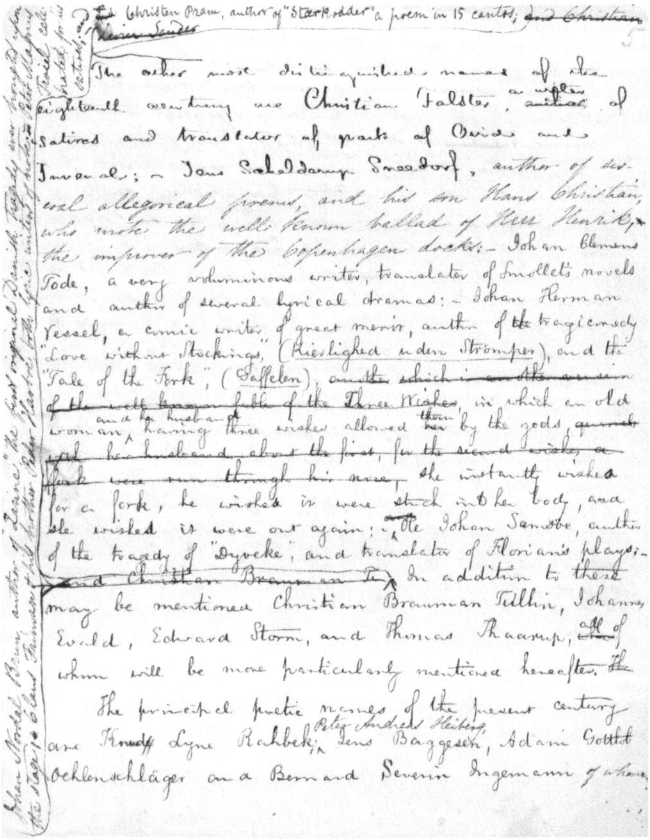
Christian Pram, author of "Stærkodder" a poem in 15 cantos;

The other most distinguished names of the eighteenth century are Christian Falster, a writer of satires and translator of parts of Ovid and Juvenal; – Jens Schelderup Sneedorf, author of several allegorical poems, and his son Hans Christian, who wrote the well known ballad of Herr Henrik,* the improver of the Copenhagen docks: – Johan Clemens Tode, a very voluminous writer, translator of Smollet's novels and author of several lyrical dramas: – Johan Herman Vessel, a comic writer of great merit, author of the tragicomedy "Love without Stockings", (Kierlighed uden Strömper), and the "Tale of the Fork", (Gaffelen), in which an old woman and her husband having three wishes allowed them by the gods, she instantly wished for a fork, he wished it were stuck in her body, and she wished it were out again; – Ole Johan Samsöe, author of the tragedy of "Dyveke", and translator of Florian's plays; – In addition to these may be mentioned Christian Braunman Tullin, Johannes Ewald, Edward Storm, and Thomas Thaarup, of whom will be more particularly mentioned hereafter.

The principal poetic names of the present century are Knud Lyne Rahbek, Peter Andreas Heiberg, Jens Baggesen, Adam Gottlob Oehlenschläger and Bernard Severin Ingemann of whom

Figure 63. Page from ms. *The Poets and Poetry of Europe*, in Longfellow's, Fanny Longfellow's and C. C. Felton's handwriting (p. 5 from folder marked "Scandinavia"), Longfellow Papers, Houghton, MS Am 1340 (66)

fingers thus far take the place of his, and I trust they will answer for the whole book unless he is restored to his natural rights" (26 December 1843; *ML* 99).

A page from the voluminous manuscript of *Poets and Poetry*—page 5 from the folder marked "Scandinavia" (Longfellow Papers, Houghton, MS Am 1340 [66], FIGURE 63)—vividly illustrates how much work Fanny and Felton had done for Longfellow. The excerpt, from the introduction to "Danish Language and Poetry," begins with a short passage in Longfellow's handwriting ("The other most distinguished names of the eighteenth century are . . . .") and continues with an addition written by Fanny Longfellow ("author of several allegorical poems . . . ."). After that, Cornelius Felton takes over ("Johan Clemens Tode . . . .") for the rest of the page, with the exception of an insert in Fanny's hand in the penultimate line ("Peter Andreas Heiberg") and a marginal note, also in Fanny's handwriting.

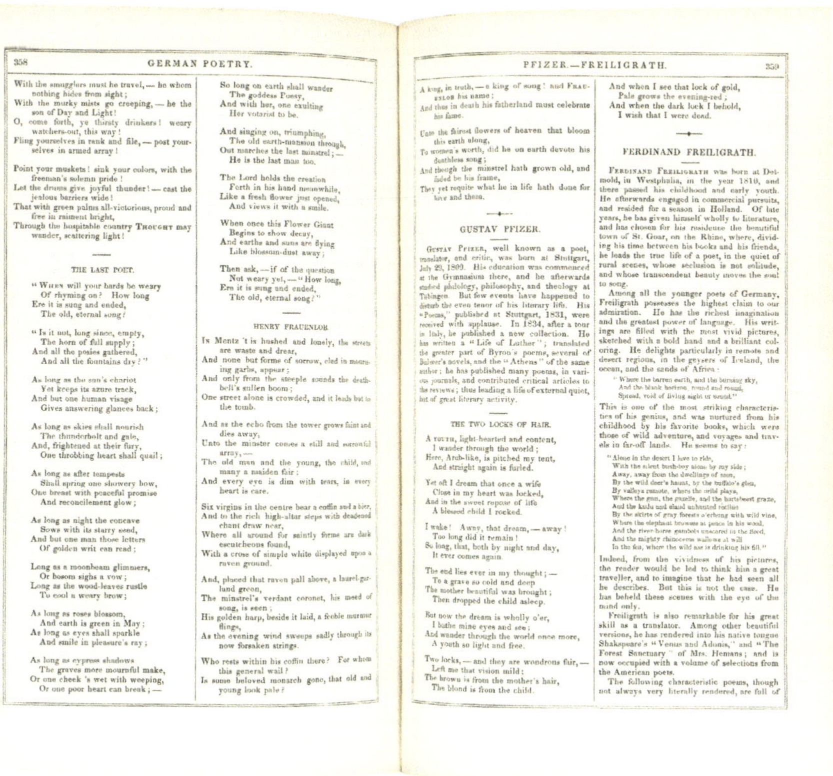

358 GERMAN POETRY.

With the smugglers must he travel, — he whom nothing hides from sight;
With the murky mists go creeping, — he the son of Day and Light!
O, come forth, ye thirsty drinkers! weary watchers-out, this way!
Fling yourselves in rank and file, — post yourselves in armed array!

Point your muskets! sink your colors, with the freeman's solemn pride!
Let the drums give joyful thunder! — cast the jealous barriers wide!
That with green palms all-victorious, proud and free in raiment bright,
Through the hospitable country THOUGHT may wander, scattering light!

THE LAST POET.

"WHEN will your bards be weary
Of rhyming on? How long
Ere it is sung and ended,
The old, eternal song?

"Is it not, long since, empty,
The horn of full supply;
And all the posies gathered,
And all the fountains dry?"

As long as the sun's chariot
Yet keeps its azure track,
And but one human visage
Gives answering glances back;

As long as skies shall nourish
The thunderbolt and gale,
And, frightened at their fury,
One throbbing heart shall quail;

As long as after tempests
Shall spring one showery bow,
One breast with peaceful promise
And reconcilement glow;

As long as night the concave
Sows with its starry seed,
And but one man those letters
Of golden writ can read;

Long as a moonbeam glimmers,
Or bosom sighs a vow;
Long as the wood-leaves rustle
To cool a weary brow;

As long as roses blossom,
And earth is green in May;
As long as eyes shall sparkle
And smile in pleasure's ray;

As long as cypress shadows
The graves more mournful make,
Or one cheek 's wet with weeping,
Or one poor heart can break; —

So long on earth shall wander
The goddess Poesy,
And with her, one exulting
Her votarist to be.

And singing on, triumphing,
The old earth-mansion through,
Out marches the last minstrel; —
He is the last man too.

The Lord holds the creation
Forth in his hand meanwhile,
Like a fresh flower just opened,
And views it with a smile.

When once this Flower Giant
Begins to show decay,
And earths and suns are flying
Like blossom-dust away;

Then ask, — if of the question
Not weary yet, — "How long,
Ere it is sung and ended,
The old, eternal song?"

HENRY FRAUENLOB.

IN Mentz 't is hushed and lonely, the streets are waste and drear,
And none but forms of sorrow, clad in mourning garbs, appear;
And only from the steeple sounds the death-bell's sullen boom;
One street alone is crowded, and it leads but to the tomb.

And as the echo from the tower grows faint and dies away,
Unto the minster comes a still and sorrowful array, —
The old man and the young, the child, and many a maiden fair:
And every eye is dim with tears, in every heart is care.

Six virgins in the centre bear a coffin and a bier,
And to the rich high-altar steps with deadened chant draw near,
Where all around for saintly forms are dark escutcheons found,
With a cross of simple white displayed upon a raven ground.

And, placed that raven pall above, a laurel-garland green,
The minstrel's verdant coronet, his meed of song, is seen;
His golden harp, beside it laid, a feeble murmur flings,
As the evening wind sweeps sadly through its now forsaken strings.

Who rests within his coffin there? For whom this general wail?
Is some beloved monarch gone, that old and young look pale?

PFIZER.—FREILIGRATH. 359

A king, in truth, — a king of song! and FRAUENLOB his name;
And thus in death his fatherland must celebrate his fame.

Unto the fairest flowers of heaven that bloom this earth along,
To women's worth, did he on earth devote his deathless song;
And though the minstrel hath grown old, and faded be his frame,
They yet requite what he in life hath done for love and them.

GUSTAV PFIZER.

GUSTAV PFIZER, well known as a poet, translator, and critic, was born at Stuttgart, July 29, 1809. His education was commenced at the Gymnasium there, and he afterwards studied philology, philosophy, and theology at Tübingen. But few events have happened to disturb the even tenor of his literary life. His "Poems," published at Stuttgart, 1831, were received with applause. In 1834, after a tour in Italy, he published a new collection. He has written a "Life of Luther"; translated the greater part of Byron's poems, several of Bulwer's novels, and the "Athens" of the same author; he has published many poems, in various journals, and contributed critical articles to the reviews; thus leading a life of external quiet, but of great literary activity.

THE TWO LOCKS OF HAIR.

A YOUTH, light-hearted and content,
I wander through the world;
Here, Arab-like, is pitched my tent,
And straight again is furled.

Yet oft I dream that once a wife
Close in my heart was locked,
And in the sweet repose of life
A blessed child I rocked.

I wake! Away, that dream, — away!
Too long did it remain!
So long, that, both by night and day,
It ever comes again.

The end lies ever in my thought; —
To a grave so cold and deep
The mother beautiful was brought;
Then dropped the child asleep.

But now the dream is wholly o'er,
I bathe mine eyes and see;
And wander through the world once more,
A youth so light and free.

Two locks, — and they are wondrous fair, —
Left me that vision mild;
The brown is from the mother's hair,
The blond is from the child.

And when I see that lock of gold,
Pale grows the evening-red;
And when the dark lock I behold,
I wish that I were dead.

FERDINAND FREILIGRATH.

FERDINAND FREILIGRATH was born at Detmold, in Westphalia, in the year 1810, and there passed his childhood and early youth. He afterwards engaged in commercial pursuits, and resided for a season in Holland. Of late years, he has given himself wholly to literature, and has chosen for his residence the beautiful town of St. Goar, on the Rhine, where, dividing his time between his books and his friends, he leads the true life of a poet, in the quiet of rural scenes, whose seclusion is not solitude, and whose transcendent beauty moves the soul to song.

Among all the younger poets of Germany, Freiligrath possesses the highest claim to our admiration. He has the richest imagination and the greatest power of language. His writings are filled with the most vivid pictures, sketched with a bold hand and a brilliant coloring. He delights particularly in remote and desert regions, in the geysers of Iceland, the ocean, and the sands of Africa:

"Where the barren earth, and the burning sky,
And the black horizon, round and round,
Spread, void of living sight or sound."

This is one of the most striking characteristics of his genius, and was nurtured from his childhood by his favorite books, which were those of wild adventure, and voyages and travels in far-off lands. He seems to say:

"Alone in the desert I love to ride,
With the silent bush-boy alone by my side;
Away, away from the dwellings of men,
By the wild deer's haunt, by the buffalo's glen,
By valleys remote, where the oribi plays,
Where the gnu, the gazelle, and the hartebeest graze,
And the kudu and eland unhunted recline
By the skirts of gray forests o'erhung with wild vine,
Where the elephant browses at peace in his wood,
And the river-horse gambols unscared in the flood,
And the mighty rhinoceros wallows at will
In the fen, where the wild ass is drinking his fill."

Indeed, from the vividness of his pictures, the reader would be led to think him a great traveller, and to imagine that he had seen all he describes. But this is not the case. He has beheld these scenes with the eye of the mind only.

Freiligrath is also remarkable for his great skill as a translator. Among other beautiful versions, he has rendered into his native tongue Shakspeare's "Venus and Adonis," and "The Forest Sanctuary" of Mrs. Hemans; and is now occupied with a volume of selections from the American poets.

The following characteristic poems, though not always very literally rendered, are full of

Figure 64. Longfellow, ed., *The Poets and Poetry of Europe* (Philadelphia: Carey & Hart, 1845), pp. 358-59; presentation copy, inscribed to John Sullivan Dwight (1813-93), Harry Elkins Widener Collection, Harvard University, HEW 7.3.3

Houghton Library owns a presentation copy of *The Poets and Poetry of Europe*, inscribed by Longfellow to John Sullivan Dwight (Harry Elkins Widener Collection, Harvard University, HEW 7.3.3, FIGURE 64). Dwight (1813-1893) was a music critic and proponent of the music of Bach, Händel, and Beethoven (he opposed the "new music" of Wagner, Berlioz, and Rubinstein, some of which Longfellow actually liked). In 1852, he founded *Dwight's Journal of Music* in Boston. He also published *Select Minor Poems from the German of Goethe and Schiller, with Notes*, which appeared as the third volume of George Ripley's 14-volume edition *Specimens of Foreign Standard Literature* (Boston, 1838). Longfellow felt Dwight's translations were not "literal" enough (to Samuel Ward, 5 January 1839, *Letters* 2: 125), but he nevertheless ended up using several of them (such as Goethe's "To the Moon," *Poets* 294-295). Dwight was a member of Brook Farm and the Saturday Club, and in November 1847 he contributed a favorable review of *Evangeline* to the Fourierist newspaper *The Harbinger*.

The illustration shows Longfellow's own translation of the German poet Gustav Pfizer's ballad "Der Junggesell" ("The Two Locks of Hair"), along with the introduction to the entry featuring poems by Longfellow's friend Ferdinand Freiligrath (pp. 358-59). The orientalist image in the first stanza of Pfizer's poem ("Here, Arab-like, is pitched my tent, / And straight again is furled") shows up again also in Longfellow's own poetry. In "The Day Is Done" (1844; 1: 246-47), poetry is described as having the power to dispel the cares of the world which, "like the Arabs," will fold their tents and silently disappear, a clear echo of Pfizer's description of Arab-like existence of the bachelor, who will settle down only to leave again:

> A youth, light-hearted and content,
> I wander through the world;
> Here, Arab-like, is pitched my tent,
> And straight again is furled.
> (*Poets* 359)

Longfellow drastically expanded and revised his largely Eurocentric image of "world literature" in a poem he finished in May 1877. "Kéramos," a poem about the making of pottery, appeared in *Harper's New Monthly* in December 1877, for which Longfellow received the princely sum of $1,000. Houghton has one of six copies of the poem that were printed and stitched together for Longfellow's personal use only (Houghton *AC85.L8605.877k [A]). In this version, the poem's refrain ("Turn, my wheel . . . .") is not italicized, as it is in *Harper's* and all subsequent reprints.

In "Kéramos," pottery, practiced by the Dutch, French, Italians, Egyptians, Chinese, and Japanese, becomes a metaphor for the global reach of poetry, as the great uniter of humankind, regardless of cultural, class, and linguistic differences:

> Turn, turn my wheel! The human race,
> Of every tongue, of every place,
> Caucasian, Coptic, or Malay,
> All that inhabit this great earth,
> Whatever be their rank or worth,
> Are kindred and allied by birth,
> And made of the same clay.

The speaker, clinging to a potter's magic cloak (an allusion to Aladdin's magic carpet), takes his readers on a *voyage imaginaire* around the world in search of examples of the potter's craft, venturing from familiar territory into ever more unknown regions, including the Chinese factory town King-te-tching and the workshops at Arita in Japan (p. 11), where Imari porcelain originates. Longfellow, in loving detail, describes a landscape he hadn't seen, imperceptibly shifting from an aerial view ("The islands . . . / Beneath me lie") to a look from the ground (sunshine is streaming through "rifts" in the smoke that rises from the workshops' chimneys). In the second paragraph of the excerpt, the scenes from nature he evokes—through sound (the leaves rustle, the reeds whisper), sight (bright flowers, bright stars, the saffron dawn, the red sunset), and movement (the waves that ripple)—are finally identified as the product of make-believe, the result of the potter's craft and craftiness. And even though we are now looking up at the sky obscured by factory smoke, the herons fly again and the skylark sings once more. Such is the trickery of art:

> Cradled and rocked in Eastern seas,
> The islands of the Japanese
> Beneath me lie; o'er lake and o'er plain
> The stork, the heron, and the crane
> Through the clear realms of azure drift,
> And on the hillside I can see
> The villages of Imari,
> Whose thronged and flaming workshops lift
> Their twisted columns of smoke on high,
> Cloud cloisters that in ruins lie,
> With sunshine streaming through each rift,
> And broken arches of blue sky.
>
> All the bright flowers that fill the land,
> Ripple of waves on rock or sand,
> The snow on Fusiyama's cone,
> The midnight heaven so thickly sown
> With constellations of bright stars,
> The leaves that rustle, the reeds that make
> A whisper by each stream and lake,
> The saffron dawn, the sunset red,
> Are painted on these lovely jars;
> Again the skylark sings, again
> The stork, the heron, and the crane
> Float through the azure overhead,
> The counterfeit and counterpart
> Of Nature reproduced in Art.

Longfellow knew about Imari from his son Charley, who had returned from Asia in June 1874 having shipped home innumerable crates of furniture, textiles, books, scrolls, games, and bric-a-brac, as well as ceramics from several different kilns in Japan including Arita ware.[231]

Longfellow's interest in the Far East, fanned by his son's travels, manifests itself also in the twenty-third volume of the mega-anthology, *Poems of Places*, the "Poetic Guide-Book"[232] which he started compiling in 1875, much to the consternation of some of his colleagues. "The world is expecting better things of you than this," Emerson had reproached him when he found Longfellow scanning the proofs of one of his small volumes. "You are wasting time that should be bestowed upon original production."[233] But Longfellow, who had "traveled all the World over" when working on his anthology, shutting out the "dull weather" outside (*Letters* 6: 364, 355), did not see it that way. In fact, *Poems of Places* allowed him to think creatively about the importance of place in literature. In each of the thirty-one small octavo volumes, place names are arranged alphabetically, a truly democratic principle that effectively erases the difference between Radicofani and Ravenna, Marseille and Le Mesnil-sous-Jumiéges. Not unexpectedly, Longfellow's biases are evident throughout the collection. New England gets two volumes and Italy, "the finest portion of the work" (*Letters* 6: 210), three, while Japan is only allowed a meager 15 pages. [234] But the fact that the Far East is represented at all in Longfellow's anthology is not without significance. The Japanese poems featured here, "Fujiyama, the Mountain" and "Niphon (Nippon) the Island" (*Poems of Places* 23: 242-43, FIGURE 65), Longfellow had discovered in an article on "Ancient Japanese Poetry" in the October 1870 issue of *The Westminster Review*.[235] Note the similarity of the first lines of the two texts: "Heaven above from earth below / Long ago the gods have parted" ("Fujiyama") and "Heaven above from earth below / Long ago the God hath parted" ("Niphon [Nippon], the Island"). Longfellow's choice of these two texts inconspicuously helps him reinforce two points the anonymous author of the *Westminster Review* article was hoping to make: first, that there is indeed a coherent body of texts that can be called "Japanese literature," with its own distinctive sets of themes and techniques, and second, that some of these themes, such as the differentiation of the original chaos into earth,

231 Arita porcelain was shipped to Europe from Nagasaki on Kyushu Island, where Charley Longfellow had traveled in March 1872, describing it in a letter home as a "great place for vases" (Charles Appleton Longfellow to Alice Longfellow, 15 March 1872, *Twenty Months* 128).

232 See Longfellow, Journal, 9 May 1874.

233 W. Sloane Kennedy, *Henry W. Longfellow: Biography, Anecdote, Letters, Criticism* (Cambridge, MA: Moses King, 1882) 116.

234 *Poems of Places: Asia, III* (Boston: Houghton, Osgood, and Co., 1878), Widener 11424.3.

235 See Christine M. E. Guth, *Longfellow's Tattoos* (Seattle: University of Washington Press, 2004) esp. 180.

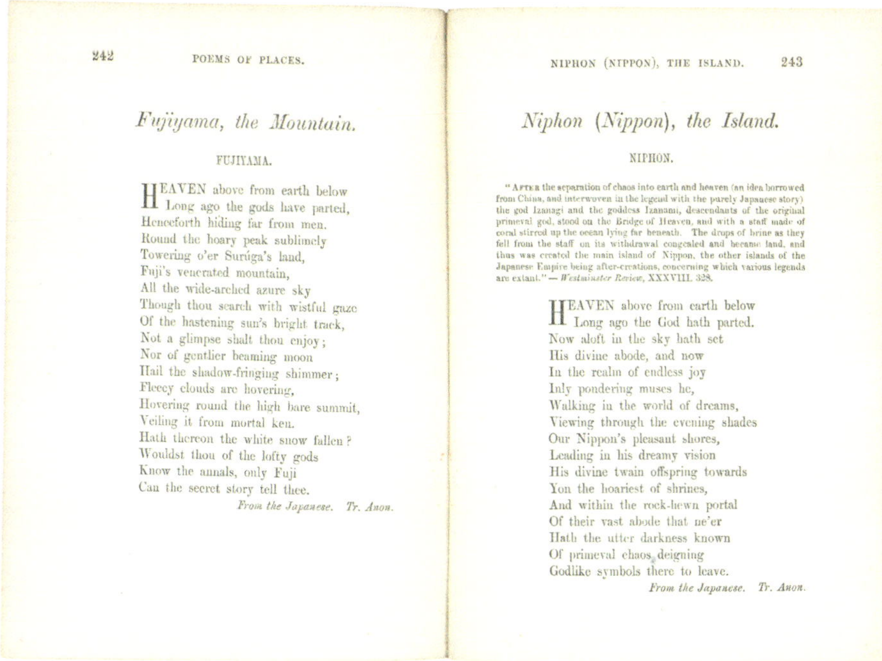

242 POEMS OF PLACES.

Fujiyama, the Mountain.

FUJIYAMA.

HEAVEN above from earth below
Long ago the gods have parted,
Henceforth hiding far from men.
Round the hoary peak sublimely
Towering o'er Suruga's land,
Fuji's venerated mountain,
All the wide-arched azure sky
Though thou search with wistful gaze
Of the hastening sun's bright track,
Not a glimpse shalt thou enjoy;
Nor of gentlier beaming moon
Hail the shadow-fringing shimmer;
Fleecy clouds are hovering,
Hovering round the high bare summit,
Veiling it from mortal ken.
Hath thereon the white snow fallen?
Wouldst thou of the lofty gods
Know the annals, only Fuji
Can the secret story tell thee.

From the Japanese. Tr. Anon.

NIPHON (NIPPON), THE ISLAND. 243

Niphon (Nippon), the Island.

NIPHON.

"AFTER the separation of chaos into earth and heaven (an idea borrowed from China, and interwoven in the legend with the purely Japanese story) the god Izanagi and the goddess Izanami, descendants of the original primeval god, stood on the Bridge of Heaven, and with a staff made of coral stirred up the ocean lying far beneath. The drops of brine as they fell from the staff on its withdrawal congealed and became land, and thus was created the main island of Nippon, the other islands of the Japanese Empire being after-creations, concerning which various legends are extant." — *Westminster Review*, XXXVIII. 328.

HEAVEN above from earth below
Long ago the God hath parted.
Now aloft in the sky hath set
His divine abode, and now
In the realm of endless joy
Inly pondering muses he,
Walking in the world of dreams,
Viewing through the evening shades
Our Nippon's pleasant shores,
Leading in his dreamy vision
His divine twain offspring towards
Yon the hoariest of shrines,
And within the rock-hewn portal
Of their vast abode that ne'er
Hath the utter darkness known
Of primeval chaos, deigning
Godlike symbols there to leave.

From the Japanese. Tr. Anon.

Figure 65. "Fujiyama, the Mountain" and "Niphon (Nippon) the Island," from Longfellow, ed. *Poems of Places*, vol. 23: *Asia*, pp. 242-243, Widener Library, Harvard University, 11424.3

air, and sky, are indeed quite interesting. As the *Westminster Review* author explains, while Japanese poems may show "quite as fertile a power of invention as the far more famous legends of ancient Greece," they are also surprisingly modern, offering, at least in these instances, an explanation of the creation of solar systems "very similar" to that given by "modern philosophy" ("Ancient Japanese Poetry," 322-23 and 333n.).

Longfellow's commitment to "Weltliteratur" inspired an item that has greatly amused some of his less charitably inclined critics, a small pitcher known as "the Longfellow jug" (LONG 5829, LNHS, FIGURE 66). The pitcher's round bulbous body features an oval portrait of the bearded Longfellow, surrounded by gilt lines, on its front and a seven-line excerpt from "Kéramos" on its back. It has a spout at the end of a straight neck, opposite a large C-shaped handle, and a flaring foot. Around the neck is a band of stylized flowers intertwined with scrolls containing the titles of some of Longfellow's works: "Golden Legend," "Tales of a Wayside Inn," "Psalm of Life," "Excelsior," "Hiawatha," "Evangeline," "Miles Standis[h]." The pitcher's body is white, covered with a cream-colored glaze, while the spout is glazed in brown with stylized floral decoration. The handle is brown and cream with overlapping fan ornamentation. Printed on the underside in underglaze black is the inscription: "Manufactured by Josiah Wedgwood & Sons Etruria / For / Richard Briggs / Boston / Registered in Great

Figure 66. The Longfellow Jug, Wedgwood, ca. 1880, LONG 582, LNHS

Britain / and France / Also in the / United States." Painted in red on the underside is the number "920," below "F." To the right is the number "6" (perhaps the gilder's number).

The jug was commissioned by Richard Briggs (1829-1893), the china decorator and pottery dealer of 137 Washington Street in Boston, as a Christmas present for Longfellow. On 30 December 1880, Longfellow thanked him in somewhat restrained language; it seems clear that the curious artifact puzzled him: "This is a very pleasant and very welcome New-Year's gift; and you have kept your secret so well, that I have been taken quite by surprise" (*Letters* 6: 671).[236] Herbert Gorman, setting the tone for future debunkings of Longfellow, saw the existence of the Longfellow jug as evidence of the inevitable deterioration of Longfellow into popular culture icon, "as the wooden Indian has become a symbol for tobacco."[237] But the jug, a precursor of the many commemorative plates, cigar box labels, busts, bookends, inkwells, and cardboard models of Craigie House, can also be seen as proof that Longfellow had succeeded in carrying the message of "Kéramos" beyond the confines of Cambridge, Massachusetts.

236 See also Regina Lee Blaszczyk, *Imagining Consumers: Design and Innovation from Wedgwood to Corning* (Baltimore: The Johns Hopkins University Press, 2000) 36-38.

237 Gorman, *A Victorian American: Henry Wadsworth Longfellow*, new ed. (Port Washington, NY: Kennikat, 1967) 349.

Figure 67. Longfellow's "Pour le Mérite" medal, indicating his membership in the "peace class" of the prestigious German order, LONG 7573, LNHS

Longfellow recognized the world in his work, and the world, in turn, recognized him. It is well-known that Longfellow's bust was included in the "Poet's Corner" in Westminster Abbey, the first and only American poet to be so honored. Less well-known is that in May 1875, Longfellow, by order of the German Kaiser, Wilhelm I, became the first American writer to be selected as a member of the "peace class" of the Order "Pour le Mérite" (LONG 7573, LNHS, FIGURE 67). The gold medal, which featured a small Prussian eagle in the center, was worn suspended from the neck. It came with a wide, silver- and black-striped grosgrain ribbon, the same type that was used for the military version of "Pour le Mérite." Both the medal and the ribbon were kept in a rectangular box covered with black paper, with white satin lining on the lid and a red velvet inset.

In accompanying letters, the Chancellor of the Order, the famous historian Leopold von Ranke, and the German chargé d'affaires in Washington, Max Freiherr von Thielmann, congratulated Longfellow on the honor. Thielmann, with characteristic German thoroughness, also asked him to confirm receipt of the insignia and to fill in and immediately return a form with his "personal data."[238] "Pour le Mérite" had originally

238 The documents accompanying the medal are part of the Henry Wadsworth Longfellow Family Papers at LNHS (LONG 27930).

been created to honor military achievements. On 31 May 1842 Friedrich Wilhelm IV, King of Prussia, established a separate division of the Order to honor prominent artists and scientists. It is not known how Longfellow, staunch anti-monarchist that he was, reacted to his appointment. But we can safely assume that this pacifist American poet would have enjoyed the fact that he now belonged to an order that, despite its military origins, had a division added to it that was devoted entirely to "peace." It had thirty permanent German members (or "knights") and up to thirty foreign members (today there are forty, in each category). Longfellow must have been pleased to see that the composer Franz Liszt, whom he revered since meeting him in Rome in 1868, was among them, as were Thomas Carlyle, Charles Darwin, Elias Lönnrot (the compiler of the *Kalevala*), and, the only other Americans so honored, John C. Frémont, the explorer, and George Bancroft, the historian. The "peace class" of "Pour le Mérite" was, in fact, the only one that survived the abdication of the Kaiser in 1918; the most recent American member to be elected was the sculptor Richard Serra.

In the document that came with the medal, Longfellow's profession was identified as that of a "Dichter," a term that carries much weight in modern German but etymologically speaking signifies nothing other than someone who writes things, a meaning Longfellow would have appreciated. To this day, Longfellow remains the only American poet or "Dichter" to have received this medal—if we don't count T. S. Eliot, that is, a poet whose Americanness has also been doubted, perhaps more justifiably so. It might be worth remembering here that in 1921 Eliot added, as Longfellow had done decades earlier in *Hiawatha*, a slew of explanatory notes to *The Waste Land*, the poem that launched his international career, that he regarded Dante as "the most *universal* of poets in the modern language,"[239] and that Eliot was, despite a well-earned reputation for elitism, a life-long fan of Groucho Marx, boxing matches, and music hall routines.[240] *Hot Corn*, the "wretched" play Longfellow and his sons saw in Boston in April 1854, might have been right up his alley.

239 Eliot, "Dante" (1929), *Selected Essays*, 3rd ed. (1932; London: Faber and Faber, 1951) 238.

240 See Lyndall Gordon, *Eliot's Early Years*, new ed. (1977; Oxford: Oxford University Press, 1988) 32, and Gordon, *T. S. Eliot's New Life* (Oxford: Oxford University Press, 1988) 256-58.

Coda:
The Longfellow Collections in Cambridge

"How will men speak of me when I am gone / When all this colorless, sad life is ended, / And I am dust?" wonders Michelangelo in a dramatic fragment never published during Longfellow's lifetime (6: 97). The hard-working, broken-nosed, homosexual sculptor was as different as one can be from Longfellow the devotee of fine wine, female beauty, and fancy clothes. Longfellow's Michelangelo was the embodiment of everything Longfellow was *not*: an artist consumed by the desire for innovation and originality. But Longfellow did share the sculptor's concerns about what would happen after his death—with an interesting difference. In "Shadows," a poem published in *The Masque of Pandora and Other Poems* (1875), the speaker is less concerned about *his* posthumous reputation than about how his children would continue to lead their lives "if I were dead." He consoles himself with the thought that the "world belongs to those who come the last" (3: 224). Luckily for Longfellow, master of self-effacement, his children did not at all subscribe to that philosophy. In 1913, Alice, Edith, Annie, and Ernest (Charley had died in 1893 from pneumonia) established the Longfellow House Trust with the goal of preserving "Castle Craigie" not only as an outstanding example of colonial architecture but also as a memorial to their father (and to another famous inhabitant of a previous generation, George Washington).

Despite the decline of Longfellow's reputation in the twentieth century, his legacy has remained more intact than that of any other American writer of similar stature. Thanks to the combined efforts of his descendants, the rangers and researchers of the National Park Service, and the staff of Houghton Library, the collections at the Longfellow National Historic Site and at Harvard University constitute one of the most complete records available of the intellectual, cultural, and social interests of a prominent nineteenth-century New England family. What the hospitable Longfellow would have especially appreciated is that his collections—the letters, journals, and books he wrote, the paintings and sculptures he owned, the furniture he bought, the smoking jacket he wore, even the pencils he used and the toys he bought for his children—remain accessible to the general public. While only about fifteen percent of the objects held at the Longfellow National Historic Site are on exhibit in the historic rooms of the Brattle Street residence, the rest of the collection is available to anyone interested in American culture and history. So are the Longfellow manuscripts and books that are now kept at Houghton.

Not surprisingly, "Castle Craigie," where Longfellow lived from 1837 to his death in 1882, has remained central to all efforts at preserving Longfellow's legacy. The last of Longfellow's children to inhabit the house, Alice Longfellow, made only a handful of changes to the house, modernizing the bathrooms and installing an elevator. After Alice's death in 1928, Longfellow's grandson, Henry Wadsworth Longfellow Dana, who had come to live with his aunt in 1917, established himself as the primary caretaker of the house. Along with Anne Thorp, the daughter of Annie Longfellow, "Harry" Dana saw to it that almost all original furnishings remained where they were. By purchasing artifacts of interest as well as by persuading family members to deposit their papers, books, clothes, and photographs, Harry Dana also added significantly to the existing collections. An authority on Soviet drama, Dana was widely known for his eccentricity. E. E. Cummings, for example, who befriended him during his Harvard days, thought he was "quite a character."[241] Dana was a committed socialist (his political views induced his uncle Ernest to strike him from his will), but he was equally passionate about the history of his family—which will seem a paradox only to those who remain oblivious to Harry's grandfather's pacifism and fairly progressive politics.

Dana's relationship with the Trustees of the Longfellow estate was strained and became even more so after he managed to get himself arrested on a "morals charge" in Cambridge, an incident that inadvertently made his homosexuality public knowledge. His personal troubles notwithstanding, Harry Dana proved to be invaluable as the first *de facto* curator of Craigie House, creating an extensive archive (765,000 items) representing over 300 years of American social history through multiple generations of the Longfellow, Wadsworth, Appleton, and Dana families.

After Dana's death in 1950, the Trustees transferred Longfellow's personal papers as well as many of his books to Harvard's Houghton Library, a move resisted by Anne Thorp, who felt that this meant "taking the heart out of the House."[242] But the collections that have remained at Craigie House are extensive enough. Remarkable for their quantity as well as for their quality are the roughly two thousand works of art in the house—paintings, drawings, prints, and sculptures by such artists as Washington Allston, Albert Bierstadt, Jean-Baptiste-Camille Corot, Thomas Crawford, George Healey, William Morris Hunt, John Kensett, and Gilbert Stuart. Of particular note are thirteen beautifully executed crayon portraits of Longfellow's family and friends by Eastman Johnson, which Longfellow commissioned in 1846.

The largest single collection of objects at the Longfellow National Historic site is the gargantuan library of approximately fourteen thousand volumes. Longfellow's own books form the core of the collection, to which were added the books once owned by Fanny Appleton Longfellow, their children, and Harry Dana, as well as fifty volumes that once belonged to Washington Allston (see the description of the library in

241 For a recent discussion of Harry Dana, see Douglass Shand-Tucci's *The Crimson Letter: Harvard, Homosexuality, and the Shaping of American Culture* (2003; New York: St. Martin's Griffin, 2004) 129-37.

242 Anne Longfellow Thorp to Francis Goodale, one of the Trustees, 30 May 1950, quoted in *Historic Furnishings Report: The Longfellow House* (see note 67) 116.

Chapter 8). Among the manuscript resources kept at the site are the Henry Wadsworth Longfellow Family Papers (an estimated twenty-five linear feet), which include the papers of Ernest Wadsworth Longfellow, daughters Edith Longfellow Dana and Anne Longfellow Thorp, as well as of his sisters Anne Longfellow Pierce and Mary Longfellow Greenleaf, and his brother Stephen Longfellow. Of particular interest are the Frances Elizabeth Appleton Longfellow Papers (four linear feet), which reveal a talented artist and shrewd observer of nineteenth-century Boston culture. Among the highlights of this collection are Fanny Longfellow's sketchbooks, made during her youth on trips across the United States and Europe, and "The Chronicle of the Children of Craigie Castle" (see Chapter 1), a lovingly detailed record of the deeds and misdeeds of her boisterous children. The Wadsworth-Longfellow Family Papers offer comprehensive documentation for the history of the two families from 1610–1971: researchers may consult the letters and journals of Henry's uncle, Henry Wadsworth, who served on the *U.S.S. Constitution* and the *U.S.S. Chesapeake*, the letters of Longfellow's maternal grandfather Peleg Wadsworth and the papers of his paternal grandfather, Judge Stephen Longfellow. This collection also contains the letters of Longfellow's father, Stephen Longfellow, and of Captain Samuel Longfellow, Henry's uncle, as well as the extensive correspondence maintained by Longfellow's mother, Zilpah Wadsworth Longfellow.

Newly processed are the papers of Longfellow's brother Samuel, a Unitarian clergyman with multiple interests, who, besides being the poet's biographer, also wrote several hymns that are still in use today. The Charles Appleton Longfellow Papers include the journals of Henry and Fanny's oldest son, which chronicle his travels in Japan, China, India, and Russia, as well as numerous rare photographs, among them those of Meiji-period Japan which are discussed in Christine Guth's *Longfellow's Tattoos* (2004).

There are different versions of how Harvard University came to own and control the rights to the Longfellow Papers. Reports of the National Park Service state that the original loan was converted into a donation in 1965[243]; Houghton Library records claim that Harvard purchased the papers and copyright in 1976.[244] According to Houghton's Finding Aids for the Longfellow collection, Harvard University, in 1976, purchased Longfellow's personal manuscripts, which it had received from the Trustees in 1954, for the nominal sum of $1.00, thereby also acquiring the copyright to all unpublished Longfellow material. The three major manuscript collections at Houghton are the Longfellow Papers (MS Am 1340), Longfellow's Letters to Various Correspondents (bMS Am 1340.1), and the Letters to Longfellow (bMS Am 1340.2). Since the vast majority of Longfellow's letters have been made available in Andrew Hilen's six-volume edition published under the Belknap imprint of Harvard University Press, Houghton's Longfellow Papers and Letters to Longfellow will be of the most value to

243 *Historic Furnishings Report* 116.

244 Only Longfellow's letters (bMS Am 1340.1) are identified as a "Gift of The Trustees of the Longfellow House Trust."

researchers today. The Longfellow Papers comprise his journals, manuscripts of poems and works in prose (many with notes and draft copies), his lecture notes, personal account books, and business papers, as well as commonplace books, scrapbooks, and newspaper clippings. Other items of interest contained in MS Am 1340 are Longfellow's manuscripts on European languages and literatures, particularly his notes on Dante's *Divina Commedia*, and the "Minute Book" of the Dante Society, of which Longfellow was the first president.

Longfellow's journals, maligned by some scholars for their alleged pedestrian nature,[245] have gradually come to be recognized as a major resource not only for understanding Longfellow's own personal and intellectual development but as a window into nineteenth-century literary culture in general. With some notable exceptions (he destroyed the 1843 journal, written when his seven-year-long courtship of Fanny Appleton finally ended), they cover Longfellow's life from his early travels to his last month. To date, only excerpts from the journals have been published, in the bowdlerized version his brother reprinted in his biography.

Despite his enlightened political views and his admiration for Walt Whitman,[246] the Reverend Samuel Longfellow shared the squeamishness of many of his contemporaries. A lifelong bachelor attracted to other men, he seems to have been particularly baffled by the mysteries of femininity. He blushingly skips entries like the one in which Longfellow reports on visiting Fanny "in her chamber" in the weeks after Erny's birth and spending some "delicious" time alone with her, like "a law student and a grisette in their *mansarde*," an allusion to George Sand's provocative novel *Horace* (1842), which describes an affair between a young man from the provinces and a Parisian working-class girl (21 December 1845). In Samuel's sanitized version of Longfellow's 1847 journal, for example, there are no references to the ether that was administered to Fanny during childbirth and ended her "pains of labor" (see Chapter 1). The entry for 7 April 1847 merely reads: "This morning was born in the Craigie House a girl, to the great joy of all" (*Life* 2: 85). Sometimes, Victorian propriety and concern for the reputation of Longfellow's contemporaries lead Samuel, a fervent advocate of temperance, to truncate and thus misrepresent entire entries. On April 15, Longfellow reports that his publisher John Owen was still ill and then recounts, shudderingly, a visit from James Russell Lowell, "quite rabid now on temperance," who wants him to destroy his wine

245 William Charvat found them "completely unrewarding" (*The Profession of Authorship in America, 1800-1870*, ed. Matthew J. Bruccoli [Columbus: Ohio State University Press, 1968] 199). For a different view, see my *Longfellow Redux* 45-50.

246 See Justin Kaplan, *Walt Whitman: A Life* (New York: Simon and Schuster, 1980) 213. Whitman claimed Samuel Longfellow admired the "Greek" (i.e., homoerotic) elements of *Leaves of Grass* (Horace Traubel, *With Walt Whitman in Camden*, 9 vols. [Boston: Small, Maynard etc., 1906-1996] 2: 502-3 [19 October 1888]). A particularly rich issue of the *Longfellow House Bulletin* is devoted entirely to Samuel Longfellow (vol. 10.1 [June 2006]).

cellar (see page 97). In Samuel's version, "Owen wants me to destroy all the wine I have in my cellar" (*Life* 2: 36). Lowell, who died on 12 August 1891, was still very much alive when the first two volumes of Samuel's biography appeared in 1886.

Most of Longfellow's manuscripts are in excellent condition, in part because he himself thought them important enough to preserve in his lifetime. Many of them were bound under his supervision. Studying Longfellow's autographs is a sheer joy, not the least because of what William Dean Howells, a frequent visitor at Craigie House, aptly called his "smooth, regular, and scrupulously perfect handwriting." Although Longfellow commonly relied on a quill when he wrote out fair copies of his poems or entries in his journals, he frequently preferred soft pencils for drafts and revisions. No matter what he used, "each letter," as Howells noted, "was distinct in shape. And between the verses was always the exact space of half an inch."[247]

The other important Houghton collection—speaking from a researcher's perspective—contains the letters received by Longfellow during his lifetime, a veritable mountain of mail (or, in library terms, thirty-seven linear feet!). Interestingly, despite his complaints about the extent of his correspondence (see the discussion in Chapter 5), Longfellow regarded the letters he had received (from family members, colleagues, or devoted fans) highly enough to have them preserved as if they were his own manuscripts. William H. Bond, Curator of Manuscripts at Houghton when the collection was received, has left a detailed description of how the archive was originally arranged.[248] Apparently, Longfellow had collected and chronologically arranged letters from 1821 to 1853. He had them bound in twenty-five volumes, all in three-quarters red leather. Unfortunately, the bindings of these volumes were subsequently broken when individual letters were extracted, often roughly so, leaving stubs or whole leaves of letters. Bond assiduously documented what was left of Longfellow's original arrangements as well as the stubs left after the removal of manuscripts. His list is preserved as bMS Am 1340.2 (6232). The empty bindings are kept in three boxes as bMS Am 1340.2 (6230). A second group of letters, dating from 1854 to 1882, had already been collected in separate file boxes, although traces of Longfellow's original ordering system were still visible, in the form of labels written by him or by Samuel and Alice that were cut from the wrappings of bundles made up by years (now preserved as bMS Am 1340.2 [6231]). A third group of manuscripts contains letters by correspondents that someone had regarded important enough to keep separate from the rest (Carlyle, Dickens, Emerson, George Washington Greene, Nathaniel Hawthorne, Oliver Wendell Holmes, Sr., William Dean Howells, James Russell Lowell, Charles Eliot Norton, Edgar Allan Poe, Charles Sumner, Alfred Tennyson, and Samuel Ward). There were also separate boxes for letters from Ticknor & Fields, letters from foreign correspondents,

247 Howells, *Literary Friends and Acquaintance* 166.

248 See the Finding Aid for bMS Am 1340.2, typescript kept in the Houghton Library Reading Room (also available at http://oasis.harvard.edu:10080/oasis/deliver/~hou00355).

letters from his children and relatives, and lastly a small collection kept in a cigar-box which Longfellow had designated as "Curious Letters."

As Bond pointed out, these arrangements had been more or less destroyed when he began working with the collection. Rather than trying to reconstruct Longfellow's original plan for the organization of the material, the Houghton staff rearranged Longfellow's correspondence, separating certain groups of letters, such as requests for autographs (bMS 1340.4) and birthday greetings (bMS Am 1340.7), from the rest. That left sixty-six boxes of letters from 6,228 identified writers, all of which are now kept in separate folders and listed alphabetically (by sender) in the comprehensive, full-text Finding Aids available through Harvard's Online Archival Search Information System (OASIS).

Longfellow freely gave out autographs of his works, as Howells noted.[249] It is therefore not at all unusual that many Longfellow items came separately to Houghton. Some of them were collected in MS Am 1370, which features drafts of poems such as "The Wreck of the Hesperus," "Excelsior," and others. MS Am 183.2 contains Longfellow autographs left to Harvard University by Annie Fields, among them autographs of "Three Friends of Mine" and "The Fiftieth Birthday of Agassiz." Miscellaneous letters have been collected as MS Am 1127.

In 2001, Houghton, with the help of the Bayard Livingston and Kate Gray Kilgour fund, purchased what must be one of the largest and most comprehensive private collections of rare books, unpublished letters, manuscripts, and photographs relating to Longfellow ever assembled, the result of 14 years of work by the Newton-based literary publicist Victor Gulotta. Among the two hundred autograph letters and documents were the second-earliest known letter from Longfellow to Nathaniel Hawthorne (1843; see FIGURE 29), letters about Laura Bridgman, and the original manuscripts of Longfellow's sonnet "Dante" (1845) and his poem "By the Seaside" (1847). A remarkable asset of Gulotta's collection were two manuscripts not written by Longfellow, an early draft and a second, longer version of an autobiography by Longfellow's close friend, Luigi Monti (see Chapter 2). The six hundred volumes in Gulotta's collection included a first edition of the *Syllabus de la grammaire Italienne*, with Charles Folsom's annotations (FIGURE 61), the "shilling edition" of *Voices of the Night* in its original paper wrappers (see FIGURES 39, 40), and one of the earliest known copies of the first edition of *Evangeline*. A special feature of Gulotta's collection are the numerous cartes-de-visite, stereoscopic images, and other photographic material, e.g., the 1893 photogravure of Julia Margaret Cameron's Longfellow portrait (see FIGURE 44).

There is no complete record of the books from Longfellow's library that were transferred to Houghton. In 1893, Alice Longfellow gave seven hundred books of American poetry to Harvard College.[250] While the fate of some of these books remains

249 "I have a good many of his poems written in this fashion . . ." (*Literary Friends* 166).

250 *Historic Furnishings Report* 107.

unknown, more recent deposits can be traced thanks to two lists of books with call numbers assigned by the staff of Houghton Library.[251] They show that in 1960 Harvard received 209 books by Longfellow, among them translations of *Hiawatha* in Ukrainian, Russian, Swedish, Danish, Polish, German, Dutch, Latin, and Finnish, as well as 192 association copies (among them Longfellow's copy of Thoreau's *Walden*, Annie Fields's poems, dedicated to her "master and friend" Henry W. Longfellow, and a 1640 edition of Hugo Grotius's *Christs Passion*). Since these books from Longfellow's library were not kept together, researchers must use Harvard's online catalogue to find individual items.

However, a combination of patience and serendipity may lead to exciting results. Not mentioned in the available lists, for example, is Longfellow's personal copy of Whitman's *Leaves of Grass*, with Longfellow's own bookplate, an extraordinary item, given the complicated relationship between the two poets (Houghton f *AC85.L8605.Zy855w). Kept in a morocco-backed and buckram-covered green slip-case and bound in dark green cloth, this first edition (among the first ones issued, but identified as "second state" because of the printed copyright and the addition of "cities and" on p. iv), the book serves as a handsome reminder of the inclusiveness of Longfellow's interests and his barrier-transcending popularity. Pasted into the book is a note from Whitman, sent from 431 Stevens Street in Camden, New Jersey, and dated 20 February 1881, to "dear Mr Longfellow." Whitman writes: "A friend in Canada—to whom I am indebted for great personal kindnesses & affections—particularly desires your autograph—could you furnish it to me, to send? & much oblige Walt Whitman."[252] Even Whitman, a shrewder and more sophisticated literary critic than he would himself admit, had to acknowledge Longfellow's popularity and relevance. When he heard that Longfellow had died, he revisited some of his old reservations, calling Longfellow a "poet of the mellow twilight of the past," suffering from a "sickness" of "verbal melody," but he also acknowledged that he had succeeded in bringing "what is always dearest as poetry to the general human heart and taste" and, as he added with perhaps some resignation, "probably must be so in the nature of things." And then Whitman used a term that he usually kept for himself: Longfellow was, he said, "the sort of bard or counteractant most needed for our materialistic, self-assertive, money-worshipping, Anglo-Saxon race, and especially for the present age in America."[253]

251 "Volumes from the Longfellow Collection at Craigie House—rec'd 1960: Books by Longfellow" and "Volumes from the Longfellow Collection at Craigie House deposited by the Trustees of the Longfellow House Trust: Association Books," typescripts kept in Houghton Library, Harvard University.

252 Whitman's Canadian friend was Dr. Richard Maurice Bucke (1837-1902), a psychiatrist in London, Ontario, an ardent admirer of *Leaves of Grass* since 1867. In 1883, he published his biographical study, *Walt Whitman*. For Longfellow's reply to Whitman ("gives me great pleasure to comply with your request"), see *Letters* 6: 692.

253 Walt Whitman, *Specimen Days & Collect* (Glasgow: Wilson & McCormick, 1883) 193-94.

Suggested Reading

Readers interested in seeing more of Longfellow's works have a choice between two editions, the *Selected Poems*, edited by Lawrence Buell and available from Penguin Classics (first published in 1988), and the Library of America edition of *Poems and Other Writings*, edited by J. D. McClatchy (New York: Library of America, 2000). Buell's introduction to the *Selected Poems* offers one of the best modern assessments of Longfellow, with special emphasis on his understanding of poetry as a profession. Since he does not limit himself to the poetry and the verse plays, McClatchy's collection is more comprehensive. However, the early *North American Review* essays, *Outre-Mer*, and *Hyperion* are not included either.

The following suggestions for further reading reflect the author's personal preferences. They include articles and books he has found helpful and enlightening, which may serve as the basic building blocks of a library for the Longfellow *aficionado*.

Aaron, Daniel. "The Legacy of Henry Wadsworth Longfellow." *Maine Historical Society Quarterly* 27.4 (1987): 42-66.

Wide-ranging, witty reflection, in sparkling prose, on the decline of Longfellow's reputation. However outmoded Longfellow's "line of goods" might seem to some today, his "continued neglect amounts to a national loss. American literature isn't all that rich and various that we can afford to discredit or forget so good a poet."

Alighieri, Dante. *Inferno*. Trans. Henry Wadsworth Longfellow. New York: The Modern Library, 2003.

A reprint of Longfellow's 1867 translation of Dante's *Inferno*, which has influenced many later translators, whether they acknowledge it or not. Edited and prefaced by Matthew Pearl, author of *The Dante Club*, and introduced by Lino Pertile.

Arvin, Newton. *Longfellow: His Life and Work*. Boston: Little, Brown, 1963.

Arvin's last book. Less a biography than a survey of Longfellow's work, colored by a basic uncertainty about whether Longfellow is worth all the critical attention Arvin bestows on him. Longfellow is the "poet of acceptance, rather than of rebellion and rejection"—a verdict that is not so different from Emerson's observation that in Longfellow the reader is always in "safe hands." Too afraid to abandon himself to the "evidence of his sensibilities," Longfellow clung to neat, moralizing lessons. Nevertheless, Arvin offers some of the best readings of individual poems.

Butler, Joyce. "The Longfellows: Another Portland Family." *The Maine Historical Society Quarterly* 27.4 (1987): 20-41.

Important biographical information especially about Longfellow's parents.

Calhoun, Charles. *Longfellow: A Rediscovered Life*. Boston: Beacon, 2004.

The standard modern biography of Longfellow. Calhoun revises earlier accounts, especially of the circumstances of Fanny's death and Longfellow's friendship with Sumner, and focuses on Longfellow as a "multicultural" poet.

Fields, Annie. "Longfellow: 1807-1882." In Fields, *Authors and Friends*. Boston: Houghton Mifflin, 1893. 3-64.

A brilliant essay by a critic and poet who knew Longfellow well—suffused with the author's admiration for him but nevertheless full of insights about the contradictions that shaped his character and his work.

Gale, Robert L. *A Henry Wadsworth Longfellow Companion*. Westport, CT: Greenwood, 2003.

Alphabetically arranged entries devoted to individual poems, other works by Longfellow, and to members of his family, friends, and colleagues. The author is not afraid to pass judgment on the objects of his investigative zeal: "Charley Longfellow ... was a spoiled and self-indulgent brat in later years." However, the reader will also find some unexpected gems here—viz. the beautifully titled mini-essay on "Friends Longfellow Knew Casually" or the entry on "Presidents Longfellow Met."

Gartner, Matthew. "Longfellow's Place: The Poet and Poetry of Craigie House." *New England Quarterly* 73: 1 (2000): 32-57.

A new look at Longfellow's career that focuses on the centrality of his life (including the house in which he lived) to his success and identifies "weariness" as one of the central themes of his poetry.

Gioia, Dana. "Longfellow in the Aftermath of Modernism." *The Columbia History of American Poetry*. Ed. Jay Parini. New York: Columbia University Press, 1993. 64-96.

The essay most responsible for the current revival of critical interest in Longfellow. The author, a practicing poet as well as a former marketing executive and current Director of the National Endowment for the Arts, bemoans the "simplified version of nineteenth-century poetry" that the modernists have passed on to us and the devaluation of narrative poetry that he sees as the main reason for Longfellow's exclusion from the canon.

Guth, Christine M. E.. *Longfellow's Tattoos: Tourism, Collecting, and Japan.* Seattle: University of Washington Press, 2004.

Drawing on her extensive familiarity with the largely untapped visual archives of the Longfellow National Historic Site, the author situates Charley Longfellow's years in Japan within the larger context of American "orientalism."

Haralson, Eric. "Mars in Petticoats: Longfellow and Sentimental Masculinity." *Nineteenth-Century Literature* 56 (1996): 327-55.

Groundbreaking study that attributes the decline of Longfellow's reputation to new and less inclusive or "feminine" models of masculinity that emerged in the latter half of the nineteenth century.

Higginson, Thomas Wentworth. *Henry Wadsworth Longfellow.* Boston: Houghton Mifflin, 1902.

The best older book-length introduction to Longfellow. Unlike many biographers, Higginson does take time to comment on Longfellow's work, in a chapter-length meditation on "Longfellow as a Poet" and in an interesting, though critical, chapter on Longfellow's Dante translations. Expresses a marked preference for Longfellow's earlier translation attempts, arguing that they are fresher and more vivid.

Howells, William Dean. *Literary Friends and Acquaintance: A Personal Retrospect of American Authorship.* Ed. David F. Hiatt and Edwin H. Cady. 1900. Bloomington: Indiana University Press, 1968.

Movingly portrays the author's relationship with Longfellow during the last decade of his life.

Irmscher, Christoph. *Longfellow Redux.* Urbana: University of Illinois Press, 2006.

The first critical study of Longfellow's entire body of work in several decades, with a special focus on Longfellow's connection with his audience and his work as a translator. My argument is based on extensive archival research, including Longfellow's unpublished journals and letters from fans.

Jarman, Mark. "A Poem of Pure Enjoyment." *The Hudson Review* 57.4 (2005): 693-99.

The poet and critic Jarman provocatively suggests that *Hiawatha*, banished from the halls of academe, might have taken on "fresh non-canonical status" and that we can now read it again "for fun, as we can no longer read *Leaves of Grass*."

Kete, Mary Louise. *Sentimental Collaborations: Mourning and Middle-Class Identity in Nineteenth-Century America*. Durham, NC: Duke University Press, 1999.

Longfellow, Sigourney, and others used the language of sentimentality to initiate an exchange of sympathies between authors and readers and to alleviate contemporary anxieties about what it meant to be American.

Longfellow, Charles Appleton. *Twenty Months in Japan, 1871-1873*. Ed. Christine Wallace Laidlaw. Cambridge, MA: Friends of the Longfellow House, 1998.

Essential for understanding the complicated father-son dynamic that is at the heart of "Charley's" insatiable desire for travel. Lively letters offer a memorable portrait of Japan during the Meiji period.

Longfellow, Ernest Wadsworth. *Random Memories*. Boston: Houghton Mifflin, 1922.

An amusing, quirky, readable account by Longfellow's conservative son "Erny," a painter of some talent but not, as he points out with characteristic self-irony, "genius." Memorable sketches of Longfellow's friends.

Longfellow, Fanny Appleton. *Mrs. Longfellow: Selected Letters and Journals of Fanny Appleton Longfellow (1817-1861)*. Ed. Edward Wagenknecht. New York: Longmans, Green, 1955.

In the absence of a full-length biography and a more comprehensive edition of her letters and journals, Wagenknecht's selection (now out of print) is the best introduction to the brilliant woman Longfellow married in 1843.

Nemerov, Howard. Introduction. *Longfellow: The Laurel Poetry Series*. New York: Dell, 1959. 7-27.

Although Nemerov, himself an important poet, remains skeptical of Longfellow's overall talent, he finds an "unyielding perception of reality" in Longfellow's work that is the hallmark of "good poetry wherever and whenever written," and he makes a special case for the importance of his late fragment *Michael Angelo*, "the equal of the best in nineteenth century poetry."

Pearl, Matthew. *The Dante Club*. New York: Random House, 2003.

The poet of Craigie House is the central character in this enormously successful mystery novel centered on Longfellow's Dante translation.

Sumner, Charles. *The Selected Letters of Charles Sumner*. Ed. Beverly Wilson Palmer, 2 vols. Boston: Northeastern University Press, 1990.

Sumner's letters—passionate, unrestrained, urgent, uncompromising—represent the other side of the most intense and interesting friendship Longfellow enjoyed.

Chronology: The Shape of a Life

Unless otherwise indicated, the quotations are from Henry Wadsworth Longfellow's (mostly) unpublished journals, which are kept with the Longfellow Papers at Harvard's Houghton Library. This chronology, though saturated with the kind of detail relevant to the theme of this book, does not strive for completeness. Readers in search of a more comprehensive timeline may turn to the one included with the Library of America edition of Longfellow's *Poems and Other Writings*, ed. J. D. McClatchy ([New York: Library of America, 2000], 805-15) or the chronologies at the beginning of each of the six volumes of Longfellow's *Letters*, ed. Andrew Hilen (Cambridge, MA: Belknap, 1966-82).

1807

Henry Wadsworth Longfellow is born on 27 February in Portland, Maine, the second of eight children of the lawyer Stephen Longfellow and his wife, Zilpah Wadsworth Longfellow.

1813

Enters Portland Academy, where he remains for eight years.

1820

17 November: Longfellow's first published poem, "The Battle of Lovell's Pond," a lament for colonists killed by yelling savages, appears in the *Portland Gazette* (signed "HENRY").

1821

Admitted to Bowdoin College, Maine, but spends freshman year in Portland.

1822

In September, Longfellow and his brother Stephen begin their residence at Bowdoin College.

1825

Graduates from Bowdoin College, in the same class with Nathaniel Hawthorne. His commencement oration, "Our Native Writers," calls for a national literature that reflects the pulse of American life: "there is nothing which so frees us from the turbulent ambition and bustle of the world, nothing which so fills the mind with glowing and great conceptions and at the same time so warms the heart with love and tenderness, as a frequent and close communion with natural scenery." Hawthorne, whose disciplinary record at Bowdoin was less than stellar, is not allowed to speak at graduation. Bowdoin offers Longfellow a professorship of modern languages, provided that he prepare himself for the position with a period of European travel, a proposition he cheerfully accepts.

1826

Leaves for France. 19 June: arrives in Paris, where he enjoys the "lightheartedness" of the people, although he finds himself drawn to the more traditional customs of people in the country. His love affair with Catholicism begins. Signs letter to his mother as "Henri," visits Rouen, Auteuil, Limoges, and Bordeaux, and hikes through the Loire Valley: "I found myself wandering about in a dirty shirt—with my travelling cap on my head—two pairs of dirty socks—with holes in the toes—together with a cake of Windsor soap stowed away in my pockets" (5 October).

1827

From March to November in Spain and Gibraltar, where he enjoys "much happiness" (undated entry, "Journal in Spain"). Visits La Mancha, made "classic" by the "memory of Don Quixote" but now a "poor, poverty-stricken country" (September 1827) and, in November, sees the Alhambra, where he is enthralled with "mirage of oriental luxury." In December he meets George Washington Greene from Rhode Island, in Europe to study foreign languages like Longfellow. Forms lifelong friendship with Greene, who would come to depend on Longfellow for moral as well as financial support.

1828

Spends Christmas in Genoa: "The 'Strada nuova' of Genoa [is] the most beautiful street I ever beheld—It is a long succession of palaces—But what misery at their gates!—The poor—the maimed—the blind!—Such splendour and magnificence seen side by side with poverty and rags 'font mal aux yeux'" (25 December). Resides in Florence and Rome, visits Naples and Rimini. 28 February: Witnesses the carnival in Rome, which ends with the lighting of wax candles (*moccoli*): "Such confusion and noise you never saw nor heard!—Lights waving up and down—extinguished—relighted—and again extinguished—and glimmering from balconies—from coaches and the crowd through a street of a mile or two in length—and the air rent with as it were but one voice—'Moccolo!'" Begins serious study of Dante. 14 December: arrives in Venice, where he resides at the Hotel Europa. Encounters Toni Toscan, a Venetian gondolier, "formerly in the service of Lord Byron," and folk poet, "one of the few who can still sing a stanza from Tasso" ("History of the Italian Language").

1829

February to June: in Göttingen, Germany, where Longfellow attends lectures at the university and reads German literature. Returns to the United States. 11 August: begins teaching French and Spanish at Bowdoin, where he also serves as the college librarian and writes his own textbooks.

1830

Publishes *Elements of French Grammar* and *Manuel des Proverbes Dramatiques.*

1831

Publishes "The Origin and Progress of the French Language" (*The North American Review,* April); 14 September: marries the 19-year-old Mary Storer Potter, the daughter of a Portland judge.

1832

Publishes three essays in *The North American Review*: "The Defence of Poetry," a review of Sir Philip Sidney (January), "Spanish Devotional and Moral Poetry" (April); "History of the Italian Language and Dialects" (October). In July, *Syllabus de la grammaire Italienne* and his anthology of Italian short stories, *Saggi de' novellieri Italiani d'ogni secolo,* are published by Gray and Bowen in Boston.

1833

Publishes his translation of Don Jorge Manrique's *Coplas por la muerte de su padre* with Allen and Ticknor in Boston: "The object of this little work is to place in the hands of the lovers of Spanish literature the most beautiful moral poem of that language."

1834

Longfellow is offered the position of the Smith Professor of Modern Languages at Harvard College and plans another European trip, this time with the goal of strengthening his proficiency in German and acquiring some Scandinavian languages.

1835

Outre-Mer: A Pilgrimage Beyond the Sea published in New York. Departs for Europe on 10 April and visits England, Denmark, Sweden, Holland, and Germany. 29 November: Mary Longfellow dies in Rotterdam from complications after a miscarriage. Though grief-stricken ("I ask myself if it can indeed be true"; to William Warren Goddard, 4 December), Longfellow sends Mary's body home in a sealed coffin and continues his travels. 7 December: meets August Wilhelm Schlegel in Bonn ("He is very much of a gentleman—and takes snuff from an ornamented box of tortoise shell").

1836

Spends the winter and spring in Heidelberg, reading Goethe, Jean Paul, and Herder. Meets the Massachusetts industrialist Nathan Appleton and his family and travels with them from Interlaken to Zurich, falling in love with Frances Elizabeth (Fanny) Appleton, who gives him the cold shoulder. He returns to the United States in October. Before his departure, he spends a few weeks in Paris and is overwhelmed with the reality of this modern metropolis: "How this great living cataract goes thundering through the streets in one unbroken roar!—A thousand currents meet and mingle" (11 September).

1837

23 May: Longfellow begins his Harvard lectures. Moves into Craigie House as a lodger. With the law partners Charles Sumner and George Hillard, the classicist Cornelius Felton, and the writer Henry Cleveland, Longfellow forms the "Five of Clubs." After being approached by Hawthorne for help, Longfellow publishes appreciative review of *Twice-told Tales* in the *The North American Review*.

1839

August: publication of *Hyperion: A Romance* and, in December, *Voices of the Night*, Longfellow's first collection of poetry. Poe begins his long critical campaign against Longfellow with a negative review of *Hyperion* in the October issue of *Burton's Gentleman's Magazine*: "Works like this of Professor Longfellow, are the triumphs of Tom O'Bedlam, and the grief of all true criticism."

1841

31 December: Publication of *Ballads and Other Poems*, which contains "The Skeleton in Armor" and "The Wreck of the Hesperus." "Blow upon blow is the word; and not let the iron cool," he tells his father (26 September).

1842

Meets Charles Dickens. April–September: On leave from his Harvard teaching job, Longfellow takes the water-cure in Marienberg on the Rhine in Germany, where he befriends Ferdinand Freiligrath, the "first and the foremost of young poets in Germany" (to Richard Henry Dana, 10 November 1842). Freiligrath radicalizes Longfellow politically. After Longfellow's return to the United States, he keeps Freiligrath's portrait by his study door and gazes at it "with *considerable tenderness*" (to Freiligrath, 6 January 1843). December: *Poems on Slavery* published.

1843

May: publishes his play, *The Spanish Student*, in book form. 13 July: marries Fanny Appleton. Nathan Appleton purchases Craigie House and transfers title to Fanny. Spends honeymoon in the Catskills and the Berkshires, accompanied part of the time by Charles Sumner.

1844

9 June: birth of Charles Appleton Longfellow. Publication of anthology *The Waif.*

1845

Carey & Hart in Philadelphia publish an edition of Longfellow's *Poems* but omit *Poems on Slavery*, for fear of losing potential buyers in the South. Begins work on *Evangeline*, my "Idyl in hexameters." 23 November: birth of Ernest Wadsworth Longfellow, "a little wandering musician with a remarkable talent for imitating with his mouth the penny trumpet and the wooden dog." Margaret Fuller launches her "bilious attack" on Longfellow in *The New York Tribune*. Attends Emerson's lectures on "Representative Men." Publishes *The Belfry of Bruges*, which "is succeeding famously well" (30 December). Finishes the year with a feeling of "Love fulfilled—the heart comforted—the soul enriched with Fanny's affection" (31 December).

1846

Translates Friedrich Wilhelm Joseph Schelling's essay "Dante from a Philosophical Point of View." Reads George Sand, Heinrich Heine, and Goethe's *Italian Journey,* and begins a new course of lectures on Dante. 26 June: visited by the African-American preacher Josiah Henson, later the model for Stowe's "Uncle Tom." Longfellow feels "mad for travel" (2 April). 19 December: goes to see John Banvard's three-mile long "moving Diorama of the Mississippi": "One seems to be sailing down the great stream; and see the boats and sand-banks crested with cotton-wood, and the bayous by moonlight." Publishes *The Estray*, a sequel to *The Waif.* Ends the year reading Emerson's poems: "through the golden mist … of fancy gleam bright veins of purest poetry" (26 December).

1847

Defines American literature as a "composite" of different national traditions, "embracing French, Spanish, Irish, English, Scotch and German peculiarities." Whoever is the "most universal" (i.e., cosmopolitan) writer "is also the most national" one (6 January 1847). Meets the Swiss naturalist Louis Agassiz ("exceedingly agreeable"), who becomes one of his closest friends. Continues to enjoy Sand ("what delicious style she writes") and reads Hans Christian Andersen. Poe accuses him of plagiarism, for which Longfellow mocks him in his journal: "In Hexameter sings serenely a Harvard Professor; / In Pentameter him damns censorious Poe" (24 February 1847). 27 February: finishes *Evangeline* and immediately begins work on a new, short novel, *Kavanagh*. 7 April: Fanny Longfellow gives birth to their daughter Fanny, the first American woman to do so under the influence of ether. The anesthetic is administered by the dentist Dr. Nathan Cooley Keep. A day later, Dr. Keep uses ether to extract one of Longfellow's teeth: "On inhaling it, burst into fits of laughter. Then my brain whirled round and I seemed to soar like a lark spirally into the air." Longfellow meets with Cuban poets and frequently attends opera performances in Boston (Bellini, Verdi, Rossini). Felton, Folsom, and Sumner look over the proof-sheets for *Evangeline*. 30 October: *Evangeline* published.

1848

27 February: feels the "approaching tread of the Stone Statue" on his 41st birthday. 28 March: welcomes the "Republic of the Poets" in France and Victor Hugo's political involvement. In July begins vacation in Pittsfield, Massachusetts. Hears Mr. Hunt, an African-American preacher in an "Abyssinian" church and transcribes his sermon on Noah and the flood. 11 September: daughter Fanny Longfellow dies after a short illness, aged 1 year and 5 months. 9 November: finishes *Kavanagh*. "I miss very much my dear little Fanny. An inappeasable longing to see her comes over me, which I can hardly control" (12 November).

1849

January: Attends Fanny Kemble's Shakespeare readings. 14 May: publication of *Kavanagh*. 25 June: "I wish we were all in Italy." Reads Thoreau's essay on civil disobedience, which he finds "extremely good." 3 August: his father dies in Portland, after "a life of suffering." 6 August: "And again the great world goes clanging on, as if there were no dead and no mourners!" December: *The Seaside and the Fireside* published. Ends the year by asking himself: "Have I advanced? Perhaps! Am I any better? Not any! Am I any worse? I hope not!" (31 December).

1850

13 June: Reacts skeptically to Agassiz's lecture on "The Races of Man," which he attends in the company of Ojibway George Copway (Kah-ge-ga-gah-bow). 23 June: Margaret Fuller drowns off Fire Island: "A singular woman was she for New England to produce." Spends the first of many summers on the Nahant peninsula. 30 August: execution of the Harvard Professor of Chemistry, Dr. John Webster, for the murder of George Parkman: "I hope this may be the last execution we shall ever have in Massachusetts! Cain the first murderer was not hanged." 20 September: Alice Mary Longfellow born. Opposes the Fugitive Slave Law as a "disgrace" (27 October 1850). Complains about the burden of teaching: "The college work is like a great hand laid on all the strings of my

lyre, stopping their vibrations. It must be taken off" (18 November). He is thrown into despair over the sudden illness of Erny ("A kind of panic and wild alarm has seized upon me," 25 November).

1851

Longs for escape from the Boston winter: "Ah me! what ills flesh is heir to in this New England climate! I wish we were all sitting under the palm-trees of the tropics" (7 January 1851). 12 March: death of Zilpah Longfellow. 24 April: Sumner is elected to the Senate. Reads Heine and Ruskin and teaches Goethe's *Faust*. November: *The Golden Legend* published.

1853

22 October: daughter Edith is born.

1854

Longfellow resigns from Harvard, giving his last lecture on 19 April. The increasing volume of his fan mail overwhelms him: "all my unanswered letters hang upon me like an evil conscience" (3 May). He is "sick and sorrowful" over the arrest of fugitive slave Anthony Burns: "We will submit to this no longer, come what may!" (27 and 30 May). Begins to read the *Kalevala*. 22 June: "hit upon a plan for a poem on the Indians, which seems to me the right one, and the only. It is to weave together their beautiful traditions into a whole. I have hit upon a measure, too, which I think the right and only one for such a theme." The tentative title is *Manabozho* (later: *The Song of Hiawatha*). He also reads Henry Rowe Schoolcraft's "ill-digested" volumes on Native American mythology. 28 July: "Nothing ever absorbed me more" than *Hiawatha*. Reads Thoreau's *Walden* and admires Harriet Hosmer's bust of the Medusa: "The agony of the face hardly mars its strange beauty" (21 October).

1855

For several months, goes to the opera regularly, often several times a week (Bellini's *Norma*, Donizetti's *Lucia di Lammermoor*, Mozart's *Don Giovanni*, Rossini's *Semiramide*, Verdi's *Rigoletto*, etc.); feels "so dissipated" that he cannot work. On his 48th birthday (27 February), he compares himself to "an old swallow with my nest close up under the roof of the old barn." 29 March 1855: beset with neuralgia, writes his poem about Portland, "My Lost Youth." 8 November: birth of Anne Allegra ("Annie"); two days later, publishes *Song of Hiawatha*. The first edition being almost sold out before publication, Ticknor & Fields immediately prints an additional 3,000. "Hiawatha makes some sensation. Sundry squibs and the like, with imitations of the metre; as if it stirred the minds of readers a little" (15 November).

1856

Hiawatha is selling at the rate of "300 a day." By February, 20,000 copies have been printed and Longfellow has earned $4,000. Longfellow lowers his royalties from 20% per copy to 15%, "so that greater discounts may be made to large purchasers" (19 March). Continues his visits to the opera: Donizetti's *Lucrezia Borgia,* Mozart's *Don Giovanni,* Meyerbeer's *Le Prophète.* 10 April: Charley maims his left hand when playing with a gun at Fresh Pond. "We eat our bread with tears" (12 April). 23 May: Sumner is caned in the Senate by the South Carolina congressman Preston Brooks. Longfellow burns "with indignation and shame" (28 May). On the way to reserving staterooms for the passage to Europe, he hurts his knee and quickly decides not to go: "The undertaking seemed too momentous on a nearer view" (June). Spends the summer on Nahant, "with Fanny watching the long emerald waves break into foam, rosy with the light of the … evening sky" (15 July). Reads German novelist Wilhelm Raabe as well as James Fenimore Cooper and is not impressed by the latter's drawn-out prose ("as if he were writing for space," 31 July).

1857

31 March: Ticknor tallies sales for Longfellow, with *Hiawatha* (50,000 copies sold) and *Voices of the Night* (43,550) leading the list. Agassiz invites Longfellow to join the Saturday Club. Reads Gaskell's *Life of Charlotte Brontë*, "so interesting, that one cannot let go" (10 May). Complains that his time is "frittered away with the nothings of everyday existence" (23 November). Begins work on his "Puritan Pastoral," initially called *Priscilla.*

1858

16 October: *The Courtship of Miles Standish and Other Poems* published. The new volume sells 25,000 copies in two months.

1860

17 January: sees Adelina Patti in Rossini's *Barbiere di Siviglia* and in Bellini's *I Puritani.* Is intrigued by Hawthorne's *Marble Faun*: "a wonderful book in its way; but with the old, dull pain that runs through all Hawthorne's writings" (1 March). 1 June: admires Rosa Bonheur's painting of the *Horse Fair* (now in the Metropolitan Museum). In December, Longfellow acquires Wetmore Cottage, Nahant, with brother-in-law Thomas Gold Appleton.

1861

Reads Dickens. His pacifism colliding with his passionate hatred of slavery, Longfellow is shaken up by the attack on Fort Sumter. "When the times have such a gun-powder flavor, all literature loses its taste" (30 April). 10 July: death of Fanny Appleton after a fire caused by a lighted match; her father, Nathan Appleton, dies on 14 July. Numb with shock and despair, Longfellow says that he "cannot record" the thoughts "that are in my heart and brain" (19 September). In October, he merely writes that other men "could bear up under even such sorrow as mine. But I cannot." Slowly, his responsibilities as a father force him to suppress his grief. On 8 November, he takes Annie to Agassiz's museum for her birthday where she admires "the butterflies and corals." 27 November: the anarchist and materialist Mikhail Bakunin visits Longfellow.

1862

26 February: death of Cornelius C. Felton. 7 March: Charley leaves on a voyage to Ship Island. 4 June: takes Charley and Erny to visit Niagara Falls and Montreal: "Niagara is too much for me. My nerves shake like a bridge of wire" (9 June). 10 July: "I can make no record of the days. Better leave them wrapped in silence. Perhaps some day God will give me peace." Dismayed by the violence that has erupted but convinced that the North needs to stand up against the South: "What an infernal thing war is!" (23 September). Works on *Tales of a Wayside Inn.*

1863

10 March: Charley Longfellow runs away to join the Union forces. "I shall not send for him," a resigned Longfellow writes in his journal on 16 March. "He is where he wants to be, in the midst of it all." The next day, he begins his translation of Dante's *Inferno*: "Mean to take a Canto a day, till it is finished." Watches Colonel Shaw lead the first black regiment through Beacon Street. "At last the North consents to let the Negro fight for his freedom" (28 May). Finishes a first draft of his translation of Dante's *Divina Commedia* in April. *Tales of a Wayside Inn* published in November. 27 November: Charley is shot through the shoulder near New Hope Church, Virginia, and Longfellow and his son Erny travel to Washington to take care of him and bring him home.

1864

Charley is discharged from the army. 19 May: death of Nathaniel Hawthorne in Plymouth, New Hampshire. Writes elegy for Hawthorne, which Fields publishes in *The Atlantic Monthly* in August.

1865

10 February: the first volume of Longfellow's translation of *The Divine Comedy* is privately published. One of the 10 copies is rushed to Italy, as Longfellow's contribution to the celebrations surrounding Dante's 600th birthday ("in commemorazione del sentecesimo anniversario della nascita di Dante Alighieri"). Longfellow is enthusiastic about "the grand event of the century," the adoption of the Thirteenth Amendment

abolishing slavery throughout the United States. "This year will always be the Year of Jubilee in our history," he writes to Sumner. "Thanks to you" (10 February).

1866

November: publishes new collection of poems, *Flower-de-Luce*. In a sequence of sonnets about the "Divina Commedia," Longfellow imagines Dante's verse as "footpaths for the thought of Italy." 13 June: last meeting of the Dante Club, which doesn't end until "the day was dawning and the birds singing."

1867

April-June: *The Divine Comedy of Dante Alighieri* published in three volumes. November: Charles Dickens visits Longfellow.

1868

27 May: sails to England, accompanied by his five children, his daughter-in-law Harriet Spelman (Ernest's new wife), his brother Samuel, his two sisters Anne and Mary, his brother-in-law Tom Appleton, and Hannah Davie, the former family governess. Receives honorary LL.D. from Cambridge University. Calls on Queen Victoria, who is astonished that her servants know Longfellow's poetry by heart: "No other distinguished person has come here that has excited so peculiar an interest." October: publication of *The New England Tragedies*. Travels to Italy for the winter.

1869

Hears "the great pianist" Franz Liszt play in Rome (to Charley, 3 January). In Sorrento, finds himself "growing a little weary of this *vita beata* of the sea-side, with nothing to do. Or am I hurried by what still needs to be done?" (11 April). Back in Cambridge on 11 September.

1870

9 June: death of Charles Dickens in London. Longfellow is filled "with inexpressible grief" (to John Forster, 12 June).

1871

March: Porter & Coates in Philadelphia print a revised edition of *Poets and Poetry of Europe*. 12 December: publishes *The Divine Tragedy*.

1872

September: publishes *Christus: A Mystery*, a uniform edition containing all three parts of his trilogy (*The Divine Tragedy*, *The Golden Legend*, and *The New England Tragedies*), with newly written introductory and transitional sections.

1873

Publishes *Aftermath*. Deeply affected by the death of Louis Agassiz on 14 December.

1874

Begins the verse play *Michael Angelo*, which remains unfinished and appears posthumously. Samuel Ward sells Longfellow's poem *The Hanging of the Crane* to *The New York Ledger* for $4,000, passing $3,000 on to Longfellow. 11 March: death of Charles Sumner, "Of what I feel … I cannot speak" (to Caleb Lyon; 16 March). Begins work on his "Poetic Guide-Book," the 31-volume anthology *Poems of Places*. 26 November: translates his sonnet "The Old Bridge at Florence" into Italian.

1875

7 July: Reads, barely audibly, "Morituri Salutamus," at Bowdoin College, in celebration of the 50th anniversary of the class of 1825. August: signs agreement with James Osgood "for ten years' right of publishing my books for $4,000 annually, in equal quarterly payments." In October, publication of *The Masque of Pandora and Other Poems*.

1876

18 March: death of Ferdinand Freiligrath. Travels to the Centennial Exhibition in Philadelphia and on 2 June meets Walt Whitman in Camden, New Jersey. As often on such occasions, Longfellow, accompanied by the Philadelphia publisher George W. Childs, is mostly silent during the visit. Whitman later said that Longfellow was "dapper and dainty and effeminate … like the lord whose wife was advised to keep him dressed well but never let him open his mouth." 10 June: Dom Pedro II, the Emperor of Brazil, the modern "Haroun al Rashid," dines with Longfellow.

1877

7 January: writes sonnet about Venice. Works on the "immense" Italian material for *Poems of Places*. 27 February: his study is "a garden of flowers" and he receives "salutations from far and near." 3 August: receives $1,000 from *Harper's* for his poem about pottery and poetry, "Kéramos." 27 September: botanist Asa Gray brings Darwin's friend, the botanist Joseph Hooker, for a visit. October: Elizabeth Agassiz reads to him her work-in-progress, a biography of her husband Louis. Emerson appears to him in a dream: "He said; 'The Spring will come again, but shall we see it, or only the eternal Spring up there!'—lifting both his hands on high" (20 October). 24 and 25 October: attends performances of Wagner's *Lohengrin* and Verdi's *Trovatore*.

1878

Continues work on *Poems of Places*. April: publication of *Kéramos and Other Poems*, which also contains Longfellow's translation of seven sonnets and a canzone by Michelangelo.

1879

Finishes *Poems of Places:* "That stone is rolled over the hill" (18 January). Sees Bizet's *Carmen*, which he finds "brilliant." 10 July: writes "The Cross of Snow," 18 years after Fanny's death: "… soul more white / Never through martyrdom of fire was led / To its repose." For his seventy-second birthday, the children of Cambridge present him with an armchair made from the wood of the chestnut tree that stood before the old smithy in Cambridge. 1 September: Richard Henry Dana IV, "my first grandchild," is born to Longfellow's daughter Edith and her husband, Richard Henry Dana III.

1880

15 September: *Ultima Thule* published. In the opening poem, dedicated to George Washington Greene, Longfellow muses on how far "the ocean streams" have swept both him and his friend from "the lost Atlantis of our youth" ("Dedication").

1881

26 January: birth of Henry Wadsworth Longfellow Dana, Longfellow's second grandchild. 26 February: publication of *The Longfellow Birthday-Book*. 24 April: death of Longfellow's publisher and close friend, James Fields. Writes a series of "Elegiac Verse": "Not in youth alone, but in age, may the heart of the poet / Bloom into song."

1882

Oscar Wilde visits Longfellow: "However fantastic he may be in public, in private he is a very agreeable and intelligent young man" (to Mary Appleton Mackintosh, 7 February). After falling ill on 17 March with peritonitis, Longfellow dies on 24 March. "A great light seemed to have gone out of my life," writes his son Ernest later. "For years I could not enter his study without a pang—the gentle presence had passed away, the affectionate greeting was no longer to be mine." *In the Harbor*, Longfellow's last collection of poetry, is published in July. The volume ends with the last lines of poetry he wrote: "The world rolls into light; / It is daybreak everywhere" ("The Bells of San Blas").

Index